THE LOVE JONES COHORT

Drawing from stratification economics, intersectionality, and respectability politics, *The Love Jones Cohort* centers on the voices and lifestyles of members of the Black middle class who are single and living alone (SALA). While much has been written about both the Black middle class and the rise of singlehood, this book represents a first foray into bridging these two concepts. In studying these intersections, *The Love Jones Cohort* provides a more nuanced understanding of how race, gender, and class, coupled with social structures, shape five central lifestyle factors of Black middle-class adults who are SALA. The book explores how these Black adults define family and friends and decide on whether and how to pursue romantic relationships, articulate the ebbs and flows of being Black and middle class, select where to live and why, accumulate and disseminate wealth, and maintain overall health, well-being, and coping mechanisms.

KRIS MARSH is Associate Professor of Sociology at the University of Maryland. Previously, Professor Marsh was a postdoctoral scholar at the Carolina Population Center at the University of North Carolina, a visiting researcher at the University of Southern California and Fulbright Scholar in South Africa at the University of Witwatersrand and the University of Johannesburg. Professor Marsh's areas of expertise are the Black middle class, demography, racial residential segregation, and education.

CAMBRIDGE STUDIES IN STRATIFICATION ECONOMICS:
ECONOMICS AND SOCIAL IDENTITY

Series Editor

William A. Darity Jr., *Duke University*

The Cambridge Studies in Stratification Economics: Economics and Social Identity series encourages book proposals that emphasize structural sources of group-based inequality, rather than cultural or genetic factors. Studies in this series will utilize the underlying economic principles of self-interested behavior and substantive rationality in conjunction with sociology's emphasis on group behavior and identity formation. The series is interdisciplinary, drawing authors from various fields including economics, sociology, social psychology, history, and anthropology, with all projects focused on topics dealing with group-based inequality, identity, and economic well-being.

The Love Jones Cohort

Single and Living Alone in the Black Middle Class

KRIS MARSH

University of Maryland

CAMBRIDGE
UNIVERSITY PRESS

Shaftesbury Road, Cambridge CB2 8EA, United Kingdom

One Liberty Plaza, 20th Floor, New York, NY 10006, USA

477 Williamstown Road, Port Melbourne, VIC 3207, Australia

314–321, 3rd Floor, Plot 3, Splendor Forum, Jasola District Centre, New Delhi – 110025, India

103 Penang Road, #05-06/07, Visioncrest Commercial, Singapore 238467

Cambridge University Press is part of Cambridge University Press & Assessment,
a department of the University of Cambridge.

We share the University's mission to contribute to society through the pursuit of
education, learning and research at the highest international levels of excellence.

www.cambridge.org
Information on this title: www.cambridge.org/9781107160101

DOI: 10.1017/9781316672754

First published 2023

A catalogue record for this publication is available from the British Library.

Library of Congress Cataloging-in-Publication Data
Names: Marsh, Kris, author.
Title: The Love Jones cohort : single and living alone in the Black middle class /
Kris Marsh, University of Maryland, College Park.
Description: Cambridge, United Kingdom ; New York, NY : Cambridge University Press, 2023. |
Series: Cambridge studies in stratification economics: economics and social identity |
Includes bibliographical references and index.
Identifiers: LCCN 2022050215 (print) | LCCN 2022050216 (ebook) | ISBN 9781107160101 (hardback) |
ISBN 9781316612910 (paperback) | ISBN| 9781316672754 (epub)
Subjects: LCSH: Middle class African Americans–Social conditions–Case studies. |
African American women–Social conditions–Case studies. | Middle class women–United States–Social
conditions–Case studies. | Single women–United States–Social conditions–Case studies. |
Living alone–United States. | Lifestyles–United States.
Classification: LCC E185.86 .M368 2023 (print) | LCC E185.86 (ebook) |
DDC 305.48/896073–dc23/eng/20221116
LC record available at https://lccn.loc.gov/2022050215
LC ebook record available at https://lccn.loc.gov/2022050216

ISBN 978-1-107-16010-1 Hardback
ISBN 978-1-316-61291-0 Paperback

To my godson Lafayette "R'Jai" Dorsey Jr.
(May 1, 1997–August 6, 2020)

Contents

Figures

Tables

Preface

I am a Black woman who is SALA – the acronym I coined for single *and* living alone – that is, without a "significant other" or romantic partner. I also use SALA to refer to those who are single *adults* living alone. I am a university professor, researcher, and businesswoman. I am friendly, bubbly, and outgoing, and I recently took up golf as a hobby.[1]

According to the Pew Research Center's "Are you in the American middle class?" interactive calculator, I am in the upper-income tier,[2] a category that 32% of adults in the Washington, DC, area (where I live) and 19% in the United States as a whole fall into. Taking into consideration my education, race, and marital status, among *all* American adults sharing the same demographics, 23% are lower income (less than $48,500), 56% are middle income (between $48,500 and $145,500), and 21% are upper income (greater than $145,500) (Bennett et al., 2020).[3] Unlike the Pew Research Center's calculator (2020), sociologist Karyn Lacy (2007) and others – looking specifically at the Black middle class – employ a lower-,

---

[1] I acknowledge that I hold several privileges. I am cisgendered, heterosexual, able-bodied, Christian, a US citizen, and a native English speaker, with an androgynous name and 3C natural hair texture.

[2] www.pewresearch.org/fact-tank/2020/07/23/are-you-in-the-american-middle-class/

[3] According to the authors of the interactive calculator, the middle class is defined as,

> Your size-adjusted household income and the cost of living in your area are the factors we use to determine your income tier. Middle-income households – those with an income that is two-thirds to double the U.S. median household income – had incomes ranging from about z (all figures computed for three-person households, adjusted for the cost of living in a metropolitan area, and expressed in 2018 dollars).

In 2018, the national middle annual income range was about $48,500–$145,500 for a household of three. Lower-income households had incomes less than $48,500 and upper-income households had incomes greater than $145,500 (incomes in 2018 dollars) (www.pewresearch.org/fact-tank/2020/07/23/are-you-in-the-american-middle-class/).

middle- (core), and upper-class typology. Professionally and personally, I prefer not to make those same demarcations. Yet, to be sensitive to the variability in the Black middle class, in this book I use the term "middle class" to signify the "middle class and beyond" to capture class variance.

In 2002, my two sisters and I purchased a home in Leimert Park, a Black suburban area in Los Angeles County, California. This area experienced, and is still going through, gentrification: In 2011, 75% of residents were Black; by 2019, this had fallen to 65%.[4] Yes, three grown women lived in one house together: it was an adventure for the ages. I only lasted three years with them, but my two sisters went on to live together for more than 15 years. During the time I lived there, a single woman and a single man, each living alone (with neither siblings nor housemates), purchased homes on our street. The demographic shift on our street resonated with me as a graduate student studying the subfields of the Black family and demography in the Department of Sociology at the University of Southern California. The anecdotal and demographic changes I saw on my street were not apparent in the literature I was reading in graduate school.

This continued to be the case as I became more immersed in the demographic and sociological literature, leading me to uncover a quandary that I felt was worth exploring. The demographic literature was clear: While marriage rates were declining for all racial and ethnic groups, this trend was even more pronounced for Black adults. In terms of the sociological literature on the Black middle class, some scholars were suggesting that the continued employment of both members of a Black married couple is required to maintain middle-class status (Billingsley, 1968; Hill, 2003; Landry, 1987, 2002; McAdoo, 2007). Thus, in their writings, it was explicitly posited that declining marriage rates may result in a shrinking Black middle class (Attewell et al., 2004; Besharov, 2005; Landry, 1987), with the implicit assumption being that the Black middle class and marriage are intrinsically connected. Something, it seemed to me, was amiss in the social science literature.

Fast-forward to 2019, when it could be seen that 45% of Black women and men in the US had never been married. I began to intellectually

---

[4] Data provided by US Census, American Community Survey, 1-Year Estimates Detailed Tables, Table ID: B02001, zip code 90008. https://data.census.gov/cedsci/table?q=race&d=ACS%201-Year%20Estimates%20Detailed%20Tables&tid=ACSDT1Y2019.B02001&hidePreview=false

unpack a compositional shift in the Black middle class away from married couples to SALA households. Though there has been considerable recent research on and coverage of singlehood, and more generally burgeoning research on the Black middle class, little of it has addressed Black adults who are both SALA *and* Black middle class.

The Love Jones Cohort: Single and Living Alone in the Black Middle Class examines the lifestyle of SALAs as members of the Black middle class. Utilizing a constellation of social science literature, as well as extensive personal insights from this demographic group, this book sheds light on the state of class and singlehood in Black America. In doing so, *The Love Jones Cohort* unapologetically focuses on Black single adults in the middle class; neither white singleness nor comparing the Black middle class to the white middle class is my area of concern here. Instead, the book offers an alternative vantage point from which to examine the heterogeneity of the Black American, and specifically the Black middle-class, experience. Throughout, the core theme is understanding how the intersecting identities of race, class, gender, and singleness inform the lifestyle choices of the Love Jones Cohort. This book suggests that members of the Love Jones Cohort are innovators, paving the way for others to navigate, survive, and thrive as middle-class and never-married adults. Put another way, the book questions whether singlehood has become easier and more accessible to everyone because of the Love Jones Cohort showing the rest of the world how it can be done.

In the past 15 years alone, there have been several noteworthy books (and countless articles) studying various aspects of the Black middle class and Black elites in America,[5] including scholarship from across the globe.[6] Similarly, various books have examined notions of growing singlehood among all racial and ethnic groups.[7] Even so, little of the scholarship has focused exclusively on the never-married Black middle class or just Black singles (Staples, 1981), or on college-educated and professional Black women's dating practices, challenges, and work/family balance (Barnes, 2015; Clarke, 2011). The *Love Jones Cohort* draws on these previously published works to understand just how unique the singlehood experience and lifestyle of a SALA is in the Black middle class.

---

[5] Banks, 2009; Bowser, 2022; Charles et al, 2022; Clarke, 2011; Claytor, 2020; Clerge, 2019; Dow, 2019; Jefferson, 2016; Jenkins, 2019; Lacy, 2007; Landry, 2018; Pattillo, 2013; Sacks, 2018; Taylor, 2017.

[6] Khunou, 2015; Khunou et al., 2019; Meghji, 2019; Melber, 2016; Southall, 2016.

[7] DePaulo, 2011; Kislev, 2019; Klinenberg, 2013.

Throughout my scholarly career researching Black middle-class SALAs, my primary focus has been to move beyond the omnipresent inquiries: "Why are Black women *not* getting married?" and "Why are there so many single professional Black women?" This line of questioning places the spotlight on Black women's individual dating practices while often ignoring the structural factors undergirding such choices, constraints, and decision-making processes. It implies a deficiency on the part of Love Jones Cohort members – specifically Black women – due to the fact that they are unmarried and child-free. As for myself, I am constantly asked why I am not married and/or whether my research can explain why so many other Black professional women remain unmarried.

I recall an incident in December 2015 at a winter bazaar in a gated community in Prince George's County, at the home of a Black SALA physician. I was presenting my work alongside two other panelists: one a dating and relationship expert, and the other a financial planner. The dating expert spoke first, I spoke second, and the financial manager spoke third. Given that I was speaking after the dating expert, my aim was to move the conversation beyond dating to discuss other aspects of being SALA, such as the friendship networks and processes for acquiring and disseminating wealth, which would then lay the groundwork for the wealth manager. I therefore opened my talk by announcing something along the lines of, "Let's switch gears and extend the conversation about SALAs beyond their dating practices."

The facial expression of a young woman sitting in the front row left me in no doubt of her displeasure. She then backed this up with a comment audible enough for me to hear: "Dr. Marsh is throwing shade." I hurriedly tried to clarify my comments by explaining that my goal on the three-person panel, as it had been throughout my academic career, was to add sociological context and texture to this demographic group while acknowledging that dating among the Love Jones Cohort is an important topic.

My research has not always been well received by those in the Black community and/or those who are pro-marriage, regardless of race or ethnicity. Some interpret my research as suggesting that young Black adults, especially women, should neither marry nor have children. To make it clear, I am neither anti-marriage nor anti-children. I am simply reporting demographic data, incorporating personal narratives from the Love Jones Cohort, and inserting several systemic factors into the conversation. I have presented data and findings on SALAs and the Love Jones Cohort in various contexts (including conferences, media interviews, and podcasts)[8] and, on occasion, have been met with angry responses, whether in person or by email. Responses range from "Dr. Marsh, you are bringing down the Black race by not promoting the Black family, Black marriages, and Black love," to "Dr. Marsh, you are a bitter single Black woman and a man-hater."[9]

These interactions demonstrate how the issue of dating among SALAs can be an emotive topic. Consequently, it can often feel like a balancing act having to juggle some people's desire to discuss "Why are Black women *not* getting married?" with my intellectual curiosity to move beyond such a question. My overarching desire is to advance a more robust structural understanding of this demographic group, as well as their presence and lifestyle in the Black middle class. This book represents my commitment to doing just this while at the same time maintaining the delicate balancing act such an endeavor requires. Next, I offer a cursory profile of the members of the Love Jones Cohort.

---

[8] Conference presentations include, but are not limited to, American Sociological Association, Population Association of America, Association of Black Sociologists. Media appearances include, but are not limited to, CNN, *The Washington Post*, and National Public Radio.

[9] It should be noted that not all the responses are negative, and that many people express enjoyment of my research. Years ago, a supporter lightheartedly nicknamed me "Dr. Love Jones."

Introducing the Members of the Love Jones Cohort

1 Adoriah (32) is a primary-grade schoolteacher and has taught in both Maryland and Washington, DC. She knew from a young age she was destined to work with children. She loves traveling, reading, shopping, and arts and crafts. Although engaged at the time of the interview, she identifies as SALA.

2 Alexandra (33) works as an analyst in a major public school system and previously worked as an assistant at an accounting firm. In her free time, she loves to write, read, and illustrate, with her favorite genre to write being young-adult fiction.

3 Alexis (31) has been a human resources manager for several years, having worked her way up from being an intern. Her favorite hobbies are running and traveling.

4 Alyssa (48) is a contractor and has a very active social life outside of work. To keep herself healthy, she loves taking hot yoga classes around the Washington, DC, area.

5 Antonio (28) is employed as an IT specialist, which entails interacting with customers at his company. He enjoys attending church, listening to music, and using his computer.

6 Ashley (29) is a program evaluator, assessing programs related to health. She holds a PhD with a background in public health. Her most recent and favorite hobby is doing arts and crafts.

7 Bianca (50) has worked for newspapers in various cities across the country and is currently settled in the Washington, DC, area. She spends her time listening to music, watching movies, and hanging out with friends.

8 Brenay (35) has primarily worked in school settings as an aide or assistant. She enjoys going out with friends and shopping and spending her downtime engaging in sports.

9 Brett (44) previously worked for the federal government and is now self-employed. He enjoys coaching youth sports and riding motorcycles.

10 Carrie (38) is currently self-employed, working in media relations. She loves creative outlets like writing, photography, music, and art.

11 Celeste (35, *estimated*) is a government employee with experience working for multiple federal agencies. Most of her responsibilities include assisting companies in implementing their action plans. Her hobbies include attending concerts or being active through recreational activities.

12 Chelesa (30, *estimated*) is a graduate student in the STEM field. While she spends most of her time as a student or worker doing research, she also attends cultural events and the theater.

13 Christine (35) has a graduate degree in counseling, which she utilizes at a therapeutic group practice. Her responsibilities vary from directing programs to providing therapy to patients. Christine enjoys traveling, reading, and spending time with her family.

14 Darren (31) works as a consultant and likes watching TV in his free time.

15 Dawn (34) currently works with adults seeking employment and has also assisted individuals in need of counseling. She likes to spend time with friends and stay active by playing sports.

16 Deborah (50, *estimated*) loves traveling to new places and cooking. She works at her alma mater and was previously employed in the nation's capital.

17 Derwin (30) works in the entertainment industry and enjoys writing in his free time. He is also a huge sports fan and lives an active lifestyle by regularly going to the gym.

18 Genesis (age unspecified) has worked in a number of establishments, from assistant to management positions. Her current occupation is in brand management. During her spare time, she listens to jazz music and plays table sports, such as ping pong.

19 Glenda (36) enjoys riding bicycles, reading poetry, and swimming. Professionally, she works for the federal government.

20 Grace (35) lives in Virginia, considers herself mildly religious, and works in the legal field. She enjoys hanging out with her friends and family, bowling, and going to happy hours.

21 Gwen (37) works for the local government in the financial sector. In her free time, she enjoys hiking and is trying to make it a more consistent habit.

22 Jamir (42) works as a federal investigator and also provides financial services during his spare time. He enjoys working out and engaging in a number of sports.

23 Jerome (30) currently works at a public affairs firm, handling projects through government contracts. Before falling into his career, Jerome worked at different hotels to put himself through school. He enjoys playing the piano, and researching, as well as reading.

24 Joanna (47) is a communications specialist and has held jobs in several industries using her expertise in writing, editing, and organizing projects. She loves a good book and being outdoors.

25 Joseph (31) is a software specialist. He enjoys researching new information during his spare time, either through reading books or with a computer.

26 Justin (32) enjoys canoeing, hiking, and watching movies. He is currently unemployed. He identifies as Jamaican.

27 Kelsey (40) works in investment and in her free time travels as much as she can. She also works out often.

28 Kendra (30) has worked as an assessment specialist for several years. Her role entails assisting teachers with professional development as well as assessment development. Her hobbies include reading, listening to music, and traveling.

29 Kevin (25) enjoys going to the gym and mentoring youth in his community. Professionally, he works in the management domain for a government entity.

30 Lafayette (52) enjoys skiing and golf and plays a musical instrument. Professionally, he works from home for a technology company.

31 LaToya (37) provides consulting expertise to small businesses and government agencies. She likes to spend her free time with a good book, with her family, and exploring museums and is an on-demand movie service junkie.

32 Layla (47) enjoys going to the spa and dancing. In her professional life, she works for the federal government in a scientific department.

33 Lillian (37) does not have time for hobbies and dedicates her time to work. She spends all of her time running her public relations business.

34 London (40) likes watching nature shows on television in her free time. Professionally, she works on contracts for the federal government.

35 Madison (35) currently works in the school system counseling students on their everyday academic and personal needs. She enjoys

listening to music and attending concerts, shopping, and spending time with her loved ones.

36 Marquez (32) works as an engineer and plays several sports in his free time in adult leagues.

37 Maurice (age unspecified) works as an instructor and in his free time enjoys going to church, listening to music, and attending different festivals.

38 Megan (26) currently works for the federal government, as she has done for most of her professional career. She enjoys spending time with members in her sorority and loves trying foods from around the world.

39 Meisha (42) spends her free time skating, writing, and biking. Professionally, she works as a government contractor and a professor at a local community college.

40 Melinda (50) carries a law degree that she uses in her occupation in the healthcare management field. She loves to entertain and cook and also attends wine tastings and spa visits.

41 Nancy (43, *estimated*) has had many jobs since she was a teenager, from working at a summer camp to interning for the government, with her most recent occupation being a program manager. During her spare time, she enjoys gardening, writing for a local newspaper in the DC area, and traveling the world.

42 Natalie (30, *estimated*) specializes in conducting program and finance audits for a consulting firm. She enjoys various forms of art, from painting to listening to music to cooking new foods.

43 Olivia (54) is an experienced attorney working for the government. In addition, she runs her own fashion business. Olivia loves to read, shop, listen to music, and travel to the Caribbean.

44 Paige (33) works as a consultant and, when she has time off, enjoys reading and hanging out with friends. She is also an avid traveler and takes international trips as much as she can.

45 Patricia (56) has spent a number of years doing investigation work for the government and is currently self-employed. In her downtime, she enjoys networking and traveling.

46 Peter (31) works for the government and enjoys playing ping pong as a hobby. He defines himself as a proud member of the LGBTQ community.

47 Rasheed (48) has worked for the government in his current position for almost 30 years. His hobbies include singing, going to the movies, and playing or watching sports.

48 Reggie (30) is a financial analyst with the federal government, who enjoys hanging out with friends and defines himself as a "outdoorsy" type. He likes go-carting, rock climbing, and zip-lining and is from a West African country.

49 Renita (52) is a social worker, who has spent her career helping underserved populations. She enjoys going on shopping sprees and occasionally watching mobster movies.

50 Richard (30) works as an administrator for a private company in the Washington, DC, area. He is an avid TV watcher and keeps up with several shows, as well as college and professional sports.

51 Rick (33) is a project administrator at a private institution of higher education. He recently moved to the Washington, DC, area where his university is located. Rick enjoys doing fitness exercises, attending networking events, and spending time with friends.

52 Robin (49) has been employed as a consultant in the technology business for over a decade. Her downtime is spent eating, reading, and engaging in STEM-related activities.

53 Serenity (50) enjoys attending jazz festivals and considers herself a wine connoisseur. She lives a very active lifestyle and works in the medical field.

54 Shannon (50) works in different jobs while concurrently enrolled in a graduate program, generally in the capacity of a research assistant. She has been playing the clarinet since a young age and also enjoys trying new things such as dancing and learning languages.

55 Sheri (33) enjoys reading, as well as taking workout classes like Zumba and SoulCycle to keep herself in shape. Professionally, she works as a contractor for a government agency.

56 Simone (33) has been employed as a project manager for several years, prior to which she worked in public schools in the Washington, DC, area. She enjoys trying new recipes either on her own or by using cookbooks and has a similar fondness for interior decorating.

57 Tanya (44) used to work in various capacities within the world of media. She is currently unemployed, but is a freelance writer and loves the outdoors. She spends her time exercising, taking pictures, and visiting museums.

58 Tina (30) lives a very active lifestyle. When she is not working, she is either working out or taking walks or finding new bike trails.

59 Tivana (31) is a policy analyst working in healthcare reform at a large consulting firm. She is active in social organizations and enjoys participating in community service.

60 Walter (age unspecified) has worked in a variety of sales positions and is currently employed as a public school teacher. Working in an educational environment has led him to enjoy learning new things. He also watches and attends sporting events in his spare time.

61 Wendy (52) currently works in accounting for the government and has in the past worked for other major finance companies. During her spare time, she enjoys volunteering at various church events, eating at new restaurants, and attending music events.

62 William (age unspecified) works as a product trainer for a major corporation and has done so for a few years. He enjoys working out at the gym and playing sports with friends.

Acknowledgments

Thank you to the Love Jones Cohort. There would be no book without your voice. Thank you to my extended research team. The contribution of Kendra Barber, PhD, a research assistant and scheduler, was beyond measure. She proved to be an essential member on this team. Thank you to the additional research team members: Janet Adesina; Kamini Anbil; Joey Brown, PhD; Jonathan Flores; Kalani Johnson; and Chris-Dé-Vaun R. Parker. Thank you to my undergraduate students who assisted with data analysis: Tamya Anderson, Bailey Covington, Samitra Harrington, Zalika Issiakou, Sagen Kidane, Tyler Sesker, Tamoni Winston, and Katarina "Kat" Yang. I thank additional colleagues and associates who helped bring this book to fruition. My appreciation is heartfelt.

The never-ending support from my parents, Deborah and William Marsh, and two sisters, Kim (Tonya Busby) and Kelli Marsh (along with my brother Stephen Jones), made this project possible. Acknowledgment goes out to the much-needed prayers and words of encouragement from my grandmother, Lillian Marsh; the memory of my grandmother, Lucy Covington; and two grandfathers, Louis Covington and William Marsh. I also thank my aunts: LaVern Moore, Bev Logan, Nancy Howard, Genela Covington, Gwendolyn Taylor, Debra Marsh, Arlene Jones, Roberta Stinson, Johnsie Logan, and Alice Logan. I thank my uncles: James Logan, Walter Logan, Howard Neal, Lorenzo Jones, and Manfred Moore. To the "original ten" first cousins – Robin Bulter, Karen McDaniels, Darren Logan, Brett Logan, Kevin Logan, Shindana Neal, and Shalamar Neal (with my sisters and I rounding out the 10) – I am bringing up the rear, and thank you for looking out for the baby. To Sammy Taylor, Jerry Taylor, Nancy Taylor, and Megan Bridges, who displaced me as the baby: Thank you for your endless support and encouragement.

To my Maryland crew: Thank you for getting me out of the house when I was stressed the most and for having wonderful conversations over dinner that did not center on sociology. Thank you for keeping me in the house and for daily text check-ins during the 2020 global coronavirus pandemic.

To my Los Angeles crew: Thank you for years of support and countless hilarious memories.

To my swimming, running, yoga, golf, and boot camp workout partners: Thank you for the many workouts. They were the fuel necessary for writing and completing this book.

To my academic twin: Thank you for paving a stellar academic path for me to follow. No more long writing days at Wegmans that turned into community meet-and-greets because of your bubbly and inviting person-ality. No more five-hour video chat calls starting at 4:00 AM with me sitting on my porch during COVID-19 while daily checking – although ill-advised – our stocks every hour on the hour.

To my writing group: Thank you for ushering me to the finish line on this project.

To my junior Black middle-class scholars: Please continue to carry the baton forward.

To my fellow Black female scholars: May this book serve as an ode to your scholarship. Whenever possible, I tried to incorporate your work into this manuscript. For those whom I overlooked, please accept my sincere apology. I know it is hard in these academic streets for us. I strive to support you as much as I can. I view this work as a "politics of citation" to #citeblackwomen – a critical praxis and global campaign that "pushes people to critically rethink the politics of knowledge production by engaging in a radical praxis of citation that acknowledges and honors Black women's transnational intellectual production" (Smith et al., 2021).

To my mentors: Thank you for your unwavering support.

To my therapists: I thank you for the conversations and questions you raised as part of my Mental Health Mondays.

To my editors: Ken Barlow, Janet Overton, and Jill Cox-Cordova, thank you for giving my words life.

To my anonymous reviewers: Thank you for your thoughtful and exhaustive reviews. When I received your more-than-15-page, single-spaced reviews, my first instinct was to cry (and I did), eat chips, and cry some more, in that order. I later realized your comments were just what I needed to make this book better. You challenged me to be a more thoughtful and mindful scholar and writer.

To my remaining family members and close friends who are too numerous to name: Words simply cannot express the gratitude I feel for every prayer you prayed, every word of encouragement you uttered, and every ounce of love you showed me through this entire process.

I would be more than remiss if I did not mention several institutions and organizations that offered support one way or another during this journey: City of Refuge; Christ Memorial Church of God in Christ; Compton Adult Day Health Care; Lynwood Developmental Care, Inc.; PJs Coffee (Bowie); Reid Temple AME Church; Wayne Curry Sport and Learning Center; OohRah Fitness; Enterprise Golf Course; University of Maryland (College Park); Carolina Population Center at the University of North Carolina (Chapel Hill); University of Johannesburg; University of the Witwatersrand (South Africa); and University of Southern California.

If I forgot to mention you, please charge it to my head and not my heart.

Now faith is the substance of things hoped for, the evidence of things not seen.

(Hebrews 11:1, KJV)

Introduction

This sociological study centers on the Love Jones Cohort, revealing the ways in which this demographic group live their lives. The term "Love Jones Cohort" originates from the movie *Love Jones* (1997) and incorporates the common demographic term "cohort," which refers to a band of people or those treated as a group.[1] The characters in the *Love Jones* movie are young, educated Black professionals who have never been married, are child-free, and live alone or with unmarried non-romantic friends.

The Love Jones Cohort: Single and Living Alone in the Black Middle Class focuses on the lifestyles of those within the Black middle class who are SALA – single *and* living alone – and how their single status shapes their decision-making processes. While much has been written about both the Black middle class and the rise in singlehood, this book represents a first foray into bridging these two concepts.[2] In doing so, it provides a more nuanced understanding of how intersecting social identities, coupled with social structures, shape five central lifestyle factors of the Love Jones Cohort: (1) defining family and friends, and deciding on whether and how to pursue romantic relationships; (2) articulating the ebbs and flows of being Black and middle class; (3) selecting where to live and why; (4) accumulating and disseminating wealth; and (5) maintaining overall health and well-being.

For this study, 62 Black adults were interviewed over the course of summer 2015, 43 of whom were women and 19 men. Ages ranged from

---

[1] This movie celebrated its 25th anniversary in 2022.

[2] Put another way, as a sociologist and demographer who has published quantitative scholarship on this topic, *The Love Jones Cohort: Single and Living Alone in the Black Middle Class* puts "metaphorical" meat on the "numerical" bones that I have published over the years.

25 to 56, with the mean (average) age being 38. Although women dominated those interviewed, I made the intellectual decision to fashion this book around single Black middle-class adults living alone, including *both* women and men. Where possible, I highlight age and gender differences.

In 2019, I attended a three-day retirement symposium for William Julius Wilson. Wilson is a well-decorated sociologist and Harvard University Professor Emeritus. Social scientists have polarized views of Wilson, with some considering him revolutionary and others viewing him as controversial and conservative. The timing, with fall semester having just started at the University of Maryland, could not have been worse for me to travel to Harvard for the event. In addition to my regular responsibilities as a professor, I was in the middle of grappling with the "so-what" question of this book; training police officers at the Prince George's County Police Department – who patrol one of the wealthiest Black counties in the country – on understanding implicit bias; and immersing myself in the golf culture by volunteering at Enterprise Golf Course (also in Prince George's County) in order to help conceptualize a research project on how Black golfers navigate racism, sexism, and classism on the golf course. However, I decided to attend Wilson's retirement symposium because his scholarship, as well as that of many of his students, were and continue to be essential to my research agenda on the Black middle class.

On the final day of the retirement symposium, Wilson clearly, concisely, and with great passion reiterated the premise of his widely popular 1978 text, *The Declining Significance of Race*. According to Wilson, the book's title garnered more attention than the actual arguments laid out within, prompting conservatives to sing the book's praises and liberals to rebuke it with stinging criticism. However, as Wilson pointed out, once people got around to reading the book, it came under heavy criticism from conservatives – in part due to his emphasis on structural impediments – while liberals gave it an enthusiastic thumbs-up. As he retired from six decades of scholarship, Wilson wanted to state for the record the theoretical assumptions underpinning his book, attempting once and for all to silence his critics by leaving no room for ambiguity. In doing so, Wilson noted that he made two distinct arguments in his book: a class-based argument and a politically driven assertion.[3]

---

[3] For the political assertion, Wilson asserts that "the center of racial conflict and tension has shifted from the economic sector, which characterized American race relations throughout most of our history, to the social political order." Wilson goes on to state that "racial tensions and a manifestation of racism are products of situations. Economic situations.

Wilson spoke passionately about the class-based argument in his closing salutation to the discipline, claiming, "Economic class has become more important than race and determines the life trajectory of Black individuals, which helps to explain the growth of the Black middle class and the increasing divide between the haves and the have-nots in the Black community."[4]

Listening to Wilson, I remembered two pivotal arguments advanced by my colleagues. First, in an interview conducted for the Washington Center for Equitable Growth in 2017, Duke professor and economist (and my mentor, coauthor, and friend) William "Sandy" Darity Jr. notes:

The core of stratification economics offers a structural rather than a behavioral explanation for economic inequality between socially identified groups. . . . Stratification economics goes against the grain of trying to argue that the kinds of differences that we observe, and economic outcomes are attributable to cultural practices or some forms of dysfunctional behavior on the part of the group that's in the relatively inferior position. . . . Economists and other social scientists must look at social structures and policies to really explain why those differences exist.[5]

Second, in the opening lines of the 2015 *Annual Review of Sociology* article, Distinguished University of Maryland Professor Emerita Patricia, and author of the often-cited *Black Feminist Thought*, Hill Collins (2015) illuminates the interdependent concerns of intersectionality as a field of study, analytical strategy, and/or critical praxis: "The term intersectionality references the critical insight that race, class, gender, sexuality, ethnicity, nation, ability, and age operate not as unitary, mutually exclusive entities, but rather as reciprocally constructing phenomena" (p. 1).[6]

It was at this point that I truly understood the sociological significance of this book. The manuscript draws on the Love Jones Cohort's intersecting identities to highlight how structural impediments, social structures,

---

Political situations. Social situations. In previous years, the situations creating racial tensions and conflict were concentrated in the economic sector. Today they are featured in the political sphere and in social situations involving housing, schooling, criminal justice and, most recently, immigration." Wilson ended this section of his symposium speech by emphatically noting that these were the arguments he was making in 1978, when *The Declining Significance of Race* was published.

[4] For a complete narrative of Wilson's retirement reflects, visit The Hutchins Center for African and African American Research at Harvard University.

[5] For the complete interview with Dr. William "Sandy" Darity Jr., visit the following website: https://equitablegrowth.org/equitable-growth-in-conversation-an-interview-with-william-a-darity-jr-sandy-of-duke-university/

[6] For writing from early Black feminists such as Sojourner Truth, Frances Ellen Watkins Harper, and Anna Julia Cooper, see Guy-Sheftall, B. (1995).

policies, and practices shape their existence, emergence, acceptance, and inclusion as a lifestyle and family within the larger Black middle class.

In 2012, a popular text by sociologist Eric Klinenberg entitled *Going Solo: The Extraordinary Rise and Surprising Appeal of Living Alone* was published in which the author addresses the well-documented rise in singlehood as a social *change*, not a social *problem*. In particular, Klinenberg finds that only a small percentage of his living alone respondents are isolated or lonely.[7] Even so, Klinenberg does not draw much attention to any specific race or class dimensions. Meanwhile, in 2019, sociologist Elyakim Kislev published a book examining the emotional well-being of singlehood entitled *Happy Singlehood: The Rising Acceptance and Celebration of Solo Living*. Kislev studies the levels of happiness of people who have been married versus those who never married *and* how the aging process influences the latter's acceptance of their relationship status. In doing so, he suggests that as they age, the never married emerge as happiest, due in part to their ability to build solid friendship networks over time (Kislev 2002a; Kislev 2022b). Just a month following publication of Kislev's book, I joined friends on a spring break trip to Jerusalem, where Kislev resides. Always up for an opportunity to discuss singlehood, I sent Kislev an email a few days before leaving the States, and upon receiving a warm response, I arranged to meet him in downtown Jerusalem.

The pending meeting had me mildly nervous, as I was concerned the criticism I was planning on leveling at his book – the omission of race – might not be well received. Yet the conversation was refreshing, bouncing around from critique to future collaborations, back to criticisms, to laughter, and to long periods of silence signaling our intense thinking. We walked away from this meeting acknowledging that singlehood might look differently for Black people in countries where they do not form the majority – globally and in the US. – compared to the dominant group, in this case white people.[8] These racial differences are due, in large part, to structural factors.

---

[7] www.smithsonianmag.com/science-nature/eric-klinenberg-on-going-solo-19299815/

[8] Throughout the book, I capitalize "Black" but not "white." My rationale stems from that put forth by the Associated Press (AP). In September 2020, AP changed its usage rules by capitalizing Black when discussing race and culture, while choosing not to do the same for whites. Their rationale was that "white people in general have much less shared history and culture, and do not have the experience of being discriminated against because of their skin color." https://apnews.com/article/entertainment-cultures-race-and-ethnicity-us-news-ap-top-news-7e36c00c5af0436abc09e051261fff1f

In 2011, prior to these two groundbreaking books on singlehood making waves in the academic and commercial worlds, Kate Bolick – later the author of a 2015 book on singlehood – wrote a piece for *The Atlantic* titled, "All the Single Ladies."[9] In the article, Bolick states:

Recent years have seen an explosion of male joblessness and a steep decline in men's life prospects that have disrupted the "romantic market" in ways that narrow a marriage-minded woman's options: increasingly, her choice is between deadbeats (whose numbers are rising) and playboys (whose power is growing). But this strange state of affairs also presents an opportunity: as the economy evolves, it's time to embrace new ideas about romance and family – and to acknowledge the end of "traditional" marriage as society's highest ideal.

The undercurrent of the article seems to suggest that white single women are *choosing* to be single by embracing an "ideology that values emotional fulfillment above all else" and "the elevation of independence over coupling" (Bolick, 2011). By contrast, *The Love Jones Cohort* considers how racism, discrimination, and gender racism make it less clear whether singlehood among Black people – especially Black women – is by choice or circumstance.

In 1987, sociologist Bart Landry wrote his seminal book, *The New Black Middle Class*. In his study, Landry asserts that Black women's best option for financial stability and reaching middle-class status is marrying and joining the labor market outside the home alongside their working husbands. Landry assumes the association between marriage and middle-class status as necessary for the economic stability of the Black middle class. *The Love Jones Cohort* provides counterevidence to some of Landry's earlier claims by asserting that a subset of Black SALA households have solid incomes, degrees, occupations, assets; are child- and spouse-free; and count themselves as members of the Black middle class.

Collectively, these theoretical frameworks, assertions, and arguments help shape the premise of this book. Given the anti-Black sentiment that exists in social institutions, as well as structural forces, systematic inequalities, institutional racism, gendered racism,[10] and stratification, the reasons

---

[9] Named after Beyonce's song "Single Ladies (Put a Ring on It)". www.theatlantic.com/magazine/archive/2011/11/all-the-single-ladies/308654/

[10] The term "gendered racism" was coined by critical race, gender, and leadership scholar Philomena Essed (1991) and refers to the notion that racism is gendered in ways that mean the everyday lives of Black women and men are impacted differently (Essed, 1991, p. 31). Although not exhaustive, other evolving terms, concepts, frameworks, or analytical tools related to intersectionality and gendered racism include: *structural gendered racism* ("the totality of interconnectedness between structural racism and structural sexism in

for singlehood can be different for Black people compared to other racial or ethnic groups. Thus, the resulting overarching theme of *The Love Jones Cohort* is to investigate the lifestyles and distinctiveness of Black women and men who are both SALA and in the Black middle class.

In writing this book, I grappled with whether to use the term SALA to refer to Black women and men who are single and living alone, or instead utilize "solo," which is more often used in the US media when naming the general population of singles. Ultimately, I decided to use SALA for two key reasons. First, the experiences of Black people are different from the general US population. Conflating the two terms essentially collapses the experiences of Black communities into a white framework, discounting the effects of institutional racism and systematic inequalities faced by Black Americans. Second, Black SALAs have traversed singlehood for decades and, percentage-wise, started outpacing their white counterparts in 1960 – a racial gap that has widened in every decade since (Ruggles et al., 2022). Specifically, at the start of the twentieth century, 16% of Black adults and 20% of white adults had never been married; by 1960, there was racial crossover; and by 2019, 45% of Black adults had never married compared to 24% of their white counterparts. (See Appendix A for an illustration of the data.) Changing SALA to solo dilutes these demographic shifts, potentially undermining the path Black SALA pioneers may have paved for the solo generation.[11]

shaping race and gender inequities") (Luna & Pirtle, 2021); *gendered anti-Blackness belonging* ("the institutionalized ideologies and everyday practices that structurally place African descendant women as out of place, and Other or nonhuman, against which whiteness is measured as structurally in place and normative (Kilomba, 2021)" (Curington et al., 2021); *structural intersectionality* ("the consequences of multiple systems of oppression, involving systematic subordination and exclusion of marginalized groups with respect to resources, opportunities, and freedoms in major social institutions") (Homan et al., 2021); *New Jane Crow* (draws from the term *Jane Crow* by Pauli Murray and "symbolizes the connection between the blatant disregard of civil liberties and constitutional protections of African Americans during the post-Reconstruction period and the current plight of women") (Goodwin, 2021); *misogynoir* ("describes the ways anti-Black and misogynistic representation shape broader ideas about Black women, particularly in visual culture and digital spaces) (Bailey, 2010, 2021; Bailey & Trudy, 2018); *double jeopardy* (to address the dual oppressions of racism and sexism that continued to disenfranchise Black women) (Francis Beal, 1988).

[11] From its inception, feminism excluded Black women. One response led to Sojourner Truth to demand "Ain't I a woman?" in a speech in 1851 delivered at the Women's Rights Conventions in Akron, Ohio. Another response was *Black Feminist Thought* by Patricia Hill Collins in 1990. *The Love Jones Cohort: Single and Living Alone in the Black Middle Class* represents a similar type of response to singlehood. The singlehood movement and scholarship seem to be taking on a similar trend of exclusion and a white orientation. An

The Love Jones Cohort seeks to address these gaps in the literature while centering the voices of those who are SALA in the Black middle class. In doing so, the book moves beyond merely exploring dating practices, marital status, and who is having children or not, by engaging in a more nuanced and intimate look at the lifestyles of the Love Jones Cohort and how structural forces shape their choices and lives.

The Love Jones Cohort Term

Recent media portrayals suggest that the Black middle class has a new face. Previously, the media stereotype for the middle class – whether Black or white – had been the married couple with children. For the Black middle class, this was exemplified by the Huxtable Family from *The Cosby Show* (1984–1992), a sitcom following the lives of a father (an obstetrician), a mother (a corporate attorney), and five happy, intelligent, and adorable children. Then, in the 1990s, a surge of television sitcoms and films arrived, depicting Black middle-class characters of a quite different demographic profile. These characters were twenty-something educated professionals who had never been married, were child-free, and lived alone or with an unmarried friend or two.

The first of these was the sitcom *Living Single* (1993–1998), which centered on the lives, loves, and careers of six Black friends living in a Brooklyn brownstone.[12] *Girlfriends* (2000–2008), another popular sitcom, revolved around the lives and loves of four Black women with a similar demographic profile to the principals of *Living Single*. More recent televisual entries centering on singles include *Being Mary Jane* (2013–2019), which followed a young Black cable news anchor, and *Insecure* (2016–2021), in which Black female best friends deal with insecurities, career and relationship challenges, a seemingly endless series of uncomfortable everyday experiences, and a variety of social and racial issues relating to the contemporary Black experience.

Meanwhile, on the big screen, films depicting this new demographic profile include *The Brothers* (2001), *Two Can Play That Game* (2001), and *Deliver Us From Eva* (2003), all of which followed in the wake of *Love Jones*

---

orientation also found in music, with the appropriation of rock 'n' roll by Elvis Presley. Yet few know the gospel singer and electric guitar player Sister Rosetta Tharpe as the godmother of rock 'n' roll and/or "the original soul sister."

12 *Friends*, following the lives of six white twentysomething educated professionals living in Manhattan, premiered the *following* year and ran until 2004.

(1997), starring Larenz Tate as an up-and-coming poet and Nia Long as a talented but recently unemployed photographer. *Love Jones* follows the two lead characters, as well as their friends and acquaintances, as they pursue careers and lovers, and deals with relationship decisions, premarital sex, personality and physical characteristic preferences, gender income differentials, and the realization that growing old and single might have health implications. The film remains a definitive, frequently referenced staple movie within Black culture. This is not only because it is endearing and well acted but also because more than 25 years later, it remains relevant.

The demographic represented in these films and sitcoms is what Sandy Darity Jr. coined, and I am calling "The Love Jones Cohort" – a term that was developed over coffee on a hot and humid summer day in 2016 in Chapel Hill, North Carolina. I was discussing with Sandy, my mentor and preceptor for my postdoctoral position in the Carolina Population Center at the University of North Carolina, how, on both the big and small screens, I was noticing a demographic shift in Black protagonists away from married couples to single adults. As we talked about the idea that *Love Jones* depicted exactly the group I was interested in studying, Sandy suggested, "Well, you can play on words by integrating your demographic training and interest in the movie by calling this group 'The Love Jones Cohort'." I quickly agreed, and just like that the term was born.

On the one hand, the terms "SALA" and "Love Jones Cohort" are not interchangeable.[13] Whereas SALA refers to household composition and can be attributed to Black households of any socioeconomic status or class group, the Love Jones Cohort directly relates to household type (SALA) *and* socioeconomic status (middle class).[14] On the other hand, two terms that are interchangeable and used throughout the book to represent this demographic group are the Love Jones Cohort and the Cohort (with a capital "C"). Likewise, never married, unmarried, single, and SALA are also interchangeably used to represent those who have never been married and are either living alone or with individuals they have no romantic connection with.

---

[13] I am not using the term "cohort" in the demographic sense of a birth cohort, but simply as a group or band of individuals who have some characteristics in common.

[14] The term "SALA" should be applied to Black groups. It can also be applied to other racial and ethnic groups that have been systematically disadvantaged – globally and in the USA – such as Indigenous and Latinx communities in America. I am also open to any group using the term SALA, as long as they are aware and actively fighting against racism in all of its forms.

In my previous quantitative work on the Love Jones Cohort (Dickson & Marsh, 2008; Marsh et al., 2007; Marsh & Iceland, 2010; Marsh & von Lockette, 2011; Marsh & Peña, 2020), I developed a Black Middle Class Index (BMCi) to measure class status. In this index, I define the Cohort as both Black women and men; aged 25 to 65; never married; no children; either living alone or with individuals they have no romantic connection with; with a professional occupation and a college or postsecondary graduate degree; with a household income at or above the median for Black households; and a homeowner (see Appendix B for additional information).

Should all these criteria be met, an individual receives the highest possible score of four, which is necessary to be considered part of the Love Jones Cohort. Any score lower than this disqualifies an individual from inclusion in the category. For example, a hypothetical young professional woman, whom we will name Aretha, makes over $150,000 a year, holds a master's degree in Marketing, works at a marketing firm, and *leases* a pricey loft overlooking the Potomac River at the National Harbor in Prince George's County. According to the BMCi, Aretha would *not* classify as a member of the Love Jones Cohort. Despite her high income and affluent lifestyle, she has no reported assets such as a home, business, stocks, or retirement accounts. This decision is steeped in the previous Black middle-class literature. Scholars argue that lack of such wealth – a stock of assets owned at a particular time and/or resources inherited across generations – produces a fragility within the Black middle class (Oliver & Shapiro, 2013) and promotes a wealth disparity across the Black and white middle class (Addo & Darity, 2021; W. Darity Jr. et al., 2021).

The original data for the BMCi derive from the 1980, 1990, and 2000 U.S. Decennial Census. Subsequential data analysis stem from the 2010 and 2014 American Community Survey (ACS). The race variable was Black only, with mixed-race individuals excluded from the original quantitative dataset.[15] The sex variable included only males and females.[16]

---

[15] In my larger research agenda, I compare various household types in the Black middle class, such as married couples versus SALA. Given this, I focus on monoracial Black households for statistical comparisons, while acknowledging that the experiences of multiracial SALAs are as important as monoracial SALAs.

[16] The Census has made progress in some areas but not in other ones. As I write this book, the U.S. Census Bureau is still investigating whether to include gender identity on future data collection (Holzberg et al., n.d.). While people have the option to identify a relationship as same sex, there are still no viable options for those who were gender nonbinary or gender nonconforming. www.census.gov/newsroom/press-kits/2020/2020-

The age variable ranged from those potentially entering the labor force (age 25) to those leaving, or preparing to leave, the labor force (age 65).[17] In several of my quantitative publications, this broad age range has also been purposeful in capturing the narrower primary childbearing age for women as well as the preretirement age for both women and men.[18] The never-married variable captured those who had never made the step from single to married.[19] Similar to including both women and men in the sample, I made the intellectual decision that there is a substantive difference between those who have been exposed to marriage, even if it has ended due to separation, divorce, or death, versus those with no exposure. The living alone variable encompasses those who are not living with a romantic partner but may have a non-romantic housemate.[20]

The Census Bureau divides households into two categories: family and nonfamily: "A nonfamily household consists of a householder living alone (a one-person household) or where the householder shares the home exclusively with people to whom he/she is not related" and "[a] family is a group of two people or more (one of whom is the householder) related by birth, marriage, or adoption and residing together; all such people (including related subfamily members) are considered as members of one family."

At the national level, using the 2014 American Community Survey data to update my original BMCi, 13% of all Black middle-class households in 2014 were comprised of the Love Jones Cohort, a percentage that has increased every decade since 1980.[21] Closer inspection of the Love Jones Cohort households reveals clear gender differences, with women making

census-lgbtq.html#:~:text=Every%2010%20years%2C%20the%20U.S.,a%20relationship%20as%20same%2Dsex.

[17] In the national quantitative data, I was able to analyze data from those aged 25 to 65. In the qualitative data, even with heavy recruitment of those over the age of 55, the age range was limited to those aged 25 to 56. Those of any age can be members of the Love Jones Cohort.

[18] In the quantitative data, I was able to determine if a child or children lived at home with an individual. I was not able to parse out whether they had children who were not present in the house. In the qualitative data, those who had children, living with them or not, were excluded.

[19] Except for one female interviewee who married "really, really young" and the marriage ended shortly thereafter, they are included in the sample.

[20] My living alone classification aligns with the Census Bureau definition of a nonfamily in reference to a child or children: "a householder living alone (a one-person household) or sharing the home exclusively with people to whom he/she is *not* related by birth (child or children), marriage, or adoption and residing together" and diverges in reference to a housemate(s) – they can be related through birth (sibling or siblings).

[21] The Love Jones Cohort was 6% of all Black middle-class households in 1990, 10% in 2000, and 13% in 2010.

up 69% of all such households, having dominated the category for the past four decades.[22]

The Study

The 62 interviews were conducted during the summer of 2015. Interviewees were targeted through professional and personal organizations, such as the National Black MBA (Master of Business Administration) Association, National Coalition of 100 Black women, 100 Black Men of America, and Black Greek organizations. The assumption was that those associated with said organizations would have at least a bachelor's degree. The aspirational sample would consist of those identifying as Black (only), aged between 30 and 60, living either alone or with individuals they had no romantic connection with; never married; and self-identifying as middle class.[23]

Potential interview interviewees were first contacted by me via email, with the purpose of the study explained as being, "To examine the experiences and perceptions of those who are single and living alone and members of the Black middle class." This advertisement email script was sent to 163 individuals and 27 national organizations.[24] Once interested individuals responded, the scheduler – a PhD graduate student in the sociology department at the time, now Dr. Kendra Barber – sent a

---

[22] For gender comparison by year, in 1980 the Love Jones Cohort was comprised of 58% women and 42% men. In 1990, these proportions remained relatively stable for both women and men. By 2000, the share of women was increasing, with the Love Jones Cohort comprising 64% women and 36% men. In 2010, women comprised 70% and men 30% of the Love Jones Cohort.

[23] On September 18, 2022, the first day of unmarried and single Americans week (September 18–24), the U.S. Census published a press release stating, "Did you know that nearly 50% of US adults are single?"census.gov/newsroom/stories/unmarried-single-americans-week.html. Within this same week is a pivotal day for Black women. In Chapter 1, the notion of equal payday is discussed. In general, equal payday between men and women is March 2022. For more information, see www.census.gov/newsroom/stories/equal-pay-day.html. According to research by the American Association of University Women, September 21, 2022, a day that also falls within unmarried and single Americans week, is Black Women's Equal Pay Day. Put differently, the average Black woman has to work a whole nine months (264 days) to make what the average white non-Hispanic male made in 2021. For more information, visit: www.aauw.org/resources/article/black-women-and-the-pay-gap/

[24] Some of the national organizations we reached out to included: Congressional Black Caucus Foundation, Inc; National Association of Black Social Workers, Inc.; National Association of Black Journalist (office on UMD campus); and National Caucus and Center on Black Aging, Inc.

follow-up email explaining our interest in interviewing single (never married) Black women and men aged 30–60. As a research team, we settled on the 30–60 age range for the initial recruitment emails. In case we received inquiries outside this age range, we were willing to expand to a five-year range on the upper and lower limits for a revised range of 25–65. This flexibility allowed us to stay within the age range for my quantitative work on this demographic group. Similarly, in our recruitment emails, as a research team, we decided not to ask about assets and to avoid being intrusive; instead, we made the assumption that the vast majority held assets – more than three quarters of the Love Jones Cohort reported one or more asset.

Interviews averaged approximately 60 minutes – though the exact time varied between interviewees – and were semi-structured, with follow-up probing questions asked. While interviewees had the right to decline being audio recorded, no one took up this offer, and all interviews were transcribed. Interviewees were constantly reassured that their identity and responses would remain confidential, and that their participation was voluntary. To protect interviewees' privacy and reassure them that their identities would not be revealed, pseudonyms were assigned. Where necessary, certain identifying markers are kept vague and/or ambiguous to ensure confidentiality – for example, the actual name of organizations where interviewees hold memberships are not provided. At the conclusion of the interview, interviewees were asked to voluntarily provide five names of friends, coworkers, associates, and/or family members who may be willing to participate in the study based on the research design's selection criteria (known in sociology as a snowball sampling technique).

All interviewees lived in Washington, DC's metropolitan area, which includes parts of Virginia and Maryland (known as the DMV). According to the Census, the DMV is the sixth most populous metropolitan statistical area in America (U.S. Census, 2021). Washington, DC, is surrounded by a "beltway" – a road that circles the city and surrounding areas. Neighborhoods inside the beltway tend to be more expensive, as they include access to many of the metropolis' amenities: multiple means of public transportation; a wide variety of entertainment, restaurants, and shopping options; educational institutions at all levels; and jobs. This metropolitan area includes some of the highest percentages of individuals living alone in the United States. Additionally, 5 of the 10 richest Black neighborhoods in the United States are in Prince George's County, Maryland, a suburb of Washington, DC (Brown, 2015).

Several interviewees had a connection to Prince George's County, with some having grown up there, others having family there, and still others currently living there. The suburb has a rich history as a research site for scholars interested in Black middle-class families and households (Lacy, 2007; Landry, 1987, 2018), and over the past decade or so has sparked additional intellectual interest around housing, policing, and governance in majority Black jurisdictions (Anacker et al., 2012; Hutto & Green, 2016; Lacy, 2012; Simms, 2019, 2021). Although one of the wealthiest Black counties in America, Prince George's County still contains structural forces and systemic factors that reinforce racial inequalities. For example, in 2015, *The Washington Post* published a three-part series on how institutional racism has played, and continues to play, a central role in the wealth of Black families following the housing crisis of 2007–2008 (K. Kelly et al., 2015).

A couple of caveats. First, while 74 interviewees were initially interviewed for this study, 12 had to be excluded for various reasons, ranging from having previously been married to having at least one child (meaning they did not fit the study's criteria). Second, although recruitment efforts were made, the sample includes only one respondent who openly identified as part of the LGBTQIA+ community.

While such theories and terms as Intersectionality; Black Feminism; Black Feminist Sociology; as well as Race, Class, and Gender evolve and are debated in scholarly communities, in the broad sense I draw from them as analytical and conceptual frameworks that inform and undergird this study, with multiple interlocking and oppressive social identities considered in tandem (Collins, 2004, 2009; Collins & Bilge, 2020; Crenshaw, 1990; Collins, 2001; Luna & Pirtle, 2021; Nash, 2008).[25] Collins's theory of "the matrix of domination" posits that systems of oppression are interlocking, not simply additive. Deborah King as well as other scholars (A. Y. Davis, 1983; T. Justin, 2021; King, 1988) articulate that multiple jeopardy, and "[t]he modifier 'multiple' refers not only to several, simultaneous oppressions but to the multiplicative relationships among them as well." Put differently, King suggests that "the equivalent

---

[25] https://time.com/5786710/kimberle-crenshaw-intersectionality/. In a 2020 *Time* magazine article, Kimberlé Crenshaw, the law professor at Columbia and UCLA who coined the term "intersectionality" 30 years previously, defines it as "a lens, a prism, for seeing the way in which various forms of inequality often operate together and exacerbate each other. We tend to talk about race inequality as separate from inequality based on gender, class, sexuality, or immigrant status. What's often missing is how some people are subject to all of these, and the experience is not just the sum of its parts."

formulation is racism multiplied by sexism multiplied by classism" (King, 1988, p. 47).[26] While relevant gender and age differences are highlighted, the general focus of the book is on the Love Jones Cohort as a demographic group, and how they assign meaning to their lifestyles based on their intersecting identities.[27]

Once transcribed, the interviews were analyzed using inductive and deductive reasoning, a methodological approach that allowed for the data to be "double fitted" with emergent theory and literature. "Double fitting" is a technique that uses empirical evidence to improve theoretical concepts, while simultaneously using the theoretical concepts to refine empirical findings. The qualitative data was analyzed through multiple iterations of the inductive and deductive coding process (Charmaz, 2006; Corbin & Strauss, 2008; Strauss & Corbin, 1997). Following my previous qualitative work (Marsh, 2013), and in keeping with open-coding techniques, no a priori categories were imposed on the Cohort's narrative data (Strauss & Corbin, 1997). Instead, themes were identified from the narratives. First, my research team, including a dozen students, both graduates and under-graduates, identified themes and developed concepts and propositions represented in the data. To minimize overlap, themes were defined, organized, added, collapsed, expanded, and redefined until an effective coding scheme was developed.

The next round of coding focused on taking the developed themes and superimposing them on the transcripts. To ensure reliability and validity within this thematic analysis – which again drew on methodological approaches in my previous qualitative work (Dean et al., 2013) – a dozen research assistants and I conducted focused coding first separately and then together to check and resolve any discrepancies in our coding. We developed a data matrix, like a spreadsheet or table, with each row reflecting a different respondent and each column corresponding to a dimension of a larger theme (Miles & Huberman, 1994). Individual cells were

---

[26] Furthermore, Angela Davis and King discuss Black women and slavery (A. Y. Davis, 1983; King, 1988). "The sexual exploitation of black women in slavery is a historical example. While black women workers suffered the same demanding physical labor and brutal punishments as black men, as females, we were also subject to forms of subjugation only applicable to women" (King, 1988, p. 47). Also see Berry 2017, Spillers, 1987, and Smith et al., 2021 for the blatant disregard for Black women and slavery.

[27] This decision is based in part on the term "womanist" coined by Alice Walker. The author and activist argues that in celebrating all women, womanists place special focus on issues specific to Black women, men, and families – of which I include SALA households (Walker, 1983).

populated with direct quotes. Additional columns were added to indicate whether a direct quote captured the dimension of the theme in question.

Chapter Breakdown and Objectives

The remainder of *The Love Jones Cohort* is divided into 10 chapters (along with a Conclusion). Chapter 1 provides an overview of the range of scholarly and historical definitions and conceptualizations of the Black middle class, before Chapters 2 and 3 turn to the voices of the Love Jones Cohort, exploring how they define and experience their middle-class status. Chapters 4, 5, and 6 then interrogate the changing demographics of the Black family, the emergence of the Love Jones Cohort, and the ways in which their single status shapes their lifestyle by exploring the SALA acronym more fully. Chapter 7 explores issues of intergenerational mobility within the Cohort, including how they intend to disseminate their wealth in the absence of children, while Chapter 8 delves into the Cohort's wealth-accumulation strategies and challenges, particularly in relation to homeownership and their SALA status. Chapter 9 probes how the Cohort's SALA status and lifestyle informs their decision-making when it comes to choosing where to live, as well as how it shapes their neighborly interactions. Finally, Chapter 10 examines the emotional and mental well-being challenges faced by those in the Cohort, and, within the context of their SALA status, what coping mechanisms they employ.

Ultimately, *The Love Jones Cohort* aims to fulfill four goals: first, to expose community members, researchers, policy makers, and business-people to the Love Jones Cohort, in the hope that they substantively incorporate this demographic group into their conversations, research, policies, and business plans; second, to push people into considering how structural racism plays a role in individual dating and marriage outcomes; third, and closely related to the previous point, to push people into thinking twice before asking the Love Jones Cohort why *they are not* married (and instead consider asking people why *they are* married); and fourth, to highlight the distinctiveness of the Love Jones Cohort relative to other Black middle-class families.

In terms of the social science literature, this book attempts to make three main contributions: first, to improve understanding of singlehood in general, and Black middle class SALAs in particular; second, to provide a more nuanced picture of the Black middle class that includes the large and growing demographic of never-married individuals; and third, to provide insight on how these experiences can influence social policy and future narratives about the Black middle class, Black family, and Black America more broadly.

While it seems increasingly clear that singlehood is becoming a hot research topic for white scholars and a way of life for much of the white population (Bolick, 2017; DePaulo, 2015; Kislev, 2019; Klinenberg, 2013; DePaulo, 2006; Traister, 2016), it is certainly not a new concept, idea, or reality for many Black adults. Generally, the singlehood movement and related scholarship seems oriented toward a white gaze. This book, then, represents an attempt to center on the voices of both Black men and women in singlehood and single studies research.

1

Scholarly Debates on Defining the Black Middle Class

Before turning to the voices of the Love Jones Cohort themselves, it is necessary to outline the scholarly debates, discussions, and controversies surrounding how the Black middle class is defined. In doing so, this chapter will paint the context for many of the key topics addressed by the Cohort in subsequent chapters related to how they view their middle-class status, and how their class status interacts with their SALA lifestyle.

I start this chapter with a quick overview of the distinction that scholars make between class and status, which sets up the necessary framework for discussing how the Black middle class has been measured over the past 120 years. Such debates raise pertinent questions on how class should be captured, if status is a more useful measure than class, whether Black middle classness should be defined separately from other middle classness, and, if so, why.

1.1 Class, Status, and the Middle Class

As mentioned previously, sociologist Bart Landry wrote his highly cited book *The New Black Middle Class* in 1987. Thirty years later, Landry (2018) wrote a follow-up book entitled *The New Black Middle Class in the Twenty-First Century*. In both works, Landry is emphatic about clarifying the distinction between class and status:

Status groups emerge out of the subjective evaluation of community members; classes are based on objective positions within the economic system. This distinction, first made by sociologist Max Weber in his critique of philosopher and economist Karl Marx, does not deny the basic Marxian dichotomy between those who own and exploit investment capital (property) for profit and those who depend on salary or wages for their livelihood (1987).

In Landry's distinction of class and status, he also points at two terms in the writings of Marx that often emerge when discussing the classes: bourgeoisie and proletariat.[1] Simply put, the bourgeoisie (also known as the ruling capitalist class) is made up of the people who control or own the means of production – the owners. The proletariat is made up of the members of the working class who must sell their labor power for a wage or salary – the workers.

In his scholarship, Landry takes a Weberian approach to defining the Black middle class, emphasizing, "Classes emerge not from the subjective values of community members but from the impersonal market dynamics and represent an individual's achieved or inherited economic position" (p. 27).[2] The subjective values Landry mentions are what he considers Weber's idea of social ranking: status. These subjective measures lie "in the criteria used to determine membership eligibility. Unlike the objective economic characteristics of class, status attributes emerge out of the values of group members and thus vary from place to place and from group to group as well as overtime" (p. 26). Examples Landry provides include "family background, address, membership in social clubs and churches, consumption patterns, education, and skin tone" (p. 26), with Landry asserting that though these are some of the "most common traits used by status groups to set boundaries ... the number of status characteristics is theoretically endless" (p. 26).

In his later work, Landry (2018) continues the conversation between Weber and Marx. Specifically, Landry states that in defining the Black middle class, he "follow[s] the approach of Max Weber, who thought of class in terms of position in the economy ... Writing at a time in the early 20th century when corporations were creating large numbers of white-collar jobs, Weber [similar to Marx] recognized the emergence of a new class, one that occupied a place between the bourgeoisie and the proletariat" (p. 2). Landry goes on to argue, "One can further distinguish between an upper middle class of professionals and administrators/executives and a lower middle class of workers in technical, sales, and clerical positions" (Landry, 2018, p. 2). As a sociologist, Landry draws class along occupation lines. Economists, meanwhile, often use income to measure class.

---

[1] Marx also writes about a petty bourgeoisie class (also known as the middle class), made up of small-scale owners as well as workers situated between the bourgeois and proletariat. Marxist theory suggests that with capitalism comes the polarization of the petty bourgeoisie class and society into two classes.

[2] For a more detailed critique of class, status, and caste by Max Weber, see Oliver Cox (Cox, 1950).

Entering the middle-class debate, economist William Darity Jr. and colleagues (2020) discuss defining a middle class starting from a classic Marxism perspective:

In classic Marxism, a "middle class" consists of those persons who lie between the two social classes that define a mode of production . . . Under capitalism, or the "bourgeois mode of production," the middle class was comprised of those persons who were neither capitalists (the "bourgeoisie") nor workers. But this conceptual approach to identification of the middle class rarely has been translated into empirical or operational criteria . . . economists have been inclined to use a narrow empirical standard based upon income for identification of the middle class: those persons in the middle three quintiles of the income distribution. (Darity Jr. et al., 2021, p. 495)

1.2 Historical Definitions and Depictions of the Black Middle Class

Given these issues of class versus status, income versus occupation, and bourgeoisie versus proletariat, as well as the differences between the upper, middle, and lower class, it is imperative that an overview of how the Black middle class has been defined is clearly laid out. Scholars have struggled for decades to decide who among the Black population should be considered middle class. W. E. B. Du Bois initiated the discussion in 1899, with St. Clair Drake and Horace R. Cayton (Drake & Cayton, 1945) later engaging with the conversation in 1945. It was not until 1957, however, that an entire book dedicated to "analyzing the attitudes, behaviors, beliefs, and values of the Black middle class" was published. The book, *Black Bourgeoisie*,[3] written by E. Franklin Frazier, made the argument – later supported by Frazier's protégé Nathan Hare (1965) – that the Black middle class, in trying to emulate their white counterparts, lived in a world of make-believe steeped in conspicuous consumption (people defining themselves by what they possess relative to their peers, and colloquially known as keeping up with the Joneses). This represented the outward expression of one's perceived or real class status (Frazier, 1957; Hare, 1965).

In 1987, Landry's aforementioned seminal book on the Black middle class was published. Both Frazier and Landry were looking at a segment of

---

[3] The website of Simon & Schuster, which more recently reissued the book, notes that *Black Bourgeoisie* was "simultaneously reviled and revered – revered for its skillful dissection of one of America's most complex communities, reviled for daring to cast a critical eye on a section of Black society that had achieved the trappings of the white, bourgeois ideal." www.simonandschuster.com/books/Black-Bourgeoisie/Franklin-Frazier/9780684832418.

Black America considered (by themselves and others) to be part of the middle class. Since the 1990s, there has been a burgeoning number of sociological books (and academic articles) focused on the Black middle class. Topics addressed include: the persistence of living with everyday racism (Feagin & Sikes, 1994); how the healthcare system is not exempt from racism (Sacks, 2018); how Black executives and professionals experience racism in the workplace (Collins, 1997; Wingfield & Alston, 2012); how neighborhoods shape social, political, and economic identities (Clerge, 2019; Gregory, 1998; Haynes, 2008; Jackson, 2010; K. R. Lacy, 2007; Pattillo, 2013); how culture and consumption is understood *within* the Black elite (Banks, 2009; Claytor, 2020); how forces of institutionalized racism continuously undermine individual security (Bowser, 2022); how children are socialized to combat these forces (Dow, 2019); and how young, gifted, and Black college students complicate issues of Black identity (Charles et al., 2022).

Over the years, the lifestyles and ways in which middle-class Black Americans presented in public were considered part of their class identity. Drawing from Frazier, this may suggest a blending in with an existing hegemonic discourse of middle classness, which assigns great value to whiteness – or close to whiteness – and acts as the rubric for all middle classness. Such a discourse calls for the self-policing, self-scrutinizing, and self-correcting of how those in the Black middle class dress, speak, and act in public, to conform to the social norms and values associated with white middle classness. This is known as respectability politics or politics of respectability.

The need to police how Black people act in public and their lifestyles is still present today. For instance, as Black activists and abolitionists protest the killing of Black women and men by law enforcement and others, there are those who have criticized the actions and tactics of such movements (including Black critics acting as self-policing agents), asserting that the Black Lives Matter (BLM) movement is non-respectable (Reynolds, 2015). Others, however, have strongly condemned such assertions.[4]

---

[4] In a *Washington Post* article, veteran civil rights leader Barbara Reynolds (2015) wrote of the lack of respectability politics behaviors employed by the Black Lives Matter movement: "In the 1960s, activists confronted white mobs and police with dignity and decorum, sometimes dressing in church clothes and kneeling in prayer during protests to make a clear distinction between who was evil and who was good. But at protests today, it is difficult to distinguish legitimate activists from the mob actors who burn and loot. The demonstrations are peppered with hate speech, profanity, and guys with sagging pants that show their underwear. Even if the BLM activists aren't the ones participating in the

Furthermore, Black women are constantly policed, by society in general and in some cases themselves, and expected to conform to a performative "lady-like" trope and/or to behave respectably (P. H. Collins, 2004; B. Cooper, 2017, 2018). Sociologist Patricia Hill Collins, in *Black Sexual Politics* (2004), argues that "controlling images" work to legitimize gendered racism in institutional spaces as well as in interpersonal interactions (Collins, 2004; Wingfield, 2007).[5] From a class dimension, "middle-class Black women are often depicted in the context of the following three (negative) categories: (1) 'Black Ladies' whose potentially unrestrainable sexuality is safely confined to a heterosexual marriage; (2) 'educated Black bitches,' who are manipulative and controlling; or (3) 'modern-day Mammies,' who uphold white dominate structures, institutions, or bosses at the expense of their personal lives" (Collins, 2004; Wingfield, 2007). Similarly, sociologist Maryann Erigha (2018), in examining the controlling images of Black women in romantic films, argues that while there has been some progress over time in the media, middle-class Black women have historically been cast in a negative light as educated Black bitches who "cannot find partners because they work too much, have unappealing traits, or do not support men effectively. While educated Black bitches defy some stereotypes, they validate others with their unstable and troubled relationship lives. As domineering matriarchs, educated Black bitches emasculate their often unemployed male partners by wielding their money, power, and sexuality as weapons of control and treating their relationships as sexual conquests. Although these middle- and upper-class character types have desirable careers, their relationship lives lack equivalent satisfaction" (P. H. Collins, 2004; Erigha, 2018; Springer, 2007). Such a depiction seems highly relevant to the challenges and stigma faced by the women of the Love Jones Cohort, as will be explored further in subsequent chapters.

Brittney Cooper, Professor of Women's and Gender Studies and Africana Studies, asserts that when Black women display themselves on their own terms, they are engaging in "disrespectability politics," which can be considered an agentic demonstration of Black women directly challenging respectability politics. In its most basic form and definition,

---

boorish language and dress, neither are they condemning it." Many responded to and condemned Reynold's article.
[5] To uphold white supremacist thinking, legitimate anti-Blackness, and for racial hierarchies sustainability, Black bodies are often characterized as closer to nature (Johnson, 2019; Shantu Riley, 2004), especially Black women (hooks & West, 2016).

respectability politics is the misguided idea that Black people should conform with mainstream (i.e. white) manners, behaviors, and appearances in order to better fit in with wider (again, white) society. Such behavior is also touted as a protective measure from prejudice, discrimination, and racism.

Even President Obama indirectly affirmed the politics of respectability in several of his speeches. In a February 2019 *New York Times* opinion piece, "Why Does Obama Scold Black Boys?," human rights lawyer Derecka Purnell writes about how the former president often talked about Black people taking personal responsibility for lifting themselves out of poverty, and about Black culture and families being dysfunctional. At the same time, Obama failed to address the systemic forces that deny equal opportunities for – among other things – homeownership, higher education, and well-paying jobs, and how these forces intersect to subjugate Black Americans (Purnell, 2019).

This discussion on respectability politics circles back to the debate on how best to define the Black middle class and the Love Jones Cohort. Several heteronormative assumptions underpin how the Black middle class is often viewed, with the typical Black middle-class family seen to consist of a married couple, 2.5 children, a dog, and a black picket fence.[6] Due to researchers equating the Black middle class with married-couple families, declining numbers in this demographic have led to predictions of a decline in the share of Black Americans who are middle class. Some scholars assert that continued employment of both partners is required for those in the Black middle class to maintain their middle-class status. Put another way, these scholars claim Black wives must participate in the labor force if they are to secure middle-class status for their families (Billingsley, 1968; R. B. Hill, 2003; Landry, 2002; McAdoo, 2007). The implicit, even explicit, message to the Love Jones Cohort that arises from this taken-for-granted focus on married-couple families is that, by being SALA in the Black middle class, they are breaking the established norms of respectability politics – essentially, they are actively engaging in disrespectability politics.

This breaking of norms has the potential to spark a broader conversation, something this book attempts to undertake. Specifically, in exploring, celebrating, and embracing heterogeneity within the Black middle class, I hope to question whether there is truly an ideal Black middle-class

---

[6] This alludes to the title of Mary Pattillo's book, *Black Picket Fences*. (The term is usually a white picket fence.)

household type when it comes to family, norms, behaviors, and lifestyles. Furthermore, this book extrapolates what, if any, measure(s) may be useful when it comes to defining the Black middle class and understanding their lifestyles.

In terms of the debate as to whether the definition of the Black middle class should be based on objective or subjective measures – or an amalgamation of both – there are structural issues with these defining variables that should not be overlooked. For example, sociologist Mary Pattillo (2013), who suggests that the parameters of the Black middle class are defined by a combination of objective socioeconomic factors (education, income, occupation) *and* subjective normative judgments. Such subjective measures may include, among other things, where people live, what church they attend, what clubs they belong to, membership of particular people in social groups, and the ability to take yearly vacations.

Objective definitions of the Black middle class often rely heavily on three variables: (1) level of education, (2) type of occupation (managerial or professional versus nonprofessional), and (3) amount of income. Yet such measures are riven with race, gender, and gendered racism constraints and contradictions, which can heavily impact their application to the Black middle class, including the Love Jones Cohort.

In general, there is a racial wage gap in the U.S. A 2020 report by the Economic Policy Institute states that the Black–white wage gap is stubborn and persistent over the last four decades. The study goes on to say, "Black-white wage gaps are large and have gotten worse in the last 20 years" (Gould, 2020). Likewise, social scientists point to a stubborn and persistent gender wage gap. This further complicates matters when it comes to the Love Jones Cohort, which is dominated by Black women who may therefore be challenged by both the gender wage gap and the racial wage gap (Wingfield, 2020).[7]

In 1995, social scientists Melvin Oliver and Thomas Shapiro made compelling arguments for adding a wealth measure as a necessary indicator for defining the middle class. In their 2020 book, however, authors William Darity Jr. and Kirsten Mullen eloquently document the devastating, systemic racial wealth disparities that lead to a fragility of the Black middle class, and even go as far as questioning the latter's existence (Darity Jr. et al., 2021; W. A. Darity Jr. & Mullen, 2020). Setting out their case for reparations for Black Americans, meanwhile, Darity and Mullen (2020)

---

[7] www.theatlantic.com/business/archive/2016/10/79-cents/504386/

boldly state that "Black [Americans] cannot close the racial wealth gap by independent or autonomous action."

While giving a brief overview of how others have defined the Black middle class, and some of the problems arising from existing definitions, as well as the differences between class (more objective criteria) and perceived social status (more subjective criteria), I have yet to explicitly explain how I define the Black middle class. I have deliberated and have varying views on how I define the Black middle class. Quantitatively, I define the Black middle class based on four strict objective measures (education, income, occupation, and wealth). Qualitatively, at the inception of this research project, my assumptions were to define the Black middle class based on an amalgamation of both objective and subjective measures. At the conclusion of this study, my assumptions did not change. Furthermore, in both my quantitative and qualitative research, I do not explicitly distinguish from the lower, middle (core), and upper Black middle class. Although I am aware of the variability within the Black middle class, in this book, and in my larger body of scholarship, I often use the term "middle class" to signify the "middle class and beyond." From my perspective, such a term captures the lower, middle, and upper middle class.

The staunch objective measures in my BMCi, which have also been used in other various scholarly definitions of the Black middle class, will assist in our understanding of how the Love Jones Cohort incorporates such measures into their definitions of the Black middle class. It is important to also mention some of the inequalities, inequities, and implications that undergird these variables that comprise some definitions of the Black middle class.

1.3 Education, Profession, Income, and Homeownership

The education indicator in the BMCi included a college degree or higher. In 2019, 26% of Black Americans, age 25 and older, held a bachelor's degree or higher – an increase from 20% in 2010. According to 2019 national data, the percentage of Black adults with an advanced degree remains abysmally small, with only 8% of Black adults, age 25 or older, having master's degrees. This percentage rate drops to a mere 1% at the professional and doctoral degrees level (U.S. Census Bureau, 2019). When this same data is disaggregated by Black women and men, both genders report similar percentages for four-year degrees (16.43% versus 16.72%) and doctorate (1.11% versus 1.04%) degree, while Black women edge out

Black men at the master's (9.30% versus 5.82%) and professional (0.86% versus 0.48%) level (U.S. Census Bureau, 2019).

The professional occupation variable in the BMCi was derived from the 1950 occupational prestige score classification (Marsh et al., 2007), in which scores ranged from 20 to 80. In 2014, the median occupation score was 23 for all Black households (Marsh & Peña, 2017). Bart Landry and I have noted (2011), despite the increasing significance of class, that race continues to depress mobility chances for Black workers, leaving fewer opportunities to attain the most prestigious and lucrative occupations (Landry & Marsh, 2011). According to the U.S. Bureau of Labor Statistics (BLS), in 2020, just 10% of Black workers held management, professional, or related occupations (U.S. Bureau of Labor Statistics, 2020).[8] Sociologists Sharon Collins (1983, 1989, 1997) and Adia Harvey Wingfield (2012), in studying the Black middle class through the lens of Black corporate executives and professionals, found that although Black professionals are given access to managerial and executive jobs, this exposure is tempered with the vulnerable nature of those positions and the discrimination, racism, and gendered racism that continues to permeate the workplaces of white corporate America.

In 2020, according to the U.S. Bureau of the Census, the median Black household income in current dollars was $45,870 (U.S. Census Bureau, 2020).[9] Sociologist Karyn Lacy (2007) has grappled with the social identity complications of the Black middle and upper middle class living and working in white environments, using income to characterize the Black middle class into three different categories: (1) lower middle class, (2) core middle class, and (3) upper or elite middle class. According to Lacy's classifications, and based on 2007 dollars, the annual earnings of these

---

[8] Black workers contend with racism, sexism, and gendered racism in the labor market. Based on limited opportunities for access and advancement in the private sectors, Black workers are often overrepresented in the public sector and various governmental agencies from the beginning to the end of their careers (Sacks et al., 2020; Wilson & Roscigno, 2010; Wilson & Roscigno, 2018). Jamir posits that a woman's occupation could be a telling gauge in determining how she might treat a man, as well as how much she might bring to the table financially: "I do see a lot of difference in certain professions. Teachers are more family oriented or loving and caring and treat men more like the head of the household. I love the way teachers treat men, but at the same time, my investment power should increase with a doctor or attorney." Jamir and his stereotypical tropes about Black women suggest that certain Black professionals – in his case Black women – can be discriminated against in the dating market simply based on the title they hold.

[9] Income in 2020 dollars, adjusted using the Consumer Price Index Research Series Using Current Methods (CPI-U-RS). Households as of March of the following year. For context, the median income for all households, regardless of race, in 2020 dollars was $67,521.

three groups are, respectively: (1) $30,000–$50,000; (2) $50,001–$99,999; and (3) $100,000+ (K. R. Lacy, 2007).[10] Landry, (2018) meanwhile, shows that income represents one of several compensation components within a job, with others including such benefits as "health insurance, paid sick leave, and retirement programs." Taken together, these components can determine a worker's life chances or standard of living. Landry asserts that the more lucrative and stable the compensation package, "the larger the potential living standard accessibility. The quality of one's house, neighborhood, children's education, health care, and leisure compensation are all outcomes of the compensation package attached to one's job" (Landry, 2018, p. 152).

However, in terms of using income as a marker of middle-class status, once race and gender are incorporated into the income measure (as well as the associated compensation package), the attempts to define the Black middle class as a demographic group become a more complicated affair. According to a 2016 *Atlantic* article, professional Black men face a racial wage gap, while their female counterparts are hit with both a racial wage gap and a gender wage gap,[11] something economist Michelle Holder terms a "double gap" (Holder, 2020). The Economic Policy Institute's *Class of 2019 College Edition* report offers stark evidence of these disparities among recent college graduates, showing that since 2000, there has been a widening of the gender wage gap among young college graduates from 11% to 13%. Meanwhile, a 2019 *Forbes* article asserts that while Equal Pay Day (in the USA, the day reflects how far into the new year the average or median woman must work to earn what the average man had earned the previous year) is nominally April 2, "For Black women, Equal Pay Day is actually August 22. This means Black women must work four months more than white women (and eight months into the new year) before earning as much as their white male counterparts made in 2018."[12]

In the BMCi, the homeownership indicator referred to all Black households that own (or are buying) a home. According to a *Washington Post* article, "In 2004, the pinnacle of homeownership in the United States,

---

[10] Roughly, based on the U.S. Bureau of Labor Statistics, Consumer Price Index (CPI) Inflation Calculator, according to Lacy's classifications, and inflated based on 2019 dollars, the crude and approximate annual earnings of these three groups are, respectively: (1) $38,233–$63,722; (2) $63,723–$127,444; and (3) over $127,445. www.bls.gov/data/inflation_calculator.htm.

[11] www.theatlantic.com/business/archive/2016/10/79-cents/504386/.

[12] www.forbes.com/sites/briannegarrett/2019/08/22/on-Black-womens-equal-pay-day-heres-how-women-are-fighting-to-close-the-gap/#4668227d5167.

nearly half of all African American families owned a home, according to census data" (McMullen et al., 2019). Since then, the Black homeownership rate has fallen to, as of the first quarter of 2020, 44% (U.S. Census Bureau, 2020). Given that in 1970, following the civil rights movement and coming into law of the 1968 Fair Housing Act (prohibiting discrimination in the housing market based on race, religion, national origin, and sex, and amended to include handicap and family status), the Black homeownership rate was 42% (U.S. Census Bureau, 2011), there appears to have been little improvement percentage-wise over the past 50 years.

Despite the persistence of structural inequalities complicating any objective measure of defining the Black middle class, based on my BMCi, a subset of Black America can nevertheless be considered middle class. Updating my original research with 2010 data, the Black middle class constitutes just under 14% of all Black households (taking into account householders aged 25–65),[13] a substantial increase from the figure of 6% in 1980. Within this demographic, Black married couples with children have fallen to an all-time low, comprising just a third of all Black middle-class households in 2010 compared to over half (55%) in 1980.

1.4 Marriage and the Black Middle Class

My quantitative research has demonstrated that a married-couple household without children has greater odds of being in the Black middle class than a married-couple household with children. More importantly for the purposes of this book, the research found that the Love Jones Cohort are increasing their share of Black middle-class households, aged 25–65. Using synthetic cohorts and aging them in 10-year intervals, we showed that as the Cohort aged, they continue to hold a steady percentage among Black middle-class households. Given this, one might conclude that the Love Jones Cohort is not some short-lived phenomenon – rather, it is an emerging household type that, if similar trends persist, may one day become *the* dominant household type in the Black middle class (Marsh et al., 2007).

---

[13] Using the 1% sample of the 1980, 1990, and 2000 Integrated Public Use Microdata Series (IPUMS) and the 2010 American Community Survey, we selected both person and household variables for non-Hispanic Blacks (alone) living in non-group quarters. This selection at the person level ensured we were examining households comprised of a Black householder (and Black spouse). For the purposes of this book, we then aggregated the person records to the household level based on a householder age range of 25–65 in order to correspond to the recruited sample.

Despite neoliberals, pro-marriage advocates, and some politicians claiming that marriage can provide the economic and financial benefits necessary to gain immediate access to the middle class, the reality is rather more complicated, especially for middle-class Black women (Council, 2021; Henderson, 2020). Sociologist LaToya Council (2021) and Literary Critic and Cultural Historian Aneeka Henderson (2020), in two separate publications, each use the backdrop of two federal laws to contextualize their arguments on marriage. The two laws in question are the Personal Responsibility and Work Opportunity Act (PRWOA) that penalizes the poor by focusing on individual responsibility for economic and childrearing well-being; and the Defense of Marriage Act (DOMA), which punishes the LGBTQIA+ community by recognizing marriage as being exclusively between women and men. Both scholars argue that these pieces of legislation have had residual consequences for other marginalized groups, in particular middle-class Black women (Council, 2021; Henderson, 2020), with Council stating, "PRWOA and DOMA legislation underscored neoliberalism, or individuals' reliance on personal effort, merit, and resources to attend to social problems beyond their control" (p. 2) – in this case, Black marriage rates. Council further suggests, "Marriage must carry some utility for Black Americans who are trying to navigate gendered racism and racial neoliberalism" (p. 9) and that "marriage provides Black middle-class women access to privileges and resources like safety and kin networks within a U.S. nation-state constrained by racism and sexism" (p. 1).

In analyzing Black art, books, film, and music to explore politicized questions around the crises of the Black marriage and ultimately the Black family, Henderson (2020) coined the term "marriageocracy." The term "unmasks the liberal fantasy that marriage, much like the American Dream, is a fair and equitable accessible competition and exposes it as a cultural logical pervading self-help relationship books, political policy, and broader cultural discourse about marriage, while upholding bootstraps courtship politics and rendering institutional structures entirely inconsequential" (pp. 8–9). Turning the discussion directly toward Black women, Henderson argues, "This nefarious line of thinking disregards their diminished and unequal capital on the marriage market, their queer identities, structural inequalities, and the compelling political and historical pressure placed on them to buckle and succumb to a legal heteropatriarchal union" (p. 9).

Thus, families (and marriages) can protect and perpetuate social inequalities. As Patricia Hill Collins (2019) asserts, "Families may be organized differently from one society to the next, yet families underpin important social functions of gaining citizenship rights, regulating sexualities, and intergenerationally transferring wealth and debt. Family rhetoric and practices organize social inequalities of gender, sexuality, race, ethnicity, religion, class, and citizenship, yet they normalize social inequalities by naturalizing social processes" (Collins 1998, 2001, p. 236).

As this quote implies, the notion that marriage equals higher income and middle-class status has deep political ramifications. The persistent gender wage gap, whereby women earn less than their male counterparts, helps explain why establishing a dual-income household – often through marriage – has generally been considered a reliable pathway into the middle class for women. However, family type in and of itself cannot produce middle-class status: A poor person marrying a poor person does not necessarily produce a middle-class couple. Nevertheless, politicians can and have presented marriage as an anti-poverty strategy.

Historian Renee Romano makes the compelling argument that promoting "marriage as a path to economic advancement for the Black community" is "both unrealistic and stigmatizing to Blacks who do not marry" (Romano, 2018). In substantiating her argument, Romano draws on the work of legal scholar Robin Lenhardt:

As Lenhardt explains, such arguments "vastly overstate the economic benefits of marriage to African Americans in particular" and especially to low-income black families (1355). Indeed, poor families often face a marriage penalty, losing low-income tax credits or welfare benefits if they marry. Moreover, by promoting interracial marriage as the solution to Black women's problems, advocates further reinforce the idea that marriage should be the yardstick for judging the health and success of black people. But "so long as marriage continues to be the metric against which all black loving relationships, married or unmarried, are evaluated, African Americans, at least given current statistics, will continue to fall short." (Romano, 2018, pp. 147–148)

From this point, Romano carried forward Lenhart's arguments,

that the narrative about Black marriage enhancing the quest for full citizenship is in fact wrong and very damaging. Instead, Lenhardt explores how the regulation of marriage has been used as a tool of racial subjugation, a way to impose standards whites consider respectable on people they consider inferior and to stigmatize nonwhite groups that in anyway deviate from these gender and sexual norms. Marriage regulations have also, Lenhardt argued, facilitated the hyperregulation of Black families and served as stigmatized blackness, whether through bans on interracial marriage that communicated that blacks were inferior or in interaction with other forms of regulation, like the welfare system. Yet there has been little interrogation of this deeply held idea that marriage is a pathway of citizenship or racial advancement, and in the contemporary U.S., Lenhardt insists, even as some forms of non-marital relationships are being normalized for non-blacks, African Americans are stigmatized as deviant and lacking in ambition for having lower marriage rates than other groups. (Romano, 2018, p. 147)

As will be seen, such issues surrounding gender and the role of marriage in perpetuating (or otherwise) the Black middle class are highly relevant to the rise of the Love Jones Cohort, particularly given that a substantial majority of its members are Black women. Next, building on the background provided in this chapter, we turn to the voices of the Love Jones Cohort themselves, and begin to unpack how its members go about defining the Black middle class and their place within this demographic group.

How the Love Jones Cohort Defines the Black Middle Class

As discussed in Chapter 1, the definition of the Black middle class has evolved over time. Traditionally, however, the earlier research underlying such definitions has principally focused on Black married-couple families with children and, in doing so, largely overlooked those who live SALA lifestyles. As such, this chapter attempts to address this gap in the literature by interrogating how those within the Love Jones Cohort conceptualize themselves as members of the Black middle class, and also how they define the Black middle class more generally.[1] It also – in conjunction with the following chapter – questions whether the emergence and presence of the Cohort complicates established definitions of the Black middle class.

Generally, those within the Cohort conceptualized middle-classness according to broader definitions of the Black middle class, in terms that align with the scholarship outlining objective, subjective, and a combination of both measures. While most interviewees did not emphasize household or family type within the definition, there was a small minority who did cite family (i.e. married family with children) as a defining measure, suggesting they may be influenced by respectable heteronormative conceptions of what being Black and middle class entails.

Seventy percent of the Cohort's narratives regarding how the Black middle class should be defined involved a compilation of objective and subjective measures. This dovetails with the findings of sociologist Mary Pattillo (2013), who suggests that the parameters of the Black middle class are defined by a combination of socioeconomic factors and normative

---

[1] The initial recruitment email for the research stipulated that we would be "*examining the experiences and perceptions of those who are single and living alone and members of the Black middle class.*" The assumption was those who participated in the study would consider themselves to be middle class.

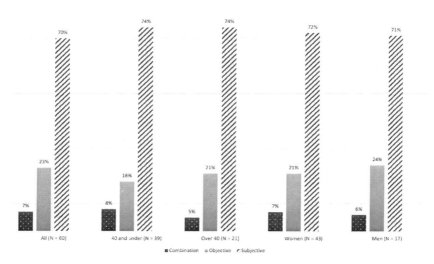

Figure 2.1. Percentage of Love Jones Cohort by age and gender who define the Black middle class with objective, subjective, or a combination of measures

judgments. Illustrative of this, Meisha listed "income, occupation, religious background, religious affiliations, and community activities" in her definition of the Black middle class (though she was one of only a few who explicitly considered religion a necessary element of the definition). In terms of elaborating on the subjective measures used by the Love Jones Cohort, this chapter will focus primarily on how Cohort members defined their middle-class status in relation to the spending of income (objectively measured) on nonessential items (subjectively measured) and securing comfort, and – for a limited number of the Cohort – their attitude toward family/household type. While various other subjective measures of middle-class status were mentioned by Cohort members – including where one lives, the car one drives, how one acts, eating out, extracurricular activities, childhood experiences, home upkeep, networks, and friends – these will be explored in greater detail where appropriate in the subsequent chapters.

Figure 2.1 provides an overview of how the Love Jones Cohort defined the Black middle class.[2] A combination of objective and subjective measures were the most cited across the entire Cohort (70%), while around a

---

[2] The coding scheme for Figure 2.1 treats answers as mutually exclusive. Therefore, the total in each set column equals 100 percent. Those that only mentioned objective *or* subjective measure were coded accordingly. Those that mention both objective *and* subjective measures were coded as a combination measure.

quarter reported only objective measures (23%) or only subjective measures (7%) in their definition. A similar trend was present within age and gender subgroups of the Cohort. This could suggest that the Cohort places value on being able to do things with their objective measures of class, such as taking vacations, joining social groups, establishing membership in particular organizations, deciding where they live, and determining how they live.

2.1 Education

In terms of those who used a combination of objective and subjective measures, Cohort members usually started by describing the objective aspects of Black middle-classness. Kendra, for example, professed that the Black middle class is "[n]ot necessarily just access to having a good job, but even accessibility to the types of colleges and universities that you can attend . . . The circles and the networks that you engage in. I would say access is a huge component [or] characteristic of middle class." For Kendra, it is not merely an objective matter of obtaining a college degree, but more subjectively about which school you go to, the assumption being that certain schools will provide the networking connections and affiliations necessary to attain and maintain middle-class status. Despite proudly proclaiming that 90% of her friends had advanced degrees, however, Kendra was hesitant to think of the Black middle class purely in terms of education or more objective measures, referring also to subjective mutual interests. Here, she cited an article that she had seen on a social media platform: "It was something like forty ways that you know you are Boujie.[3] It was talking about [going to] brunches . . . [and] different poetry events and all these other sorts of things." Kendra admitted to liking these types of activities, and associated such subjective interests with being part of the Black middle class.

Melinda, though happy with her level of educational attainment and its contribution to her middle-class status, cautioned that the success of college-educated Black women created an imbalance in their relationships with Black men: "I see a lot of insecurity with them [Black men]. Because of how Black women have exceeded them in so many ways from education

---

[3] Boujie (a shortened version of the term bourgeoisie) is a slang term meant to suggest that someone appreciates the finer things in life. The word can have negative connotations and is sometimes used interchangeably with such words as pernickety or stuck up, implying the subject of the word is not in touch with the larger Black community.

to money. I think women's [rights] has done a disservice to [Black] women. I'm very much a traditional person. I appreciate the fact I have my own education. I have my own money . . . but I think that in some way's society is off balance right now. In some ways we can go back to the Betty Crocker[4] days because men felt needed."

Thus, despite highlighting her own objective educational and economic attainment, Melinda (50)[5] felt driven to advocate a return to a patriarchal and oppressive family formation that would seem more closely aligned with previous iterations of how the Black middle class was defined. In doing so, her comments echo historical and theoretical assumptions that marriage and dual-earners are required in order to maintain the respectability and success of the Black middle class (Higginbotham, 1994; Landry, 1987). This, I would argue, only goes to validate the necessity and relevance of an intersectional lens when it comes to revisiting how the Black middle class is studied and defined. This demographic group allows for the vantage point of looking simultaneously at advantage (class) and disadvantage (race and gender), given that it helps us to understand how and why inequality is maintained over time and that "inequality mainten-ance proceeds (and is often challenged) based on the actions of persons constrained and motivated by the interlocking (rather than side-by-side or additive) nature of their race, class, and gender statuses" (Clarke, 2011, p. 4). Like sociologist Averil Clarke (2011), sociologist Cassie Pittman Claytor (2020) uses college-educated as a criterion determining member-ship in the Black middle class, rationalizing her decision thus: "Having a college degree dramatically improves Blacks' life chances, while also conditioning their cultural taste and consumption" (p. 24).

Regardless of Melinda's concerns about a perceived gender imbalance and problematic gender dynamics, education remains a central factor in how those in the Love Jones Cohort objectively conceptualize the Black middle class. Gwen acknowledges that "there's an income threshold" in defining the Black middle class and quickly interjects that "there's an education component" to the definition too. Brett, a second-generation member of the Black middle class, considers his parents middle class, who both hold four-year college degrees, while he has a master's degree, and

---

[4] Betty Crocker was a white fictional character developed in the 1920s. She was consistently in the kitchen baking desserts and other foods. For more information, see: www .bettycrocker.com/menus-holidays-parties/mhplibrary/parties-and-get-togethers/vin tage-betty/story-of-betty-crocker. Some might view her as the housewife in heteropatriarchal union.

[5] When I think it is useful, I will state the ages of the quoted Cohort members.

views formal education (and degree attainment) as central to defining the Black middle class.

2.2 Income, Consumption, and Comfort

Shannon, who speaks various languages, slipped between subjective and objective measures to define the Black middle class, referring to "[b]eing a certain grade above the poverty threshold," before going on to list lifestyle measures such as childhood clarinet and tennis lessons: "I personally believe that it's values that define who you are in your income status." Being financially solvent – both in terms of being able to pay for necessities and being able to splurge on the luxuries subjectively perceived as being consummate with a middle-class lifestyle – came up repeatedly among those in the Cohort, with Olivia describing those who are middle class as being "[s]elf-sufficient financially. Able to pay their bills and still have money left over for fun things without having to rob Peter to pay Paul."

Ashley emphasized the fact that objectively middle-class status involved a clear distinction with those at the bottom rungs of the economic ladder (and those at the very top): "It's not that you are living paycheck-to-paycheck; or you don't know where that next meal is coming from. You certainly aren't super rich and you can go on vacation whenever you feel like it." Grace also referred to "not living paycheck-to-paycheck," and placed the emphasis on the subjective items above-and-beyond bare subsistence that formed a key part of her middle-class lifestyle: "If I want to go buy a purse, I can buy a purse. If I want to go on a vacation, I can go on a vacation." In terms of how this played into her SALA status, Grace noted, "I plan for myself and not for the family."

Again, echoing the above sentiments, London observed that those in the middle class "don't worry about the lights being on. They have money to travel. They have money for leisure activities. They have money to put aside for their savings. They're comfortable they're not living paycheck-to-paycheck." This idea of not having to live paycheck-to-paycheck appeared to be a running theme, with Paige describing middle class as having "enough income where I'm not necessarily living paycheck-to-paycheck. I can take advantage of activities that I don't necessarily either (a) have to budget for, or (b) feel as though it's hurting the bank." It is notable that in terms of using income as an objective measure, many Cohort members referenced what Black middle-class status was *not* ("living paycheck-to-paycheck") before going on to reference the (modest) luxuries having a higher income involved.

LaToya – a consultant for the federal government – was explicit and specific in giving income as a key element of Black middle-class status, citing a figure of "anywhere from $120,000 on up to $350,000." It was not clear whether this range was based on an individual or household income. Beyond annual income, LaToya considered herself to be middle class based on her assets and wealth (something explored in greater detail in Chapters 7 and 8). One of her assets was her home, which she referred to as "a gold mine and I'm not going to pull it [equity] out. I bought it for $250,000 and it is worth $400,000 and I'm not touching it until it's time for me to buy other properties." In addition, LaToya had IRAs, mutual funds, stocks, and savings.

In determining what income level constitutes middle-class status, Jamir cited geographic context as being a relevant factor: "So, $125,000 would be significantly different in Atlanta or the Midwest, like Cincinnati, Ohio. If you were making $85,000, you might make it [thrive] in Atlanta, but $85,000 is nothing in San Francisco, New York, or Washington D.C." Gwen, meanwhile, acknowledged that while she would count as solidly middle class in the South, she was unsure if she would classify herself as middle class in the Washington, D.C.'s metropolitan area. Similarly, Bianca asserted that middle-class status can depend on "which part of the country you live in." In connecting middle-class status to geographical context, Jamir, Gwen, and Bianca are alluding to the fact that it may be easier for those in the Black middle class – whether SALA or not – to live comfortably in certain locations in America compared to others, and that those who may consider themselves to be middle class in one place may not be considered so in another. This points to another difficulty in applying income as an objective measure to define the Black middle class, especially in conjunction with subjective measures.

Related to the aforementioned insistence that middle-class status involves not just living "paycheck-to-paycheck" but being able to purchase small luxuries, a number of the Love Jones Cohort gravitated toward subjective ideas concerning lifestyle, comfort, and the avoidance of struggle. William, for example, talked about the fluidity of his middle-classness, claiming while laughing, "I'm not feeling like middle class today. A couple weeks ago, I was feeling like I was middle class, so it really just changes, day by day and week by week. Those unexpected obstacles that come up." Meanwhile, Marquez, in defining middle class as upwardly mobile with "[a] tax bracket between poverty and rich," added, "If they're not struggling." This conception of middle-class status as enabling the avoidance of "obstacles" or "struggling" points to a subjective understanding of middle-classness as granting a certain degree of material and mental comfort.

Carrie, Madison, and Joanna were more explicit in placing comfort at the center of their conception of middle-class status, though they were keen to emphasize that such comfort was not to be equated with financial extravagance, which (subjectively) would fall under the purview of the rich. As Carrie proclaimed, middle-classness equated to "A comfortability in your lifestyle. That you have beyond what you need to meet your basic needs, yet you're not rich or living extravagantly, so you're in the middle." Madison, meanwhile, described a middle-class individual as "[s]omeone who isn't financially comfortable or stable but is striving to live a comfortable lifestyle," while Joanna cautioned "there's a certain comfort level [of lifestyle] there, but you're still at risk of overspending."

As can be seen in some of the previous comments, many in the Cohort used subjective measures, such as small luxury items, vacations, or extracurricular activities, as variables determining Black middle-class identity. In other words, the ability to access these items or activities is a key element of what separates the Black middle class from the wider Black community. This is not to say that those in the Cohort regard purely objective measures as being more or less important in defining whether someone is middle class; rather, their perspective implies that a person's income (objectively measured) plays a role in financing subjective outcomes associated with a perceived middle-class lifestyle and status. This suggests that those in the Cohort are not strictly bound by rigid objective measures of income and education, but instead draw on more dynamic and expressive attributes that are reflective of their SALA lifestyles and the activities they pursue as part of their SALA status.

This line of inquiry is relevant to the notion of "conspicuous consumption" mentioned in the Introduction of this book. While it was economist Thorstein Veblen who initially coined the term in his 1899 writings (W. Darity Jr. et al., 2021; Veblen, 2009), it was sociologist E. Franklin Frazier (1957) who popularized the term and applied it to the Black middle class. However, sociologist Cassi Pittman Claytor (2020) has called into question the pejorative use of this term in the scholarship on the Black middle class and their consumption patterns, arguing that "[f]ocusing only on middle-class Blacks' desire for and acquisition of high-status goods, such as designer handbags or expensive footwear, insufficiently addresses the creative, expressive, and experiential function of their consumption, while also underplaying their *strategic* use of consumption" (p. 29). Claytor goes on to say that "[f]or members of the modern Black middle class, consumption is a means to indulge their middle-class sensibilities and to display their personal style and taste" and "offers them a way to deftly construct an image of who they are and to express their personalities." These words certainly appear to ring true for many of the Cohort interviewees who, in living a SALA lifestyle, have the independence, space, and resources with which to express themselves via these means.

2.3 Family

As has previously been mentioned, heteronormative family structure of traditional household or family type – married with a child or children – have often been regarded as a central tenet of earlier definitions of the Black middle class, in part to the exclusion or invisibility of SALA households. It is notable, therefore, that relatively few (6%) of the Cohort interviewees used family as part of their definition of the Black middle class. This may be because that – contrary to the more historical work of Black middle-class scholarship – for those living a SALA lifestyle, this focus of middle-class status is of lesser concern. Alternatively, it may also be a reflection of the fact that societal presumptions about family formation are taken as a given, and so not brought up for discussion by Cohort members, especially given the sensitivity of the topic.

Kevin, Chelesa, Alexis, and Joseph were the only Cohort members who referred to the concept of family – if only tangentially or in passing – in defining and describing the Black middle class. Kevin described middle-class status as being "Where you can live comfortably. Where you can maintain a family and still have a social life." Such thoughts were echoed by Chelesa: "A person who has obtained a certain level of education, let's say, post-high school, college level, who has an income that can support living and having a house, potentially a family, where they own property." Alexis was the most explicit in placing family – particularly having children – at the center of her conception of the Black middle class: "Being in the Black middle class is you setting a foundation for your future family or you're setting a foundation for others to aspire to. I look at middle class as a step to make sure that eventually my children's children will be taken care of because I created some type of inheritance or some legacy for them." Much less explicit, Joseph, while attempting to quantify a middle-class income, brought family into his definition: "If I had to put a number on it, I really couldn't put a number on it because I think it would depend on the person, the family, what kind of lifestyle they were after."

This chapter has looked at how education and income are central to the way Cohort members judge their (and others') middle-class status. This involves both objective measures regarding level of education and income, and associated subjective measures, such as education-related networks and the lifestyle commodities, as well as activities that a middle-class income provides. Chapter 3 builds on the discussions presented earlier to delve deeper into what it means to those within the Cohort to be Black *and* middle class in contemporary America, and how their SALA status influences (or otherwise) such perceptions.

The Love Jones Cohort and Black Middle-Class Identity

This chapter addresses how those in the Love Jones Cohort discuss being Black and middle class, and in doing so addresses several ideas raised by William Julius Wilson in his retirement speech – in particular, the possibility that the growth of the Black middle class is causing a growing divide between the haves and the have-nots in the Black community. As we will see, from our Cohort interviewees, the tension engendered by this divide often took the form of expressing a degree of responsibility to the larger Black community. Christine and Simone were two Cohort members who explicitly discussed how gender is a central component of how they experience being Black and middle class, further emphasizing the necessity of applying an intersectional lens. Most of the Cohort were hesitant about explicitly incorporating their SALA status/lifestyle as a key aspect of how they perceived being Black and middle class, with only 10% of the members of the Cohort expanding on how their singleness plays a role in shaping their Blackness and middle classness. Despite this reticence, I argue that SALA status – in conjunction with race, class, and gender – should be regarded as one of the interlocking identities shaping what it means to be Black and middle class. While some Cohort members used interracial comparisons in discussing being Black and middle class,[1] the bulk of this chapter highlights how their perceptions relate to the intragroup relationship between the haves and have-nots within the Black community.

Figure 3.1 shows that across the Cohort, 81% of members view being Black and middle class in terms that are relative to the wider Black

---

[1] While this book is emphatically not a comparative work exploring how the Black middle class and Black singles compare to their white counterparts, I acknowledge I must be sensitive to the data where it is relevant.

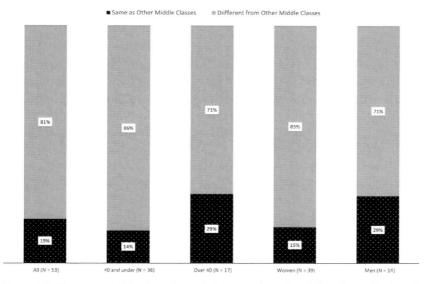

Figure 3.1. Percentage of the Love Jones Cohort members that defines being Black and middle class as the same or different from the other middle classes

community, rather than equating their middle-class status with other non-Black middle-class groups. Those in the Cohort who were 40 and under (86%) and women (85%) reported an even higher percentage than the overall Cohort. The Cohort spoke of these comparisons based on several factors: responsibility, racism, gendered racism, struggle, and inter-generational transference of wealth and trauma.

3.1 Colorblindness

Robin, Tanya, and Richard were among those who perceived being Black and middle class as no different from being middle class in any other racial or ethnic group. Robin observed: "I don't weed out white middle class and Black middle class and label it. If I were picking a label, I would just say middle class. When I say middle class to myself, I'm including whites in it as well, not just only the Blacks." Tanya proclaimed, "People are people regardless of what their socioeconomic background is," while Richard was emphatic that "I'm a middle class person who happens to be Black. I don't think that there's a difference between a Black middle class and a white middle class because I only separate them by way of income. It doesn't really matter the race or whatever gender."

To a degree, Robin, Tanya, and Richard's inability or refusal to acknowledge any racial difference across America's middle class aligns with the idea of colorblindness, colorblind ideology, or colorblind racism. In their 2020 article drawing on the work of sociologist Eduardo Bonilla-Silva pushing for a global theory of colorblindness, sociologists Jean Beaman and Amy Petts lay out the central frames of the colorblind ideology:[2] "Colorblindness is an ideology that enables people to ignore the persistence of racism by providing nonracial explanations for enduring racial inequalities." Furthermore, Bonilla-Silva defines the four central tenets of colorblindness as "minimization of racism," "cultural racism," "naturalization," and "abstract liberalism" (Beaman & Petts, 2020; Bonilla-Silva, 2006, 2015). While Robin, Tanya, and Richard are not stating that racism does not exist, the underlying implication of their comments is that people should be defined according to class alone, with issues of race set aside. Such a perspective plays into the tropes of colorblindness and overlooks the harsher systemic, structural, and institutional conditions that Black Americans must endure to secure and maintain their socioeconomic status as well as the disparate outcomes of their status relative to other middle classes.[3]

3.2 Inter-class Responsibilities and Tensions

Various research has been conducted on social identity and how it plays out in the Black middle class (Banks, 2009, 2010; Harris & Khanna, 2010; Lacy, 2004, 2007; Meghji, 2019; Moore, 2008). I argue that being Black while holding middle-class status presents the middle-class Black person with an identity conundrum – a conundrum that, in the case of the Love Jones Cohort, is further complicated by their SALA status. This assertion draws on aspects of sociologist Karyn Lacy's (2004) notion of strategic assimilation theory. It suggests that in relation to mobility, those within the Black middle class seek to stay intentionally and consciously connected to the wider Black community. Furthermore, the theory explains,

The processes by which middle-class blacks from two suburban communities negotiate the racial dualism that accompanies having to shift incessantly

---

[2] Bonilla-Silvia acknowledged that other scholars have described colorblind racism using various other terms, including new prejudice laissez-faire racism (Bobo et al., 1996), competitive racism (Essed, 1991), and symbolic racism (Kinder & Sanders, 1996).

[3] The mental health and well-being of the Love Jones Cohort is addressed in chapter 10 of this book.

from the black to the white world ... many middle-class blacks with access to majority white colleges, workplaces, and neighbourhoods continue to consciously retain their connections to the black world; through their interactions in these black spaces, middle-class blacks construct and maintain black racial identities. (Lacy, 2004, p. 910)

Thus, the class status of the Love Jones Cohort (and their singleness) may make them objects of suspicion by others in the Black community, while their race (and singleness) may lead to them being unwelcomed in white spaces. Sociologist Kesha Moore (2008) articulates a similar point:

The habitus of the Black middle class is theoretically important because it represents a group that experiences non-concordance on the systems of racial and class stratification. In the class system of stratification, the middle-class strata represent a higher status group; while in the racial system of identification, blackness represents a lower status category. Such incongruence situates middle-class blacks in a functional position to explore the relationship between the two systems of stratification (p. 495).[4]

Furthermore, in Moore's three-year ethnographic study of 35 Black middle-class residents near downtown Philadelphia, she explores two "competing forms of black middle-class identity (multi-class and middle-class minded) and the tensions between them" (Moore, 2008). On a basic level, a multi-class minded identity can promote connectedness, racial solidarity, and community. A middle-class minded identity affirms the ability to cross class boundaries and can be based on the degree of acceptance of white middle-class ideology (Martin, 2010; K. S. Moore, 2005, 2008).

Thus, some members of the Black middle class may, given their class standing, feel socially disconnected with their Black Folks[5] or counterparts of a different class status. This disconnection may sway those in the Black middle class – and those in the Love Jones Cohort in particular – toward a middle-class minded identity. Among the Cohort interviewees, Olivia and LaToya provided comments that potentially offer some insight into this

---

[4] Moore provides a detail of the term "habitus" that was made popular by the French sociologist Peter Bourdieu's (1984) concept of habitus (Bourdieu, 2014; Gieseking et al., 2014). She noted that habitus "encapsulates the importance of culture and cultural identity in both class identity and the process of class stratification. Habitus is defined as the relationship between two capacities: the capacity to produce culturally specified products and actions, and the capacity to differentiate and appreciate these culturally specified products and actions" (p. 496).

[5] E. Patrick Johnson uses the term "folk" in his 2003 book, *Appropriating Blackness*, Duke University Press, to represent the Black working class (E. P. Johnson, 2003).

viewpoint. Olivia, in setting out what being Black and middle class meant to her, seemed to reflect a more middle class–minded mindset: "[The Black middle class] have an opportunity to extend their connections, their professional and personal connections, that can translate into opportunities and good marriages, good pairings, and just a solid network that a person without means may not have ... feeling that one can even have dreams and goals that maybe people in lower socioeconomic situations may find more difficult to embrace." Here, Olivia alludes to the fact that middle-class Black people are afforded a degree of socioeconomic power that working-class Black people do not have access to, and that this allows them to "embrace" middle-class goals that may be rejected by their working-class counterparts.[6] It also touches on ideas of personal ambition and responsibility, of being justly rewarded for hard work, something that LaToya addressed more directly.[7]

Upon being asked "what does being Black and middle class mean?" LaToya's immediate response was, "a Republican mindset." She then proceeded to explain, "A lot of people, including myself, my peers, when we think middle class and we think African American and what we expect from other people in lower classes than us ... You work for it and earn it. We're not going to give it to you." LaToya confessed that she believed many Black Americans feel the same as her: "We talk about it behind closed doors, but publicly we say we're Democratic."

While some scholars contend that middle-class Blacks form a multi-class identity that links them with the larger Black community (K. S. Moore, 2005), others suggest that Black Americans will take on a white orientation to ascend the mobility ladder, a behavior that can directly or indirectly distance them from the larger Black community (Fordham, 1996, 2011; Fordham & Ogbu, 1986). In terms of the latter view, a 2013 study I coauthored with Angel Harris challenged the highly refuted assumptions in anthropologists Signithia Fordham and John Ogbu's (1986) arguments. They argue that a major reason Black students have

---

[6] An aspect of this type of middle-class mindedness might evolve into questions of authenticity. Other scholars have grappled with the tension related to linking racial identity, such as "authenticity," and the Black middle class (Collins, 2004; Harris & Khanna, 2010; Lacy, 2007; Moore, 2005).

[7] Some cohort members ascribe to such an idea – personal responsibility and pulling one's self up by their bootstraps – Scholar Mavis Sanders (1997) retorts: How does one pull themselves up with the bootstraps when they do not have boots? (Sanders, 1997; Watkins-Hayes, 2009). This is a nod to structural forces and systemic factors, not simply individual accomplishments, that determine outcomes and life chances.

relatively low school achievement is that Black culture is antithetical to mainstream society, and negatively sanction those who attempt to perform well in school. Furthermore, they posit that "high-achieving Blacks often choose between either adopting behaviors that reinforce Black culture and compromise their achievement (e.g., reduce effort, use nonstandard Black English or 'Ebonics') or risk having their Black peers question their legitimacy as members of the Black community and accuse them of 'acting white'" (Fordham & Ogbu, 1986). Using the Maryland Adolescent Development In Context Study (MADICS) data set, we found that Black students with a strong racial identity and connection to their Blackness – as opposed to a race-neutral profile – had higher educational aspirations and achievements (A. L. Harris & Marsh, 2010).[8] Elsewhere, sociologist and scholar of the Black middle class, Patricia Banks (2010) has set out a compelling history of Black middle class and their responsibility to the larger community, and how they enact racial unity through Black art participation:

For middle-class Blacks, racial unity has often been understood and experienced as a responsibility to advance the race. In the late nineteenth and early twentieth centuries, we see this with middle-class Blacks who aimed to uplift the race through their professional work and volunteerism (Higginbotham, 1994; Gaines, 2012). In more recent decades, a sense of duty to advance the group has also been evident among middle-class Blacks. (P. A. Banks, 2010, pp. 274–275)

Among the Cohort, Carrie's perspective mixed a middle class–minded identity and multi-class-minded identity. In terms of the former, she said, "Being Black and middle class in America I think means that you have attained some level of success. The American Dream." However, she then went on to explain her belief of taking advantage of this success to pay it forward within the collective Black community: "I have a responsibility to continue to build a legacy for people that are coming after me because we're here on the backs of people that came before us." While Carrie expressed her self-contentment with her SALA status and the success she had personally achieved, she felt that "[a] lot of people are able to continue

---

[8] Building upon this work, I was the lead author on two additional qualitative publications related to this topic. I published a paper on the demonstration of racial identity and womanhood among a group of young high-achieving Black women (Marsh, 2013) and another publication on the strengths of strong racial identity among high-achieving Black high school students in a racially diverse setting (Marsh et al., 2012). These publications illustrate that education remains a pathway for social mobility but suggests that Black students, potentially the next generation of the black middle class, do not have to renounce their racial identity, known as racelessness (Fordham, 2011), in lieu of academic success.

to be upwardly mobile because they're getting married." In equating marriage with upward mobility, Carrie's comments point to how her SALA status, in conjunction with dominant narratives surrounding the politics of respectability, shape her perception of what it means to be middle class and her perceived responsibility to the extended Black community.

Maurice was explicit about the wider responsibilities and implications of being Black and middle class, proclaiming that it "[m]eans that we are a core group of people that have made many strides in the history of this country, and we have opened doors that were closed to us before, previously, in many different professions." Kevin echoed these sentiments ("It kind of comes with a certain sense of responsibility"), which in his case were informed by having grown up poor. Kevin felt that many Black professionals understand what it means to be poor, and that gaining a sense of a middle-class status presents them with a fork in the road: "Some choose to either give back or some choose to turn their back." The path chosen by Kevin was clear; he insisted that the relative comfort afforded by being Black and middle class incurred a responsibility to assist and mentor others: "At least try to give back. Or at least direct someone in the right direction and let them know that it is possible to [be a middle-class Black person]."

Carrie, Maurice, and Kevin perceived that obligations toward helping less-affluent Black community members is, in some respects, reflective of W. E. B. Du Bois's Talented Tenth ideology – the broad idea being that the 10% of the Black community who have cultivated the necessary intellectual skills have a responsibility to lead and uplift the Black masses.[9] Sociologists Juan Battle and Earl Wright II (2002) took a quantitative assessment of the idea of the Talented Tenth; for the purposes of their investigation, they defined the group as college-educated African Americans. They drew from

---

[9] Writing before W. E. B. Du Bois, and Booker T. Washington, and alongside Sojourner Truth, Ida B. Wells, and Mary Churchill, to name a few, was Anna Julia Cooper. Cooper argued for a bottom-up approach for racial uplift. Philosopher Joy James (2014) noted that "rather than focus on the Black intellectual male elites, Cooper asserted that we must pay attention to the conditions of the working class and poor Black women." The reasons why Cooper might not be as well known as Du Bois is that Cooper was overlooked as a canonical figure among early Black philosophers. Cooper struggled to get scholarship into the mainstream due to "racialized, gendered, and class power dynamics" in the publication process (James, 2014). To get a glimpse into the relationship between Anna Julia Cooper, Du Bois, and publishing, see (Moody-Turner, 2015). See https://plato.stanford.edu/entries/anna-julia-cooper/ for additional information.

Du Bois's original conceptualization of the term.[10] In doing so, they asserted that the Talented Tenth and Black middle class are not synonymous terms, despite the tendency of many scholars to use the terms interchangeably (p. 658). "It is very possible that through hard work, determination, and pure effort, one can become a member of the Black middle class without obtaining a college education. It is not possible, however, to become a member of the Talented Tenth by any means other than obtaining a college education. For this reason, the usage of the term Talented Tenth is not synonymous with Black middle class" (Battle & Wright, 2002, p. 664). The scholars used data from the National Black Politics Study to examine the attitudes of today's Talented Tenth concerning their responsibilities as leaders of their respective communities. Using multivariate analysis, they found "that among other things, the Talented Tenth report being more politically active and more involved in their communities and are suspect of the motives of the Black middle class" (J. Battle & Wright, 2002).

In addressing the idea of a Talented Tenth, Tina did, however, equate middle-class status and privilege with the following concept: "[I]t means that you're doing a little bit better than 90 percent of Black people in America, so [being Black and middle class] must be different than being something else and middle class ... Comparing the Black middle class to white and middle class, the one thing you think is different is, possibly, responsibility? ... That means doing things like mentorship for people who aren't as privileged."

Nancy, meanwhile, viewed the impact of middle-class privilege in a more negative light, highlighting a perceived class tension between the haves and have-nots in the Black community: "I think other members of the Black community, when they perceive that you're doing well, they tend to shun you or think that you think that you're better than them." Antonio alluded to a similar type of tension: "As Black individuals, we're not in a community where we're helping each other out to build. Why is everybody selfish?" Antonio goes on to say, "If we're helping each other out, we'll all be the middle class and be comfortable. People are selfish ... I'd rather everybody be in the middle class than the upper class and lower class. Then, we know that we're continuing to rise. We're not rising individually, but we're rising as a whole [Black community]."

---

[10] The authors acknowledge, "This use of Du Bois's original conceptualization does not take into account his attitudinal or conceptual change toward the Talented Tenth over the course of his life" (p. 658).

While Nancy suggests the Black middle class is shunned, Antonio might be alluding to a possible equal level of suspicion, selfishness, and potential shunning on both sides. Kendra asserts that the Black middle class are doing the shunning: "There is a very small percentage of African Americans who have achieved, but as opposed to setting ourselves apart ... [it is our] duty to come back, remove the judgment." Kendra argues that the tension or "the rub with the Black middle classes [is]: do you really want to help people? Do you really want to welcome more people to expand the Black middle class?" Kendra is clear that the Black middle class can be an exclusive group that shun certain people and "where some people are allowed in and then some are not."

3.3 Struggle

Several members of the Love Jones Cohort mentioned struggle as a key element of being Black and middle class, particularly in contrast to how other races experience being middle class. Madison, for example, claimed that being Black and middle class means "Someone that still has to try really, really, really hard. I believe ten times harder than someone in a different race, to have a comfortable lifestyle." Rick described being Black and middle class as "Someone who is working very hard to achieve a goal, but their circumstances don't match that they're trying to achieve," while Justin explained, "I still think that as a race we're still trying to kind of prove ourselves in trying to get the same benefits as everyone else." Meisha echoed the sentiments of Madison, Rick, and Justin in citing a common mantra referred to by Black people for many years: "We have to pay what I call the Black tax which means we have to work harder than the other people and still get the same pay."[11] For these members of the Cohort, it was clear that being Black *and* middle class was a very different proposition – both practically and mentally – to simply consider yourself middle class without consideration of color. Their comments also suggest an anxiety that, should they not work sufficiently hard and engage in constant struggle, their middle-class status may be at risk.

---

[11] This notion of struggle is not unique to Black Americans. There is some research to suggest that British Black middle class also face racist work environments (Meghji, 2019). Similarly, the South African Black middle class struggle with the complexity of belonging in their larger community and "the effects of being racially othered in interaction with whites and white spaces" (Khunou, 2015).

Other members of the Cohort also referred to the anxieties provoked (or at least not mitigated) by being Black. Shannon spoke of how navigating integrated spaces had been a huge turning point for her: "I realized my own insecurities. Even though I subscribe to the middle class, I just had this mentality of inferiority … We live in an anti-Black culture." Kendra, meanwhile, in discussing her feelings about being Black and middle class, used white privilege as a point of comparison, arguing that white people feel like, "Damn it, I got this white privilege … I know it's wrong, but what do I do to evoke change? It's similar in that way where we have economic privilege, and that makes a hell of a difference regardless of race [but] when we go out into society, you feel Black. Right now … it does not matter about what your 'pedigree' is. We're still in the 'struggle' socially."

Here, Kendra is acknowledging that being middle class does not buy the Love Jones Cohort out of their Blackness when it comes to experiencing racism. This is particularly the case in terms of the workplace – which for many SALAs, who cannot draw on the resources of a partner, is the sole source of income that provides their middle-class status. Black professionals are often confronted with having to make their workplace presence more palatable to non-Black colleagues (McCluney et al., 2021).

In terms of the struggle to receive appropriate financial rewards for workplace endeavors, Deborah spoke with frustration in her voice of having to return to education to increase her (restricted) chances of advancement: "I'm going back to school to get another degree to get myself to another level financially. I think in our society it's still a struggle because it [the degree] could open doors for me, maybe kick down doors for me. I still have to continue to fight to get an opportunity, just a small opportunity."

Beyond the struggles involved in simply being Black and middle class, applying an intersectional lens reveals how certain members of the Cohort face additional challenges. One such factor is whether the Cohort member has immigrant status, with Simone, as the lone example in the Cohort, remarking, "I think I have three strikes against me – I'm Black, Caribbean, and middle class … Since I have an accent, people think where I come from, we lived in mud huts. So I have to fight to prove that I'm educated, that I have the means, that I can sustain the way I live."

While Deborah and Simone did not specifically cite gender as a factor in the struggles they faced to maintain their middle-class status, other women in the Cohort were more explicit. Relevant to this aspect are the words of Adia Wingfield (2019), made in her Sociologist for Women in Society presidential address: "Black women are playing an essential role transforming workplaces, media, and politics in the current moment . . . Black women are 'reclaiming their time' by making efforts to change systemic racial and gendered processes that render workplaces and organizations particularly unwelcoming spaces" (Wingfield, 2019).[12] Such a perspective was reflected – though perhaps not so directly – among some of the Cohort, with Joanna, for instance, asserting that being Black and middle class "[m]eans being fortunate and having had probably a really good education in order to even allow me to get to this point. Interestingly enough, I think it just means being able to really kind of fend for myself as a Black woman." Christine, meanwhile, was emphatic in placing gender at the center of her response: "I don't think about Black middle class versus other races of middle class. I just think about being a woman and being a Black woman."

Natalie, as one of only four Black women in her office, said she "better be ready to work hard, very hard. Each level that you move [up the mobility ladder] you have to work even harder so don't think it's going to get any easier just because you're making progress. Because when you are making progress new level, new devil so that's all it's meant to me. Because every time I've moved from a job gotten better pay, new level, new devil, it's been something else." Natalie also discussed the struggle to stay true to herself as a Black professional woman, "but the politics are different and change . . . and means being adaptable, but not to the point where you are sacrificing yourself in a way that does not benefit you. That, I think, is the most difficult thing to find balance in, understanding how not to sacrifice yourself in that way."

3.4 Black Middle Class as the New Normal

Although many members of the Love Jones Cohort regarded being Black and middle class as involving unique and specific challenges, there were

[12] A befitting example of Wingfield's reclaiming their time efforts of Black women and changing systemic racial and gender processes is the Creating a Respectful and Open World for Natural Hair Act or more commonly known by some as the CROWN Act of 2021, that was introduced in Senate on March 22, 2021. "This bill prohibits discrimination based on a person's hair texture or hairstyle if that style or texture is commonly associated with a particular race or national origin." Scholars Saran Donahoo and Asia Smith (2021) chronicled the legal battles to professionalizing Black hair. Their work, along with the critical race analysis of the CROWN act by Britney Pitts (2021), provides strong support for the passage of such legislation at the federal level (Donahoo & Smith, 2022; Pitts, 2021). Sociologist Chelsea Johnson argues, "Hair straightening, adornment, cutting, covering, and styling are all strategies that Africana women have used to reimagine Black femininity and critique inequality through their bodies" (2019, p. 16).

some who simply regarded being Black and middle class as normal. Lillian – second-generation Black middle class – for example, proclaimed, "To see a lawyer and a doctor as parents in a black family, it actually wasn't a surprise to me." She referred back to how her experiences growing up had shaped her thinking: "My parents were from the segregated south where those types of jobs are normal for us because we were the only ones that could service us. We were our own bankers, doctors, lawyers, teachers." Lillian did not "feel like I'm special or better" for being Black and middle class, instead regarding her socioeconomic position as "to be expected and I don't sign up for it." For Lillian, her Black middle-class identity was something to be accepted and normalized, rather than agonized over or dissected. Dawn similarly emphasized the normality of her middle-class lifestyle: "Most of us are probably educated [with a] bachelor and above a bachelor's [degree]; living somewhat comfortably. Just living a normal, Black American life." Brenay – also first-generation Black middle class – observed, "I see it as the norm, in some circumstances. I define it as Black humans, human beings just living to make it happen, doing the best that they can."

These latter comments are reflective of how Cohort members' previous experiences, including childhood upbringing, can shape their views on what it means to be Black and middle class. Here, the class status of Cohort members' parents is extremely relevant – in other words, the question to be asked is whether a Cohort member is first-generation middle class or not, and how this affects their perception of being Black and middle class (such as whether it is regarded as a "struggle" or "normal").

Overall, this chapter has shown us that the majority of the Love Jones Cohort are wrestling with similar notions regarding being Black and middle class as their non-SALA counterparts: namely, feeling a degree of responsibility to the wider Black community and awareness of the tensions that exist between the haves and have-nots within that community. Also clear is that most – though not all – regard being Black and middle class as involving greater struggle compared to other groups claiming middle-class status. Though the interviewees were generally reluctant to cite their SALA status (or did not feel it was relevant) in discussing what it means to be Black and middle class, it would be a mistake to think it does not constitute a relevant factor. Instead, the impact of their SALA lifestyle on their middle-class status was made explicit in more indirect terms, in their discussions of their lifestyles, wealth decisions and so forth, which will be discussed in the remainder of this book.

4

The Rise of Never-Married Black Singles

Marriage as a social institution is changing in the United States. One consequence of this is the rise of Black never-married singles as a demographic, in particular those who may also be middle class: in other words, the Love Jones Cohort that forms the subject of this book. Through the deployment of quantitative data and discussion of the various theoretical assumptions that have been put forward to explain declining marriage rates among Black Americans – especially women – this chapter sets out a framework for understanding how and why the Cohort has begun stepping into the limelight, and what the implications of this might be. In doing so, the chapter engages several members of the interviewed Cohort, drawing on their words to emphasize and reinforce the points being made.

4.1 The Retreat from Marriage

Over the past decade, the overall percentage of US adults marrying has fallen steadily, as has the number of people having children. Obviously, as marriage rates decrease, the number of never-married people increases. A 2019 Pew Research Center report documents just over half (53%) of Americans as saying that by 2020, people will be less likely to get married, with just under half (46%) saying people will be less likely to have children (Horowitz et al., 2019). And for the most part, those predictions held. As of 2021, half of the women of all races and 48% of men, over 15, were unmarried (that includes never-married, widowed, and divorced) and close to a third were never married (33% versus 37%). When this same data is disaggregated by race (householder whose race was reported as only one race), Black women are slightly edged out by Black men in the never-married category (48% versus 52%) (US Census Bureau, Decennial

Censuses, 1950–1990, and Current Population Survey, March and Annual Social and Economic Supplements, 1993–2021).

An apparent "retreat from marriage," combined with a rise in singlehood, can be seen across all racial and ethnic groups over the past three decades.[1] Nevertheless, as journalist Joy Jones points out in a 2006 *Washington Post* article entitled "Marriage is for White People," the Black population in general, and Black women in particular, have the lowest marriage rate of any racial or ethnic group in the United States. As a consequence, Black women are leading the way in carving out alternative strategies for establishing emotional, sexual, nurturing, and reproductive needs (R. J. D. Barnes, 2015; Craigie et al., 2018; Jones, 2006) Glenda – one of our Cohort interviewees – offers an example in this regard. Glenda is a lawyer for the federal government, a swimmer, and self-professed avid reader. In my two-hour interview with her, Glenda maintained a joyful disposition – it often felt like two girlfriends having a light-hearted, gossip-filled conversation over Sunday brunch. Glenda discussed how she considered her neighbors to be friends, even family, and how she envisioned "having sort of a 'Friends' type of relationship with my neighbors where we would all hang out together." As such, and regardless of her single status, Glenda has established a network of neighbors and friends to meet her needs.

The prevailing explanations offered for the trends related to decline in marriage range from the economic and demographic to the social and cultural; and cast explicit or implicit light on the structural impediments to mate availability among the Cohort, and larger Black family formations (Cross et al., 2022). Tanya was among the Cohort members who noted the rise in Black singles and the related challenges of finding a partner: "All these educated Black women who can't find a mate or have chosen their career first before thinking about having a mate, settling down, raising a family."

Figure 4.1 illustrates the percentage of never-married Black women and men between the ages of 25 and 65, from 1880 to 2019. Two interesting trends are illuminated.[2] First, over the decades examined, the proportion of

---

[1] Social scientists have debated the "retreat from marriage" for decades. See Lichter et al. (1992) and Wilson (2012b) to contextualize the conversation. The retreat from marriage involves a decline in marriage rates, an increase in cohabitation, a delaying or forgoing of marriage, and an increase in divorce.

[2] In Figure 4.1, socioeconomic variables such as level of education, professional/managerial position, and full-time employment *are not taken into consideration.* Figure 4.1 is generated using Integrated Public Use Microdata Series (IPUMS), survey documentation and analysis (SDA) tool, and the online data analysis system. Data are derived from multiple samples, United States, 1850–2019. Variables include year (row, 1850–2019), marital status (column), person weight, age (25–65), race (Black), and sex (male and female). Data for 2020 were not available when this book was written.

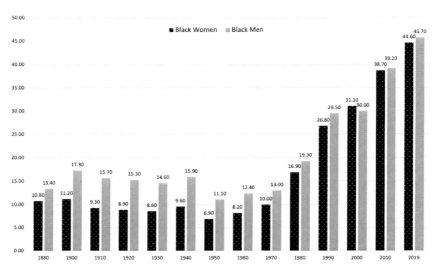

Figure 4.1. Percentage of Black women and men aged 25–65 who have never been married, 1880–2019

never-married people more than tripled for both Black women and men. In 2019, just under half of Black women (45%) and men (46%) were never married.

Alyssa (48) was among those who had no reservations regarding her decision not to marry or have children. "It's been my choice not to have kids, not to get married because I wanted things to be a certain way, so I live with no regrets. I'm very happy, I'm content."

Second, at the start of the twentieth century, a larger percentage of Black men (17%) were never married compared to Black women (11%). Midcentury, the percentages decreased along with the gap between Black never-married women and men, and by the end of the century, there was relatively little difference in percentages between the two groups.

4.2 Education, Occupation, Income, and Homeownership

Figures 4.2–4.5 illustrate how Black singles fare in terms of education, occupation, income, and homeownership. Figure 4.2 shows the percentage of never-married Black women and men aged 25–65 who had obtained a bachelor's degree *or higher*, from 1940 to 2019.[3] In 2019, roughly a quarter

---

[3] Figure 4.2 plots the percentage of those that completed four or more years of college for never-married Black women and men. Figure 4.2 is generated using IPUMS' SDA tool and

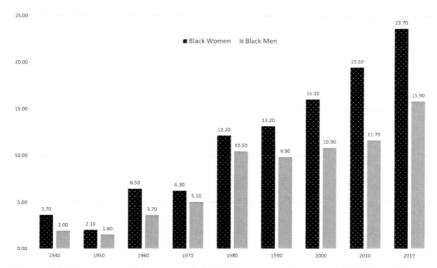

Figure 4.2 Percentage of never-married Black women and men aged 25–65 with a bachelor's degree or higher, 1940–2019

(24%) of never-married Black women and 16% of never-married Black men had completed four or more years of college.[4] For each year represented, a larger percentage of never-married Black women than Black men had a college degree or higher, a gap that began to increase in 2000 and seems on course to continue widening.

Despite the apparent gender imbalance in education, the Cohort's women were hopeful that if they did decide to partner, it would be with an educated Black man. Dawn, for instance, who expressed that she was open to a serious relationship once her financial situation improved, noted her two main preferences in relation to a possible suitor in the following terms: "I would prefer them not to have any mental health illness. I would prefer them to have some kind of education." In terms of her latter comment, Dawn is alluding to the notion of homogamy: people wanting to marry or partner with people in their same social and economic class

the online data analysis system. Data are derived from multiple samples, United States, 1940–2019 between only decades reported. Data are not available before 1940. Variables include year (row, 1850–2019), education (column, recoded for under four and four or more years of college), person weight, age (25–65), race (Black), sex (male and female), and marital status (never married).

[4] For the education, occupation, and income variables, data are based on the scores of the householder.

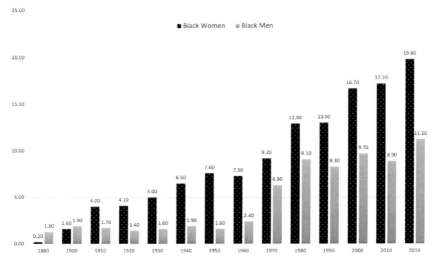

Figure 4.3 Percentage of never-married Black women and men aged 25–65 with a professional occupation, 1880–2019

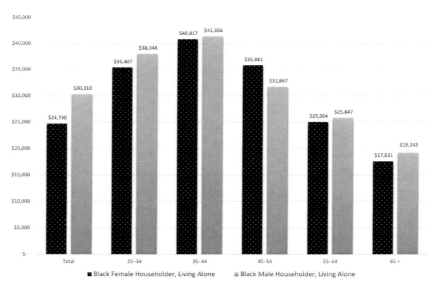

Figure 4.4 Median income of Black female and male householders living alone, aged 25 and over, in 2019 dollars

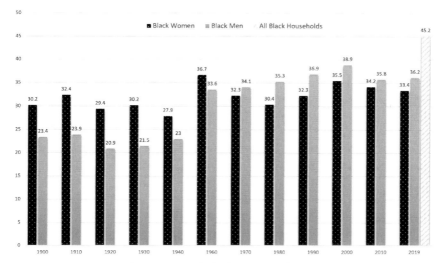

Figure 4.5 Percentage of never-married Black women and men aged 25–65 who own or are buying a home, 1990–2019

(Kalmijn, 1998; Schwartz, 2013). However, given that Black women are outpacing Black men in higher education, especially advanced degrees, this increases the likelihood of a disparity between the two parties in terms of having comparable resources and social standing.[5]

Figure 4.3 highlights the percentage of never-married Black women and men aged 25–65 with a professional occupation, from 1880 to 2019. As can be seen, as of 2019, one in five (20%) never-married Black women and roughly one in nine (11%) never-married Black men hold professional occupations.[6]

---

[5] There is a meme that has been circulating the Internet since 2016, suggesting that the Black woman is the most educated group in the USA. When comparing the educational attainment of all Black adults, aged 25 and above, Black women edge out Black men for four-year (15.19% versus 10.87%), master's (5.10% versus 2.63%), doctorates (0.61% versus 0.47%), and professional-level (0.47% versus 0.22%) degrees (U.S. Census Bureau, 2019). *Intra*-racially, we, Black women, are more educated than Black men, especially with advanced degrees. *Inter*-racially because of structural racism, we, Black women, are not outperforming all other groups. See my University of Maryland colleague Phil Cohen's blog for a detailed explanation about this misinformation: "No Black women are not the 'most educated' group in the US," 2016 (https://familyinequality.wordpress.com/2016/06/07/no-black-women-are-not-the-most-educated-group-in-the-us/).

[6] Figure 4.3 includes data from IPUMS' SDA. Variables include year (row, 1850–2019), occupation (column, based on the OCC1950 scores), person weight, age (25–65), race (Black), sex (male and female), and marital status (never married). According to IPUMS

Figure 4.3 also shows two stable patterns: first, an increase in the percentage of never-married Black women with a professional occupation over time; and, second, a relatively stable gap between never-married Black women and never-married Black men holding professional occupations since 2000.

For some women in the Cohort, this disparity in the number of professional Black women and Black men was a potential issue, with Sheri, for example, proclaiming, "The occupation does matter in some respects, yeah. I feel like me and a mechanic aren't going to have much to talk about unless we got some similar interests outside of work." Others, such as Patricia, were more open to compromise: "People in my age group [mid-fifties] are retiring so it really doesn't matter what your education, occupation was at that point. People are just looking for companionship." Conversely, having previously worked in accounts management, Tanya was now unemployed, which she felt directly impacted her current SALA status and lifestyle: "It's hard out there for people who are unemployed to feel worthy in a relationship, especially in the DMV [the D.C. area]. People want to meet a mate who is their equal."

Figure 4.4 documents the median income of Black female and male householders over the age of 25, living alone, in 2019 dollars.[7] The total median income is slightly higher for Black male householders than for their female counterparts. Within the age categories, Black female householders aged 45–54 are the only age group with a (slightly) higher median income than their male counterparts. Otherwise, the difference in median income can be seen as indicative of a gender wage gap (Barroso & Brown, 2021).

---

website, "OCC1950 applies the 1950 Census Bureau occupational classification system to occupational data, to enhance comparability across years. For pre-1940 samples created at Minnesota, the alphabetic responses supplied by enumerators were directly coded into the 1950 classification." Occupation scores were based on OCC1950 scores, where 0–99 was considered professional, and 100–999 nonprofessional occupation scores. See "*Series, IPUMS. Integrated occupation and industry codes and occupational standing variables in the IPUMS*" or "US Bureau of the Census (1950): Alphabetical Index of Occupations and Industries (1950)" for a more detailed description of the occupational classifications.

[7] Source: U.S. Census Bureau, Current Population Survey, 2021 Annual Social and Economic Supplement (CPS ASEC). According to the Census, "Numbers in thousands. Households as of March of the following year. Median income is calculated using $2,500 intervals." For additional information, see www.census.gov/data/tables/time-series/demo/income-poverty/cps-hinc/hinc-02.html. Like Figure 4.1, in this figure socioeconomic variables such as level of education, professional/managerial position, and full-time employment *are not considered.*

These income differentials can potentially impact relations between the sexes. According to one of the Cohort's male members, Kevin, women want "[t]o feel like they're with someone who can protect them and provide. Women want a man that exudes a certain provider level . . . A certain level of education or make a certain amount of money." Madison, meanwhile, asserted that men want "[b]ig butts, light skin, long hair, or like an exotic type of look.[8] Some get intimidated by women that are considered doing well occupation-wise, financial-wise. Some men want you [women] to have your own money."

Building on these comments, there are quantitative studies that set out to test the association between perceived attractiveness (based on interviewer reported scores) and wages (Goldsmith et al., 2006; Monk Jr. et al., 2021). Sociologists Ellis Monk Jr., Michael Esposito, and Hedwig Lee (2021) find that "[a]mong Black women and Black men [especially Black women] the wage penalties associated with perceived physical attractiveness are so substantial that, taken together, the earnings disparity between the least and most physically attractive exceeds in magnitude both the Black–white wage gap and the gender gap" (p. 221). Put another way, the study finds that Black women, on average, are rated as less attractive than white and Latinx women – calling into question the relationship between complexion, attractiveness, labor market, and health outcomes (Diette et al., 2015; A. M. Landor & McNeil Smith, 2019; Stewart et al., 2020) – and results in lower wages for these Black women. Studies also suggest that, on average, lighter complexioned individuals, relative to their darker skinned counterparts, tend to have higher wages, higher education attainment, and more likely to be employed in white collars jobs (Goldsmith et al., 2006, 2007; Monk, 2014; Monk Jr. et al., 2021; Rosenblum et al., 2016).[9] These are factors that might improve their

---

[8] The underpinnings of Madison's statement could be based on the idea of "colorism" – a system of prejudicial or preferential treatment of the people (can be of the same race) based solely on skin tone or skin color in relation to socioeconomic status, mobility, marriage, and other interrelated variables (Hunter, 2005, 2007). Alice Walker is often cited as the first to coin "colorism" (Harris, 2018; Walker, 1983). A "colorist" is someone who harbors biases or prejudicial attitudes, conscious or unconscious, toward individuals based on their skin color and other often synonymous features with whiteness (Jennings, 2022), for example, "good hair" (versus "bad hair") – a term that has a long history in Black America and remains a juggernaut in misguided contemporary standards of beauty (I. Banks, 2000; Byrd & Tharps, 2014) and slim body frames (T. A. Justin & Jette, 2022).

[9] This research relates to two interrelated and relevant theories: the beauty queue and halo effect. Hunter (2005) theorizes that the beauty queue "describes how skin tone affects a symbolic rank-ordering of women by skin tone, with the lightest women who gain the

standing in the dating market as well as their ability to accumulate wealth.[10]

As a potential wealth-building asset measure, Figure 4.5 focuses on the percentage of Black never-married women and men aged 25–65 who own or are buying a home, from 1900 to 2019. In terms of the homeownership rates shown, two noteworthy aspects emerge.[11] At the beginning of this timeframe, a larger percentage of never-married Black women were homeowners (30%) than Black men (23%), a trend that persisted until 1970. Since then, the opposite has held true: in 2019, 36% of never-married Black men owned a home compared to 33% of Black women. For context, the 2019 homeownership rates for both male and female Black never-married people are lower than that seen for all Black households (45%).

Attitudes to wealth varied within the Cohort, with Reggie, for instance, asserting, "I don't care too much about that [wealth]. If you're happy with whatever it is you're doing and you're doing a good job about it . . . wealth is going to come regardless." Alexis, meanwhile, professed that though having wealth is great, it was not a deciding factor in her mate selection. Nevertheless, she was emphatic that "[i]t's important that you have great credit."

4.3 Sex-ratio Imbalances and Interracial Dating

Figures 4.2–4.5 separately reveal the variables I compiled in order to create a Black middle class index (BMCi). Over several subsequent quantitative publications, I found such gender differences were reflected in – in fact, were even more pronounced among – those classified as the Love Jones Cohort. In 2020, I coauthored a book chapter (with Dr. Jessica Peña) in an edited volume on the middle class in world society. In our data analysis for that chapter and this book, we determined that, as of 2014, the Love Jones Cohort comprised approximately 13% of all Black middle-class

---

most privilege near the front of the queue and the darkest women who experience the most discrimination near the back" (M. Hunter, 2016; M. L. Hunter, 2005). Hunter hypothesizes that "[t]he halo effect is a propensity to allow positive evaluations about one trait in a person (often physical attractiveness) to influence the appraisal of other aspects of that person's characteristics, such as intelligence, kindness, and likeability (Nisbett & Wilson, 1977)" (M. Hunter, 2016, p. 56).

[10] See the following report on the implications of skin tone and wealth in Los Angeles: "The Color of Wealth in Los Angeles." https://socialequity.duke.edu/wp-content/uploads/2021/08/50074_LA-Report_8-17-21.pdf.

[11] Data prior to 1900 and 1950 for ownership of dwelling (tenure) were excluded for the United States 1850–2019 dataset developed by the IPUMS online data analysis system.

households.[12] In terms of the gender breakdown of the Cohort category, there was a 70/30 split in favor of women, a trend that has been relatively consistent over time (Marsh et al., 2007; Marsh & Peña, 2020).

Meanwhile, my 2008 article "The Love Jones Cohort: A New Face of the Black Middle Class?," coauthored with Lynda Dickson, provides potential theoretical frameworks and explanations for the decrease in Black marriage, the rise in Black singlehood, and changing Black families.[13] In our paper, we showed how prevailing explanations for the rise in Black singlehood range from the economic and demographic to the social and cultural (Dickson & Marsh, 2008). Economic explanations are often cited, suggesting that limited employment opportunities for Black men make them poor marriage prospects – also known as the "shortage of marriage-able Black men" or the "marriageable male" hypothesis (W. A. Darity Jr. & Myers Jr., 1995; W. J. Wilson, 2012a). Another frequently cited economic-demographic–based explanation concerns the female "marriage squeeze," which refers both to the *quantity* of available Black men and their *quality* (A. D. James et al., 1996). In essence, there are not enough men for the women to marry. One of the consequences of the unequal sex ratio of quality Black men to Black women is nonmarital childbearing, with premarital childbearing found to have a delaying effect on, and in some cases putting a brake to, future marriages for Black mothers (Graefe & Lichter, 2002).

Though the demographic literature posits this sex-ratio imbalance as one of several theoretical frameworks explaining the rise in singlehood among Black Americans, the Love Jones Cohort complicates any such theoretical explanation. While some in the Cohort actively choose to remain single, other members of the Cohort feel a marriage squeeze (something that will be expanded upon in Chapter 5).

Maurice was among those questioning the sex-ratio imbalance in the Cohort, asserting that although "There are more Black women than there are Black men. There are quite a few [Black men], even some of my contemporaries, who aren't married, no kids, or have kids, but they don't want to get married. And there are others like me who want to get

---

[12] We used the nationally representative 1% sample of the 1980, 1990, 2000, Integrated Public Use Microdata Series (IPUMS) as well as the 2010 and 2014 American Community Survey (ACS). The ACS is an annual nationally representative survey that is designed to replace the decennial census long form in 2010 and thereafter.

[13] See our article, The Love Jones Cohort: A New Face of the Black Middle Class? In the journal *Black Women, Gender & Families*, 2(1), 84–105 for more detailed explanations (Dickson & Marsh, 2008).

married." Marquez, meanwhile, claimed, "[D]espite the whole ratio of women to men blah blah blah. There are a lot of guys who may be ready for a relationship but it's just as rough out here for guys as it is for women." William, age unspecified, appeared to concur with this perspective: "I wake up every day and I'm like, wow, I can't believe I am really single at this point in my life."

Among the women of the Cohort, some appear to support the "marriage squeeze" hypothesis that there is a lack of quality men, and these women are remaining single due to lack of suitable dating options, rather than through active choice. A frequently expressed point of view was that their dating options were limited by the fact that the men they encountered were "playboys" or "cheaters" (Nancy); "immature" (Sheri); "douchebags" (Simone); or financially irresponsible (Megan). According to Olivia, "Solid, successful African-American women are totally outnumbering their male counterparts," with the result being a shortage of men that leads to an issue of supply and demand. As Olivia argues, if a man has "means and education, is fairly attractive, got most of his hair, unless he just chose to go bald, got most of his teeth, limbs, he is prime property. He's a premium in numbers."

The higher out-marriage rate – marrying outside of one's own race and/or ethnicity – of Black men is yet another explanation offered for the dramatic decline in marriage among Black women. Some sociological studies suggest that not only are Black men more likely to marry non-Black women than Black women are to marry non-Black men, but the *quality* of the Black men who outmarry (as measured by education, income, and occupational levels) appears to be higher than is the case for either Black men who marry Black women or single Black men (Crowder & Tolnay, 2000; Qian, 1997; Tucker & Mitchell-Kernan, 1990).

Law professor Richard Banks (2012) suggests interracial dating and marriage as a possible solution to the rising rates of singlehood, especially for Black women. This was a major topic among the Cohort, with the vast majority (82%) reporting that they would date [interviewees were not explicitly asked about marriage] someone of another race or ethnicity. Of those who provided more detail about why they would date interracially, half (53%) said they were open to dating anyone they found a connection with. However, roughly a tenth of all the Cohort willing to date another race stipulated that they would not date a white person, the assumption being that they would be unable to find a connection with a white person. While Banks (2012) asserts that Black women should consider marrying non-Black men, by placing the onus on Black women to seek non-Black partners, he neglects to consider, among other things, that Black women are perceived as the least desirable in the dating market.[14]

Social media and associated technologies are a central part of our social world and dating. When scholars examine dating in the digital age, gendered and racial exclusion emerges, with Black women bearing the brunt of this marginalization and gendered racism (Adeyinka-Skold, 2020; Curington et al., 2021; Hwang, 2013). Just over a quarter of the Cohort reported using online dating sites at the time the interview was conducted, and of those, just under 40% stated they no longer used such platforms. Among those who had used dating sites, the following themes emerged: A quarter expressed a preference for meeting someone in person; a quarter found such platforms unproductive; and 18% noted that online daters or their profiles were dishonest.

Sociologists Celeste Vaughn Curington and colleagues (2021) conducted a comprehensive study drawing from a mainstream dating website, archival research, and over 75 in-depth interviews with daters of diverse racial backgrounds and sexual identities, leading them to coin the term "digital-sexual racism." According to these scholars, the term refers to the fact that Black daters are rendered "simultaneously hyper-visible and invisible . . . They are contacted on dating sites specifically because they are Black but also ignored on other user sites entirely because they are Black" (pp. 123–124).[15]

Sociologist Sarah Adeyinka-Skold (2020) found similar results when drawing on interviews with slightly over 100 Asian, white, Black, and Latinx heterosexual college-educated women. Adeyinka-Skold's respondents felt that men are intimidated by their professional accomplishments, a further impediment to dating on top of the gendered racism and sexual racism encountered by Black women. Madison was one of the women in the Love Jones Cohort to touch on such sentiments, noting, "Some [Black] men, they're either intimidated or jealous by the one [Black women] with education."

[14] In 2018, National Public Radio (NPR) devoted a show to the subject, "Least Desirable? How Racial Discrimination Plays Out in Online Dating." Based on 2014 data from OkCupid, the show suggested most men, regardless of their race and ethnicity, rated Black women as less attractive than women of all other racial and ethnic groups, and ultimately less willing to date (Hwang, 2013a, 2013b).

[15] Research also finds that skin tone and hair texture stratify Black women in many spaces including dating experiences and their representations in the media (M. L. Hunter, 2013; C. Johnson, 2019).

Many of the Cohort's female members held ambiguous views of inter-racial dating, despite often having dated outside their race in the past. Ashley, for example – who has an advanced degree and has worked in public health – revealed with a chuckle in her voice but a deep sense of sincerity that, while she had dated a white guy when she was younger, she now wanted "little chocolate babies. I can't have that little chocolate baby with a man that's not chocolate." My interaction with Ashley reminded me of the work of sociologist Eduardo Bonilla-Silva (2006), who asked respondents how they felt about interracial marriage. Bonilla-Silva argued that his respondents did not want to appear racist, so made comments intended to appear empathetic along the lines of "I am ok with people marrying who they want to marry, I am just worried for the children" (Bonilla-Silva, 2006). An alternative perspective, for Ashley, might be that she wants to bear, nurture, and affirm Black children in an America she feels continues to lack kindness toward Black children.

While Olivia was open to considering other racial and ethnic groups ("I've never dated a Caucasian, and I doubt that I would, but I have dated a Puerto Rican"), she went on to say that she interracially dates with caution: "I've been very cautious about racial groups in which women are subju-gated or treated as second-class citizens. That's not how I was raised. I'm too vocal and too forthright for that. So, I've kind of not even considered certain races for that reason." For Olivia, the parameters of what she is willing to accept in terms of interracial dating are limited by what might be perceived as a race/gender/class, intersectional, or a Black feminism identity.

Simone – who lived with her younger brother and had moved to Prince George's County from the Caribbean – had also dated outside of her race but gave a somewhat scathing assessment of a website for interracial dating: "My cousin found her [white] fiancé on [said website]. He's a millionaire, but he's a douchebag, too ... He pays for everything, the apartment, the lights." Simone explained that one day her cousin's fiancé wanted out of the relationship: "He goes, 'I don't want to be with you anymore. Just leave.'" From Simone's point of view, such websites serve primarily to objectify Black women's bodies: "On [website], those guys like Black chicks with big butts."

Despite her cousin's experiences, Simone's own dating escapades involved dating several men outside her race: "From high school [to] guys I dated in college [they] were outside my race." However, the reason she gave for this was not that she found people outside her race more attract-ive, but "because the guys inside my race, they didn't find me attractive."

While Simone's comments speak to Bank's assertion that Black women need to widen their dating preferences, it is pertinent to question the motives of the non-Black men she dated. Research suggests that in many such situations, it is not so much that non-Black men find Black women physically attractive, but that it appeals to their sense of achieving a sexual conquest or public spectacle (Giddings, 2011, 2014; Lloyd, 2013; Ndlovu, 2011).[16] Relatedly, Collins (2009) discusses how white people often perceive Black women and men as being hypersexual or having an excessive sexual appetite – a misnomer that stems from slavery – where whites assumed their African enslaved descendants were prone to high sexual prowess (Berry, 2017; Collins, 2009; Davis, 1983; Spillers, 1987).

Sheri, meanwhile, appeared to present interracially dating a last resort as very much, conceding, "I'm just open to anything at this point. Hoping that maybe my desire to marry this tall Black man isn't really what's set for me." Going further, Renita – an upbeat person who loves shopping and gangster movies, and who radiated pride when talking about her parents – was unequivocal that she would only date Black men: "I don't date outside my race. I'm prejudiced. I have a great [Black] man in my life; that's my daddy. I think all Black men should be like him ... I just don't like anything outside of Black."

While almost all the Cohort's women stated a strong preference for a Black partner, there was greater variability in the views expressed by the men. Joseph was one of those who did assert that he was "more attracted to Black women," and provided both political and personal reasons for his preferences: "I'm not trying to be with white girls. In my opinion, it's not a racist thing. It is in line with my political views in terms of where Black America is right now, the state of Black America, the future outlook of Black people in America and around the world. I think if I had kids, they would be put in a conflicting situation."

We met Peter at his office on Capitol Hill, where he has worked on presidential campaigns and on the fundraising side of Congress. Peter openly acknowledged he is gay, proclaiming a preference for Black men but retaining a degree of open-mindedness: "I think it's good to keep an open mind, to a certain degree. I do prefer Black and certain Latino guys. Could I see myself in a long-term relationship with a white guy? No. Could

---

[16] This narrative resonates with the life and story of the South African woman Sara Baartman (other names include Hottentot Venus, Saartjie Baartman, Hottentot Venus, and Venus Hottentot), who was grossly objectified for her large buttocks. For more information on Baartman, see Ndlovu, S. G. (2011).

I date a white guy? Sure. I have done it before." Again, it is worth noting that – similar to views expressed by other members of the Cohort – while Peter would date a white person, he precludes a long-term relationship, perhaps hinting at similar political and personal views to those of Joseph, and/or the lack of connection such an interracial coupling would have in his eyes.

Rasheed, despite proudly proclaiming "I love my Black sisters, love them, love them, love them," went on to qualify this purported preference for Black women with the assertion, "If I date outside my race, on a scale of one to ten, she got to be a twenty-five to a thirty. She got to be the baddest thing you ever seen."

Amongst the other men, there were those who appeared equally at ease dating outside their race. Justin, who is Jamaican, had dated interracially ("I actually lost my virginity to a white girl"), while Derwin said he dated outside of his race as a "matter of convenience" (claiming it was because he was attending a historically white institution of higher education in Maryland).[17] The relative openness and ease with which the Cohort's men approach interracial dating compared to the women is perhaps a reflection of the previously mentioned point that, in contrast to Black men, Black women are perceived as being the least desirable in the dating market.

In a 2017 report commemorating the 50th anniversary of the US Supreme Court ruling of *Loving* v. *Virginia* – the ruling that struck down state laws banning interracial marriage in the United States – researchers at the Pew Research Center found one in six newlyweds are married to someone not of their own race or ethnicity (Livingston & Brown, 2017). The report goes on to say that Black men with a college degree (30%) are more than twice as likely as Black women to marry outside of their racial

---

[17] Predominantly white institutions (PWI) are often used to describe institutions of higher learning in which the white make up the majority. Bonilla-Silva and Peoples (2022) argue that most colleges in the United States *are* "HWCUs (historically white colleges and universities) with a history, demography, curriculum, climate, and a set of symbols and traditions that embody and reproduce whiteness and white supremacy" (Bonilla-Silva & Peoples, 2022). Paying attribution to one of my graduate students, Ashley Hixson, who so eloquently in her dissertation proposal defense argued that it is imperative to use HWI or HWCU instead of PWI to emphasize the violence, terror, and oppressions associated with white supremacy in higher education (Hixson, 2022; Wilder, 2013). Furthermore, there has been extensive research on higher education as sites where Black students and faculty, in particular, experience various forms of racism, including gendered-racism (Castañeda et al., 2015; Dancy et al., 2018; Fries-Britt & Kelly, 2005; Griffin & Reddick, 2011; Harper, 2012; B. T. Kelly et al., 2021; Lewis et al., 2013; Zambrana et al., 2017).

group (13%). While some may suggest that interracial marriage represents racial progress, others have pushed back on drawing such blindly positive conclusions. For instance, sociologist Chinyere Osuji's (2019) book, which provides an in-depth look at 103 Black and white interracial couples in the USA and Brazil – offers a structural argument that even within such partnerships and families, white supremacy can be reinforced and maintained (Erickson, 2020; Osuji, 2019). Thus, despite Banks's assertion that interracial dating and marriage offers a solution to Black singledom, it may be that Black people are actively choosing SALA status in preference to this option due to – as suggested by the Cohort's observations – personal, political, and practical reasons.

4.4 The Benefits of Black Marriage versus Staying Single

Turning from interracial dating to Black marriages, some scholars have suggested that the benefits of marriage and the ability to maintain the institution may not be as great for Black married couples compared to other racial and ethnic groups (Broman, 1993, 2005; Cherlin, 1998; Dillaway & Broman, 2001), though others have challenged this claim (Council, 2021; Henderson, 2020; Marks et al., 2008; South, 1993; St. Vil et al., 2018). In the essay, *Working on Single Bliss*, Distinguished University of Maryland Professor Emerita of English Mary Helen Washington, indirectly draws on the question of the benefits of marriage by quoting the words of social scientist Anna Julia Cooper. Anna Julia Cooper, one of the first Black women to obtain a PhD, dismissed the question of marriage as a false issue:

The old, subjective, stagnant, indolent, and wretched life for woman has gone. She has as many resources as men, as many activities beckon her on. As large possibilities swell and inspire her heart. Now, then, does it destroy or diminish or capacity for loving? Her standards have undoubtedly gone up. The necessity of speculating in "chawnces" [pronunciation spelling of chances] has probably shifted. The question is not now with the woman 'How shall I cramp, stunt, simplify and nullify myself as to make me eligible to the honor of being swallowed up into some little man?' but the problem, I trow [to think, believe, or trust], now rests with the man as to how he can so develop his God given powers as to reach the ideal of a generation of women who demand the noblest, grandest and best achievements of which he is capable; and this surely is the only fair and natural adjustment of the chances. Nature never meant that the ideals and standards of the world should be dwarfing and minimizing ones, and the men should thank us for requiring of them the richest fruits which they can grow. If it makes them work all the better for them. (Cooper, 1988, p. 31; Washington, 1995, p. 345; Plott & Umansky, 2000, p. 188)

Regardless, many scholars have emphasized that it is important to look at Black marriage through the intersections of race, gender, class, age, culture, identity, and nativity (Blackman et al., 2005; Bryant et al., 2008; Chaney, 2010; Chaney & Marsh, 2008; Clarke, 2011; Jenkins et al., 2020; Johnson & Loscocco, 2015; LaPierre & Hill, 2013; Mouzon et al., 2020; St. Vil et al., 2018). Beyond this, the processes and structural forces undergirding the "matrix of domination" (Collins, 2009) and the inequalities of love (Clarke, 2011) must play a salient role in how any such discussions are conceptualized.

Social scientists Belinda Tucker and Claudia Mitchell-Kernan use the 1989 Southern California Social Survey (SCSS) to examine issues related to mate availability and values attached to marriage. Based on their sample – which included over 1,000 Black, Latino, and white adults – Tucker and Mitchell-Kernan (1995) find that in general, all racial and ethnic groups, including Black respondents, value marriage. Interestingly, when the scholars did observe racial differences, Black respondents seem to value marriage more than their white counterparts (Mouzon, 2013, 2014 ; Tucker & Mitchell-Kernan, 1995; Waite & Bachrach, 2000). Furthermore, Tucker (2000) finds that the greatest difference by race and ethnicity centers on the economics of marriage: "African Americans believed most strongly that having an adequate income was critical for marital success and were most likely to see an economic benefit to be derived from marriage" (p. 180). Within the Cohort, this view linking marriage with economic stability was reflected by Maurice's assertion that, if he were to one day marry, having found an appropriate partner, he would want "to make sure our financial status is intact." Sheri also alluded to marriage and economic stability, though in a slightly more indirect way, emphasizing that she would like her potential mate to "have their own and buy their own. I mean either their own house, their car, something. Own something."

In order to better understand the emergence of the Love Jones Cohort, I draw from the economic and sociological literature, and consider social exchange and rational choice theories (Grossbard-Schectman, 2019). The general tenants of social exchange theory assert that social interactions between individuals involve a series of estimates of the rewards (gains) and punishments (losses) arising from exchanges of valued resources. This theory is based on *interpersonal transactions*, with people engaging in rational, self-motivated transactions as a means to maximize gains and minimize losses, thereby promoting their own personal goals. Rational choice theory, meanwhile, is focused on *individual* behaviors and actions, with actors utilizing certain means to achieve a desired end, with everyone afforded the same opportunity structure to achieve their desired ends. Thus, social exchange theory can be seen as the practical application of an individual making rational choices within social interactions.

Against this context, Genesis made the choice to not date for the immediate future, instead prioritizing a drama-free lifestyle: "Right now, I'm more content with being single due to other priorities. And just the whole stress of dating and that whole drama. It's all about the peace, which is very important to me. Unfortunately, dating is not really a priority." Similarly, Rick gave self-imposed life goals as his reason for not pursuing a romantic relationship, professing, "I'm content with being single right now. I'm a little bit more motivated to pursue certain goals." This view was also reflected by Alexis, who was adamant that her single status was the outcome of active decision-making: "Right now, for where I'm at in my career and my phase in life, this single living intentionally is definitely a choice."[18]

While rational choice theory has been criticized on a number of counts (Hechter & Kanazawa, 1997), it has increasingly been applied to individual decision-making around mate selection, fertility, divorce, and other family formations (Friedman et al., 1994; Hechter & Kanazawa, 1997; H. L. Smith, 1989). I argue that due in large part to structural impediments and anti-Black sentiment in various social institutions, many Black adults – especially Black women – lack the opportunity (Hamilton et al., 2009), and moreover may not wish, to exchange their resources for marriage (Blackman et al., 2005; Clarke, 2011). Despite this, they are increasingly achieving (maximizing) middle-class status, leading to the swelling ranks of the Love Jones Cohort.

Relevant to exploring the motivations behind Cohort members making the choice to remain single is the argument that the very institution of marriage – at least as it is practiced and idealized in the USA – rests on implicitly racist assumptions. English professor Candice Jenkins, for example, has challenged the frequently deployed term "nuclear family,"[19] framing a portion of her argument around the Distinguished University Professor Emerita of English Hortense Spillers's 1987 essay, "Mama's Baby,

---

[18] See Hill (2020) on how both men and women "privilege career pursuits, women are more likely to report opting for singlehood, by intentionally delaying romantic relationships, marriage, and family formation until they have met career goals."

[19] Her essay appears in *Keywords for American Cultural Studies, Third Edition*, a hybrid print-digital publication that includes 150 essays, each focused on a single term such as "America," "culture," "diversity," or "religion." https://keywords.nyupress.org/american-cultural-studies/.

Papa's Maybe: An American Grammar Book." Jenkins quotes Spillers's observation that the nuclear family is "a discursive and ideological institution deeply implicated by histories of white supremacy and racist violence" (Jenkins as quoting Spillers (Giddings, 2011, 2014; Lloyd, 2013; Spillers, 1987)), before going on to argue that Spillers's work "[s]poke back to and paved the way for other Black women's writing on 'family' that highlighted the institution's fraught history and the ways that the word 'family,' particularly in its narrowest senses, has operated as a disciplinary term –with those who are disciplined by the concept overwhelmingly Black women."

Meanwhile, as professors Christiana Awosan and Ijeoma Opara (Awosan & Opara, 2016) assert, though, "A few quantitative studies examined demographic factors ... [contributing] to the 'shortage of eligible or marriageable Black men' and rise in singlehood among Blacks ... these studies do not aid in understanding never-married heterosexual Black men and women's qualitative experiences of romantic involvement and relationships" (p. 446). Along with my work on the Love Jones Cohort, there is a growing body of research on college-educated Black women and the social drivers behind the barriers to romance they face, their reproductive decisions, and how they form families. Sociologist Averil Clarke (2011), for instance, drawing on 58 in-depth interviews with college-educated Black women (under the age of 50 to focus on those of child-bearing age) supplemented by survey data from the National Survey of Family Growth, provides a comprehensive study on the dating practices of, challenges faced by, and outcomes achieved by these women. In line with similar scholarship, Clarke concludes that due to constraints and inequities arising from class, gender, and race, Black women are often deprived of loving, sexual, and reproductive relations. Instead, they find themselves floating in and out of sexual relationships that provide little to no companionship or commitment (Clarke, 2011; Hill, 2013; Landor & Barr, 2018).

Building on these findings, Clarke challenges scholars to examine how family formations are often a manifestation of social inequalities, and how even the most intimate lifestyle arenas of Black women are subject to the effects of their intersecting social positionalities. Clarke's scholarship both provides a necessary intersectional approach and casts a light on the structural constraints affecting marriage decline among the Black middle class, especially educated Black women. While the Black women in Clarke's study desire upwardly mobile lifestyles, the messages they receive around relationships, family formation, and fertility are often steeped in respectability politics, which may result in negative impacts on their psychological well-being.

In applying social exchange theory to mate selection, the underlying argument is that men exchange their economic resources and/or social status for women's physical attractiveness, sex, or household service (Becker, 1991). This, though, overlooks how intersections of race, class, and gender can intersect to affect such exchanges (Clarke, 2011; Collins, 2004; Crenshaw, 1990; Landor & Barr, 2018). Scholars Antoinette Landor and Ashley Barr (2018) argue "[a]ny critical approach to family research – whether it be a gender perspective . . . a critical race perspective . . . or a more explicitly intersectional perspective . . . demands attention to symbolic structure" (p. 333). This symbolic structure (Bourdieu, 1989, 2001) is permeated by symbolic violence – the exercise of control and domination not by force but the cultivation and widespread dissemination of cultural rules that maintain social hierarchies – against Black people and families (Landor & Barr, 2018).

Collins (2004) points out that, in the spirit of respectability politics, Black women often submit to Black male dominance. This can result in unfulfilling and even toxic relationships conducted in order to maintain an image of good wife and mother (Collins, 2004; Landor & Barr, 2018), with Black women constantly admonished that they must be "respectable" (Collins, 2004; Cooper, 2017, 2018; Cottom, 2018). On this point, Landor and Barr (2018) draw out Clarke's observations on the rationality (or otherwise) of unhealthy or unfulfilling relationships, noting that Clarke (2011) "contended that the decision to return to or maintain relationships 'already calculated as pointless' was neither rational nor irrational, as 'rationality is of little use when weighing the costs and benefits of the various ways of remaining unfulfilled'" (p. 150).

Scholars drawing on an intersectional lens may theorize that Black women are faced with two competing "rational" choices (Clarke, 2011; Collins, 2004; Landor & Barr, 2018). On the one hand, they can submit to the oppressive nature of respectability politics by engaging in relationships and marriages. This means being fully aware that such relationships may be shaped by gender inequality, inequity, capitalism, heteronormativity, patriarchy, and gendered racism. On the other hand, these women can challenge respectability politics by forgoing unfulfilling romantic relationships, making a rational and agentic decision to carve out a SALA lifestyle that includes fulfilling and gratifying non-romantic relationships with friends and family members. From this point of view, choosing a SALA lifestyle may be viewed as challenging the politics of respectability, even demonstrating a level of disrespectability politics (Cooper, 2017).[20]

Landor and Barr (2018) put it as follows: "For many African American women, then, the purported choice seems to be between enhancing collective respectability and assuming a personal 'tax,' or avoiding the personal tax and forgoing respectability." In other words, you're darned if you do and darned if you don't, but you darn sure need to understand that structural factors can constrain individual opportunities. This often leaves Black women grappling with choosing between the lesser of two evils. Thus, the "rational" choices open to professional Black women are predicated on "irrational" policies, practices, and processes that undervalue and even express open disdain for Blackness. This directly and indirectly has the propensity to shape the intimate spaces and romantic relationships (or lack thereof) open to the Love Jones Cohort.

The fact that a growing number of Black women[21] – and men – seem willing to forgo respectability politics and actively choose singlehood is perhaps one reason underlying the rise of the Love Jones Cohort. In this regard and bearing in mind the earlier discussion of rational choice theory, Kendra's recounting of how she ended an unfulfilling relationship, and how her now ex-boyfriend responded, is telling: "He told me that I was so cold. Detached from emotions. He said everything that I did was based on logic and rational thinking. And it was all true." Kendra acknowledged, "That was not the best relationship" but that was ultimately, she learned, "[a] lot and I knew exactly what I did not want."

This chapter has set out some of the quantitative and theoretical rationalizations that have been put forward or may be relevant in explaining the rise of Black middle-class SALAs in the USA, backed up by relevant narratives from interviewed members of the Love Jones Cohort. In the next chapter, I delve deeper into whether the members of the Cohort have assumed SALA status through choice, circumstance, or both.

---

[20] In her research, Scholar Aneeka Henderson (2020) suggests that "no amount of respectability is able to reverse reports and representations implying that Black women are considered to be the least desirable on the marriage market or capable of erasing the racialized sexual and gender pathology appended two Black women's flesh" (p. 9). Henderson argues that through fictional depiction, such Black women are encouraged "to suffer through abuse and assault in order to sustain a facade of bourgeoisie nuclear family" (p. 9).

[21] For an example, visit the podcast, Unchained. Unbothered. with Keturah Kendrick, http://unchainedunbotheredpodcast.com/.

5

Choice, Circumstance, or Both?

Sociologist Eric Klinenberg has argued that the rise in singlehood should be regarded as social change, not a social problem. His work, however, draws little attention to the race or class dimensions of this demographic shift. Similarly, in examining the emotional well-being of singlehood, sociologist Elyakim Kislev asserts that never-married people are happier than those who have been married, but fails to include a nuanced discussion of race. Social psychologist Bella DePaulo's research highlights how singles are stereotyped, stigmatized, and ignored, but again provides scant context on race and ethnicity. Journalist Kate Bolick, meanwhile, hypothesizes that *white* single women are choosing to be single by choice. Collectively, this scholarship overlooks how systemic inequalities, including racism and gendered racism, shape singlehood among Black adults, especially Black women. Such shortcomings are particularly relevant when it comes to looking at whether Black individuals are single through choice or circumstance (or both) and what the implications of this are for the Love Jones Cohort, particularly, and the Black middle class, more generally.

Among the interviewed members of the Love Jones Cohort, 62% say they are actively dating. Figure 5.1 unpacks the question of whether a person considers their singlehood to be a choice, the product of circumstance, or a mixture of the two, especially for those in the dating market.[1]

---

[1] Figure 5.1 represents an attempt to categorize those interviewees who explicitly used choice, circumstance, or both when initially describing their SALA status. As the interview continued, interviewees often offered explanations that slipped between choice and circumstance and/or an amalgamation of both. Thus, this figure captures interviewees' initial responses regarding their SALA status, before additional information was provided in their narratives.

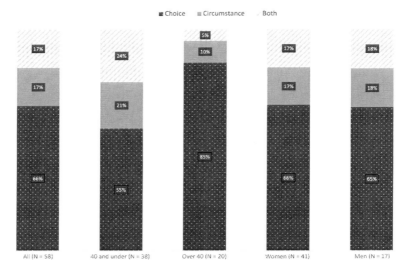

Figure 5.1. Percentage of Love Jones Cohort, by age and gender, who classify their SALA status as being due to choice, circumstance, or both

Overall, two-thirds of the Cohort claimed to be SALA by choice, with the remaining third equally split between those who considered their SALA status to be the result of circumstance and those who saw it as resulting from an amalgamation of choice and circumstance. Once the figures are broken down according to age and gender, a couple of interesting stories emerge. Among members of the Cohort aged 40 and above, an overwhelming 85% reported being SALA by choice, compared to a much lower figure of 55% for those under the age of 40. In terms of gender, it is pertinent to note that the responses given by both women and men reflected the same percentages across the entire Cohort; that is, two-thirds claimed to be single by choice, with the remainder equally split between circumstance and both.

5.1 Circumstances Constraining Choice

Nancy – who remained pleasant and engaged throughout our two-hour interview and spoke with a hint of Southern drawl – was one of those in the Cohort who explicitly brought up the issue of choice early on in our conversation, asserting, "I don't choose to be single, but I choose to be respected and in a relationship with someone who has the same mindset [to respect her]." Nancy was adamant that "I'm not going to stand for . . .

opportunistic men who just want to play around on you" and went on to say that her single status "is definitely by choice." Pointing her finger as she dismissed "those type of men," she clarified, "I don't choose to be alone; I choose to live alone." Thus, though Nancy ultimately claims her single-dom is by choice, it appears that this choice has been constrained by previous failed relationships with men who were unfaithful or disrespect-ful. Moreover, though Nancy did not specifically mention any issues of racism, sexism, or gendered racism as reasons for her singleness, it may well be that such forces impacted the dating pool she had to choose from.[2]

My interview with Carrie felt like a comfortable conversation among friends, and with a hint of sarcasm and humor, she told me, "I'm single and I live alone. To me it just means that I'm single. I don't know what else." Carrie went on to elaborate that her single status is by choice, yet compli-cated. Speaking with a hint of nostalgia in her voice, she explained, "I've made clear choices. I was engaged when I was younger and called that engagement off . . . So that's why I say it's by choice, because as I've gotten older, I've definitely got a clearer sense of where I'm going in my own life." While she admitted that "at this time, it just so happens" that the right person was not in her life, she asserted, "I believe that he'll come." Elsewhere, Glenda, while in some ways echoing Carrie's perspective, veered toward saying her SALA status hadn't been driven by choice, as she hadn't been offered a sufficiently attractive alternative: "I'm living alone because life hasn't presented me with a better alternative . . . I'm thirty-six, I kind of feel like at this point it's a big if, because there's some really weird people out there, but if life presents me with a viable alternative, then I'll give it a go, so it's not necessarily by choice."

Nancy's and Carrie's stories – as well as those told by other members of the Cohort – clearly suggest that their current SALA status, decisions, hopes, and views of the future are informed by their previous circum-stances. Thus, the explicit assertion on the part of many in the Cohort that they are SALA by choice is tempered somewhat by the implicit acknowledgment that their previous dating experiences and circumstances are woven into the threads of their SALA status. Referring back to the work of Clarke (2011) and Collins (2004), Nancy, Carrie, and other women in the Cohort appear unwilling to exchange their resources for the

---

[2] Given that Nancy's reply is quite ambiguous, she opens by saying she didn't choose to be single, then goes on to say that her SALA status is by choice, I struggled with which category to classify her into for Figure 5.1. However, I settled on the classification of *both* for Nancy. Please take this into consideration when you review Figure 5.1.

under-maximization of unfulfilling relationships. Put another way, these women are suggesting that the issue is that they are unable to find a fulfilling relationship to commit to and/or exchange their resources for.

5.2 Institutional and Societal Constraints

While it is possible that Nancy and Carrie are aware that the oppressive institutional constraints facing Black Americans – specifically Black men – are greatly relevant, whether directly or indirectly, in preventing these two Black women and others like them from partaking in fulfilling and rewarding romantic relationships, it is not something they publicly discuss in their interviews. In relation to this, drawing on theories related to rational choice, social exchange, and critical race that highlight how race, racism, and anti-Blackness permeate social institutions, we wanted to explore how the criminal record of a potential suitor might shape Cohort members' dating preferences. Of those who touched on the subject, the vast majority (80%) mentioned that they were willing to date someone with a criminal record, though 7 out of 10 of these Cohort members were explicit that it would "depend on what they did."

At the extreme end of the scale, Sheri recalled that, back when she was a teenager, she had dated a man before becoming aware – on their third date – that he was on probation, yet she continued to date him: "The guy told me he shot somebody. I was like, 'What? Oh, wow. Okay' ... I dated him for three [or] four months [but the relationship] didn't last long. It had really nothing to do with that [the probation], it more so had to do with his cleanliness." Moreover, 14% of the Cohort who were willing to date someone with a criminal record explicitly brought up the fact that anti-Blackness and discrimination in the criminal justice system and policing have the potential to produce spurious criminal records, with Shannon, for example, proclaiming, "Because of our judiciary, our legal system is not in favor of Black men ... We live in a society where, just in [Washington] DC, you had Black men going to jail for marijuana. Now that there's an influx of non-Black people moving into the city, now marijuana is legal." This discriminatory criminalization of Black men is one possible factor constraining the choices Black women make when it comes to their dating status, in turn leading to a rise in the number of SALA women.

Tanya, who had recently been laid off, spoke of how her current circumstances as caregiver had a direct bearing on her SALA status. Tanya's long-distance romantic relationship had ended nearly 18 months prior to our meeting, and she explained her single status since then in the context of her caregiving responsibilities: "It's more so by circumstance. Some people will probably tell me, 'You're lying; it's by choice.' No, circumstance more so, in the sense that being a caregiver for my mother has overtaken my life . . . my life does not allow me to free up emotionally and physically for another person." Meanwhile, Olivia, who we spoke to for over two-and-a-half hours at her massive ranch home in Prince George's County, admitted she had purchased the house "a little under duress" in 2003. One of her parents had lost their legs to diabetes, and as their caregiver, Olivia required a one-level home accessible to her parents.

Historically, Black women have been tasked by the wider Black community with mothering and caregiving responsibilities (Barnes, 2015; Collins, 1998, 2004; Ellick, 2021). Even when Black women are not biological mothers, as is the case for those in the Love Jones Cohort, expectations are often placed upon them (whether directly or indirectly) that they should assume such caregiving responsibilities where necessary. Research suggests that aging Black Americans heavily rely on informal systems of caregiving, with Black caregivers more often a child (presumably a daughter) or other family member than a spouse (Chadiha et al., 2004; Fabius et al., 2020).

Various researchers have explored the coping abilities and strategies of Black women caregivers (Dilworth-Anderson et al., 2002; Ellick, 2021; Williams & Dilworth-Anderson, 2002), with Sharon Wallace Williams and Peggye Dilworth-Anderson (2002) conducting a quantitative study of 187 Black caregivers (82% of whom were women) of impaired elderly family members. The study examined the social support for the caregivers, which they found often relied on a combination of informal, formal, and church systems. Williams and Dilworth-Anderson note the implications of their study: "Cohesive family networks and network size are important factors that help determine what support caregivers receive. African American caregivers may be at risk for negative health outcomes because they are less likely to use formal support as care recipients' activities of daily living limitations increase" (p. 224).

Other scholarship has also shown how Black women such as those in the Cohort often feel obligated to help others, including their extended family and fictive kin, even when this may have detrimental effects on their financial, physiological, and psychological well-being (Chiteji & Hamilton, 2002; Higginbotham, 2001; Woods-Giscombé, 2010). Health scholar Cheryl Woods-Giscombé (2010) sought to develop a conceptual framework for the Superwoman Schema (SWA) by conducting focus groups with single (no spouse or children) Black women, aged 25–45 (a demographic Tanya would fit into). Woods-Giscombé found that within these women's familial and extended networks, there was often an expectation that they had more time to take on certain roles and responsibilities, and that often they found it uncomfortable to push back against such assumptions. A similar trend was evident among a number of members of the Cohort, who found themselves providing financial and social support to the detriment of their own social, physical, and financial health (something that will be explored further in Chapters 7 and 10). These perceived societal obligations and the consequences arising from them can have clear impacts on an individual's dating choices – that is, whether their SALA status is by choice or circumstances. The persistence of such expectations within the Black middle class, therefore, represents a potential factor in women joining and remaining within the Love Jones Cohort.

As outlined in Chapter 4, rational choice theory is focused on individual behaviors and actions, while social exchange theory is based on interpersonal transactions. From a rational choice theory perspective, the Cohort's narratives suggest that the growth of singlehood may be a conscious choice – in other words, people behave in logical and internally motivated ways. However, this theory pays little direct attention to the powerful structural and societal forces that potentially constrain choice and lead to individuals choosing SALA status as their best available option.

5.3 Respectability Singleness

Regarding those women in the Cohort who are circumstantially single, I argue that in many cases they engage in *respectability singleness*. While they may want a relationship, they have made an active choice not to pursue a man or ask him on a date. As Olivia (54) explained, "Well, it's unlikely I'll be pursuing anything. I am content being single, but if I were being pursued—" Stopping mid-sentence, Olivia quoted the Bible scripture (Proverbs 18:22): "*For he who finds himself a wife finds himself a good thing.* Which means he's pursuing; I would not be opposed to that. I'm always open to being caught." Kelsey (40) expressed a similar perspective, explaining she was content to leave her fate in the hands of a higher power: "I am interested in [having] a serious relationship with the right person. If I don't meet that right person, then I'm fine with being single. One thing I don't want to do is be in a relationship with the wrong person. I'm trusting God for that right person."

Other women in the Cohort across the age spectrum also embraced their circumstantial singleness or respectability singleness, expressing that though they would be interested in a relationship if the right person approached them, they were not open to pursuing a man simply for the sake of being in a relationship. For these women, their SALA status and lifestyle is informed by a belief that pursuit should take the form of man-to-woman, not woman-to-man, a conviction that is very much in line with respectability politics. For them, being the protagonist or initiator in a romantic relationship is simply not acceptable or appropriate. Scholars have argued that Black women are constantly subject to pressures to conform to a performative "ladylike" trope or to behave respectably (Collins, 2004; Cooper, 2017, 2018; Cottom, 2018; Higginbotham, 1994).

As psychologist Lisa Bowleg and colleagues (Bowleg et al., 2004) put it: "A prevailing gendered cultural scenario for African American women is that they must be traditionally feminine in their intimate heterosexual relationships, and also be nontraditional in terms of their workforce participation" (p. 71). Bowleg then goes on to provide an alternative explanation: "[W]omen, recognizing the mundane racism that their male partners experience, allow men to control some aspects of relationships as a way to compensate for the fact that their partners fall short of hegemonic masculinity ideals such as economic and professional prowess" (p. 72).

Meanwhile, public policy and sociology scholar Maria Johnson (2013), in her work on Black daughter–father relationships, highlights that respectability politics is steeped in Black women (and girls) having to conform to the standards of white middle-class femininity, which include "piety, purity, submissiveness, and domesticity (Moore, 2011)" (Battle, 2016; Johnson, 2013). The pressure to meet such societally imposed standards was implicit in what many of the Cohort's women said, suggesting that it plays a significant role in why so many Black women are choosing or being pushed into long-term SALA status.

Sheri was one of those among the Cohort who suggested an internal deficit – that they were somehow lacking something – among the circumstantial reasons explaining why they were not in a serious relationship. Sheri spoke in absolutes as she described her SALA status. "I would like a serious relationship; I just don't know how to go about it. I've had so many fails [relationships]." She went on to acknowledge that men would say to her, "You make me feel bad about myself," or "You're insecure," or "You're jealous," and admitted that she had a "fear of being alone," which she pointed to as being "one of the reasons why I'm always having these setbacks and I'm always alone." At the time of the interview, Sheri was involved in another dysfunctional relationship: "I'm with a guy, he's 10 years younger than me, and he's annoying. I'm just with him because: primarily, he puts up with me and I put up with him … he tends to do some immature things like creating a Plenty of Fish [online dating site] profile while we're dating."

Sheri's comments show that she is fully aware that she is forsaking her own mental well-being for an unfulfilling, ultimately pointless relationship (Clarke, 2011; Collins, 2004). In doing so, it can be argued that Sheri is grappling with the internal pressures of respectability politics (Landor & Barr, 2018) and assuming a personal tax of being in a relationship for the sake of public respectability rather than choosing to assert her singlehood. Such is the power of the all-pervading societal ideals that lead people – especially women – to accept that being partnered or married is necessary to be a "respectable" adult (and, to some degree, a member of the middle class).

Carrie's comments on dating echoed Sheri's sentiments: "Internal pressures sometimes lead to people – mostly women – to settle for sub-par behavior from a dating partner while seeking a suitable mate." This suggests that unproductive relationships may sometimes be used as a placeholder until a respectable and suitable partner becomes available. Carrie added this qualifier: "I'm definitely content with being single. It sometimes takes work to get to that place because I think society is all about being coupled up, especially for women. Being in a relationship somehow validates you." She went on to discuss using dating hiatuses in order to recharge herself from exposure to the dating market, stating, "I talk with my friends all the time who [see] me going through a dating hiatus and have said, 'I really admire you. You are in a place where you're just focused on yourself.' … That's not to say it's easy, but I just get to a place where I'm not settling."

5.4 Looking to the Future

Turning to the Cohort's men, Kevin commented:

I think I might wish one day when I'm an old man sitting in my chair and think damn, I remember when I could just come home to nothing. No kids, no wife, no nothing, and I could just sit down and be with myself. That's why I try to embrace the time that I'm in [being SALA]. When that other time comes [marriage], then I'll have something to kind of think back on.

Thus, Kevin's contentment with his SALA status seems predicated on anticipated future changes in his circumstances. Juxtaposing Kevin's comments with those of Carrie and Sheri points to an apparent gender-related difference in the outlook of the Cohort's men and women. While Kevin is *assuming* that appropriate opportunity will eventually present itself, Carrie and Sheri are left *hoping* it does. In other words, Kevin is waiting for the time to come, while Carrie and Sheri are conscious that their time may already be up.[3] Age, of course, may play an important role in these perspectives: Kevin was 25 at the time of the interview, while Carrie and Sheri were in their early thirties.

For many in the Cohort, including those unable to provide a clear-cut answer to whether their SALA status was due to choice, circumstance, or both, the future played a salient role in their explanations. Specifically, while content with their current choice to be single, they anticipated being in a relationship, among other things, once a certain degree of personal growth had been achieved. Madison's response exemplified this attitude: "Staying single allows me more time to feel more complete and whole as a person, as an individual ... Once I start feeling more complete as an individual and once I start doing more of the things I find personally fulfilling, achieving personal goals and dreams and aspirations ... I feel like I'll meet someone."

In some ways, the line of future thinking expressed by Madison – and reflected by many others in the Cohort – about finding a long-term partner and so leaving the Love Jones Cohort challenges one of my research's assumptions that SALAs will maintain or grow its share of Black middle-class households over time. Such prognostication also challenges some of the social science literature suggesting that for Black women, having an advanced degree or a successful career significantly reduces, from a statistical perspective, their chances of getting married or having a child. Sociologist Jennifer Lundquist and colleagues (Lundquist et al., 2009), for instance, assert in their quantitative study on race and childlessness in America from 1988 to 2002 that "[c]ontrary to common arguments regarding the cultural normativity of nonmarital childbearing among all Black women, highly educated Black women, similar to their White counterparts, are still more likely to remain childless than their less educated peers" (p. 753).

A possible solution to this conundrum perhaps lies in the fact that while some in the Cohort would ideally like to marry and have children, they are, however, unwilling to do so at any price. Paige was one of those who made

---

[3] This point is further explored in relation to wealth accumulation in Chapter 8.

clear that she was unwilling to rush into a relationship just for the sake of changing her SALA status: "If it doesn't feel right, if it's not right, if it's going to advance into something that's right, that feels right, [if not] then I'm not interested." Renita concurred, saying that despite the fact that she expected to marry one day, "I'm very secure in who and what I am, and I know I won't settle for anything. A lot of times people think because you're single that you're desperate. I'm not desperate." Grace also expressed similar opinions, stating, "If I find somebody, great. If I don't? I'm happy and I've learned to be happy … It's hard to incorporate somebody into your world when you are comfortable with certain things, in my opinion."

Meanwhile, London was among the most explicit in expressing the viewpoint that though marriage remained a hoped-for outcome, her preference was to remain SALA if the right person failed to present himself:

I want a husband, so I am content … if someone was to say they wanted to get married tomorrow and I felt that way about that person too, then I would change it, but it has to be a good fit for me. I'm 40 and … been by myself long enough, I rather wait and find the right person to just have somebody to say I've got somebody.

While such attitudes were commonplace – to a greater or lesser degree of certainty – among the Cohort's women, it is notable that comparable discussions about marriage and settling (or otherwise) for the sake of it did not come up with the Cohort's men. This is not to say, though, that the men showed no ambivalence to their SALA status, with William, for example, stating that he didn't "necessarily think the pros outweigh the cons. It's the other way around." In comparing his SALA lifestyle with those of his married friends, he conceded, "When I look at my friends and their situations, there's part of me that thinks, wow, that's really good; you have a solid foundation, the kids, the wife, and the things that you have endured."

This chapter has looked at the degree to whether the women and men of the Love Jones chose their SALA status and how systemic inequalities, institutional constraints, and societal pressures play a role in such decision-making (or lack thereof), particularly among the Cohort's women. It suggests that while many hope or anticipate that they will one day marry and so leave the Cohort, this is not something they are willing to pay any price to achieve. As a consequence, some will likely remain SALA into middle age and beyond, bolstering the numbers of Black middle-class members of this demographic. Next, we turn to the lifestyle attributes and characteristics of those in the Love Jones Cohort in order to determine what light they can shed on America's Black middle class.

6

Lifestyle Ebbs and Flows

The existence of the Love Jones Cohort, whether members belong to this demographic by choice or circumstance, offers a fresh lens with which to explore the lifestyle characteristics of the Black middle class. Earlier research on the Black middle class – which has often been equated with married-couple families – asserts that they face the ongoing problem of having to stabilize their class position. This can take one or more of five forms: (1) purchasing and maintaining a house in a "good" neighborhood; (2) developing and maintaining strong institutional ties (e.g. attending the "right" church, belonging to alumni associations, participating in politics); (3) securing and keeping positions commensurate with middle-class status (family stability, white-collar occupations, and high levels of education); (4) attaining high levels of education; and (5) developing and exemplifying behavior patterns and lifestyles appropriate to the middle class (Durant & Louden, 1986; Frazier, 1957). In looking at the lifestyle strategies and attributes of the Love Jones Cohort, this chapter examines how the decision to not marry and instead continue to live alone may impact such attempts to stabilize their class position.

Based on the narratives provided by our interviewees, own space and life, freedom, and self-reliance are central aspects of the Cohort lifestyle, as is – for many in the Cohort – loneliness. In addressing this latter issue, the Cohort lifestyle places great emphasis on the human interaction and companionship provided by family, friends, and social networks. The interviews also shed light on how the perceptions of and pressures emanating from family and friends help shape how members of the Cohort understand their lifestyles, and to navigate the ebbs and flows that arise.

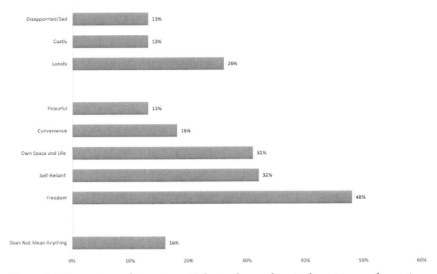

Figure 6.1. Percentage of Love Jones Cohort who used neutral, positive, and negative words to describe their lifestyle

6.1 Neutral, Positive, and Negative Views of Being SALA

Descriptions provided by interviewees of the Love Jones Cohort lifestyle fit into three broad categories: neutral, positive, and negative.[1] Figure 6.1 reports these three areas. A neutral response is that the SALA lifestyle is not perceived as being of relevance to the Cohort member. In terms of a positive response (what I would describe as the *flows* of being SALA), the most popular terms used were "freedom" (mentioned by nearly half of the Cohort), "self-reliant" or "independent," and "own space and life." Conversely, in terms of a negative response (the *ebbs* of being SALA), the most commonly used terms were "lonely" (touched on by a quarter of the group), "disappointed/sad," and "costly." Cohort members often used multiple indicators to describe their lifestyle.

Among the Cohort, 16% felt that their SALA status and lifestyle did not have any wider meaning; that is, it was "neutral."[2] This, of course,

---

[1] The categories are not mutually exclusive; over the course of the interview, a Cohort member may have described their lifestyle in ways that fell into one or more of the categories.

[2] I am using *does not mean anything* response as a neutral classification.

is not to suggest that they see SALA lifestyle as meaningless. Rather, the point these Cohort members appeared to be making was that their lifestyle was not a political or social statement aimed at public consumption, with no connection made between their SALA lifestyle and structural forces, systemic racism, and declining Black marriage rates. Nor did they appear to view their SALA lifestyle as in any way being an affront to Black love, Black marriage, Black relationships, Black women, or Black men. Generally, the feeling expressed by these individuals was that they did not give the basis of their SALA lifestyle much attention, nor did they want to spend much time discussing the subject during the interview.

Layla was one of the more self-reflexive interviewees, taking a long pause to think about her SALA status and lifestyle before weighing up the pros and cons. On the positive side, she pointed to the freedom afforded her by being SALA (something mentioned by 48% of the Cohort interviewees): "It means I have freedom to make decisions that I need to make; I don't have to consult with anyone." However, she caveated this statement by acknowledging that the SALA lifestyle "has its pluses and minuses. But, you know, I make the best of it."

Layla's ambiguous phrase "I make the best of it" was echoed by Lillian, who observed, "It's just what I have to do." In both these cases, the wording used could imply discontent with their SALA status, that they are making the best out of a less-than-ideal situation and/or that they do not want to ruminate over their current relationship circumstances. However, Patricia, who used a similar phrase to describe her status – "it's just the way it is" – was explicit in putting a more positive gloss on her situation, claiming she had "no problems with living alone" and pointing to the life-skills this had provided her with. Here, Patricia is among the 32% of Cohort interviewees who mentioned self-reliance as a positive aspect of their SALA status: "There are people in my age group [50s] that are now going through divorce. They don't have the skills to make decisions because someone has taken care of them all their life. To find yourself in this age group and suddenly alone is not a good situation for them compared to me." Patricia's comments resonate with one of the central tenets put forth by Kislev (2019) – namely, that those who have been living alone long term are often better equipped to handle their single status later in life than people who suddenly find themselves returned to single status following separation, divorce, or death of a partner (Kislev, 2019, 2022a, 2022b).

6.2 Friendship, Freedom, and Situational Loneliness

Among the Love Jones Cohort, friends are often perceived as an extension of their families, cast as daily characters with starring roles in their SALA lifestyles and emotional well-being, and can serve to counter bouts of loneliness. Members of the Cohort expressed how their friends met various aspects of their social needs, whether this be workout friends, golf buddies, and/or foodie fellows. Such social networks are particularly relevant in the case of the Cohort given that the most cited negative aspect of SALA status was "loneliness" (mentioned by 26% of interviewees). In concert with the book *Family Life in Black America* (Taylor et al., 1997), sociologist Tetyana Pudrovska and colleagues (2006) point out in this regard: "Black persons are less likely than white adults to depend upon and interact with members of the nuclear family only and instead maintain more diffuse social networks that may provide an important source of instrumental and expressive support as older Black individuals adjust to the strains of singlehood" (Pudrovska et al., 2006, p. 320).

Also relevant to this aspect of the ebbs and flows of SALA life, particularly for Black women, is the work of my previous graduate student, Kecia Ellick, and my previous undergraduate student, Nina Page. Family science scholar Kecia Ellick (2021) uses intersectionality as an analytical tool to explore the coping strategies of 24 highly educated (PhD, ScD, PsyD, MD, EdD, etc.) Black women in Georgia – some of whom were single and never married – arguing that a key coping mechanism for these highly educated Black women is to lean on friends and family for emotional support. These Black women "[c]ultivated sister circles of other Black women with whom to commiserate about shared experiences, seek advice, or simply vent their mutual frustrations" (Ellick, 2021).[3]

Nina Page (2020), meanwhile, uses singleness as an analytical framework to provide a literary analysis of playwright Ntozake Shange's work, showing how the writer conveys "love like sisters," and how, through togetherness and healing, Black women supported one another in the face of adversity (Page, 2020). In building her singleness analytical framework, Page draws on English Professor Mary Helen Washington's 1982 essay, "Working at Single Bliss." In this essay, Washington (1982) asserts that single Black women should view their singleness as an attitude,

---

[3] Several scholars discuss how beauty salons, and related digital communities, serve as sites for friendships, sisterhood, activism, entrepreneurship, and self-care for Black women (N. T. Battle, 2021; Gill, 2010, 2015; Jacobs-Huey, 2006; Wingfield, 2008).

not a status, thereby allowing them to focus on strengthening their non-romantic relationships with other Black women (Page, 2020; Washington, 1982). These types of relationships – often referred to as using such terms as reciprocal nourishment, sister-circle of friends, sorority sisters, sisterhood, sistah-circle, and/or sister-friend (Davis, 2019; Davis & Afifi, 2019; hooks, 1986, 2000; Washington, 1982) – challenge the restrictive definition of the family used both in the Census and elsewhere. Even as these types of close friendships do not technically count as familial relations, they undoubtedly offer family-type relations and social support, something attested to by the women of the Love Jones Cohort.

Relevant to this discussion are the findings of an empirical study that used the National Survey of Families and Households and the General Social Survey to test competing arguments about the merits of singlehood, marriage, and social integration (Sarkisian & Gerstel, 2016, p. 377). The study found support for the view that singlehood "is associated with greater social involvement. Compared to those married, the singles are more likely to contact and receive help from their parents or siblings. Single people are more likely than those married to give help to, get help from, or socialize with neighbors or friends" (p. 377).

Time and again, female members of the Cohort emphasized the high value they placed on friendships and the importance of these social networks in providing support for their SALA lifestyles. Nancy, for example, asserted, "My friends and family tend to check on me even more [because she is single]." Tanya, meanwhile, while acknowledging there are ebbs and flows to her SALA lifestyle, stressed the role of her friends in extenuating the positive: "It's a wave. I think the importance of a lot of us having a support system, hanging out with friends, and having an outlet with them is helpful." Kelsey was another member of the Cohort who, rather than dwell on the negatives of living alone, highlighted the benefits of socializing with friends: "Just because you live alone, doesn't mean you're always alone. Because you have friends you can always go out with, invite over, or go to their homes."

Turning to the men, sociologist Robert Staples (Staples, 1981) suggests in his book on Black singles, "Single males have fewer meaningful friendships with either sex than most women ... Women are more likely to be socialized into a nurturant role that compliments the friendship role. Men maintain a certain emotional distance from other men due to the fear of being labeled homosexual or weak" (p. 122). Whereas women see their female friends as sources of emotional support, Staples argues that men view their male friends primarily as sources of practical help or people to do things with (activities). One possible implication of this in terms of the Cohort and being SALA is that Black women comprise a much higher proportion of the Cohort and are more likely than their male counterparts to need the emotional support that friendships provide them both in the present and into later life.

Within the Cohort's men, Reggie, Rick, and William mentioned their friends. Reggie's reference to his friendship circle perhaps reflects a more pragmatic outlook: "My friends come over . . .We have a rooftop pool and different stuff like that. They'll come over and want to hang out and chill." Rick also mentioned that he enjoys spending time and doing things with his friends and works to maintain the relationship, "[p]articularly as you get older when you're not really making friends anymore." William enjoys playing sports, presumably with his friends, as he spoke often of spending time with them.

As touched on previously, freedom was a prominent feature in the lifestyle scripts of many in the Love Jones Cohort (with 48% explicitly mentioning freedom), as was, relatedly, having one's "own space and life" (mentioned by 31% of interviewees). Walter, for example, whom we talked to at his home in a quiet suburban area on the outskirts of Prince George's County, was emphatic that his lifestyle "[m]eans freedom. It means flexibility. It means liberation. It means comfortability. It means individuality. It means independence." For Walter, this positive aspect of the SALA lifestyle was not just about the freedom *to* move within his own space, but signaled freedom *from* other people and their emotional baggage: "Freedom from having to deal with other people's anything." This latter comment perhaps also speaks to the point made earlier about single Black men viewing friendship in a different light to Black women.

Like Walter, who laughingly observed, "when I come home, I know that everything that I left there is to be where I left it." Layla enjoyed the freedom and control of knowing, "I have my space. I only have myself to blame if I can't locate something. I don't have to worry about going to particular rooms in the house if I don't want to talk to a partner or something." Nancy and Glenda, meanwhile, extolled the freedom afforded them by their SALA lifestyle in relation to food. Nancy observed, "If I want to eat popcorn and have a glass of wine for dinner, then that's what I do." Glenda lightheartedly described playing a self-invented game of "Create a Meal," which entailed looking for things in her house with which to make a meal, with the result that she sometimes ended up with donuts for dinner. Elsewhere, LaToya linked her SALA status with her freedom to travel, proclaiming, "I love traveling and that's really what I spend my money on."

The freedoms around the ability to predict the placement of the Cohort's intimate space and personal items, traveling, and having an eclectic dinner were some of the random aspects of freedom expressed by the Cohort.

Despite freedom reoccurring as a positive theme, for some Cohort members this attribute of the SALA lifestyle was tempered by the (mis)perceptions of family and friends. Lillian, for example, expressed frustration that "[e]verybody thinks I'm Carrie Bradshaw [narrator and central character of TV show, *Sex and the City*, which revolves around the dating lives of four white women in New York City] . . . They think it's just going on dates all the time. Party all the time. Live this free life and it's not realistic." In refuting such misnomers, Lillian touches on the most commonly cited (26% of the Cohort) negative aspect of the SALA lifestyle: "They don't see the other side of that where I'm like, 'Yeah, nobody has said good morning to me in six months. Nobody says hello to me when I get home.'"

Kislev (2019, 2022a, 2022b), in exploring the growing acceptance of single life, using cross-sectional and panel data, examined the level of happiness and loneliness of four groups: married, never married, widowed, and divorced. Overall, he discovered that "widowed and divorced/separated people are the least happy in comparison with both married and never married people." Furthermore, he found that married people remain "the happiest and the least lonely of all the groups, at least in subjective terms," though "incidents of loneliness among couples rises with age." Yet a meta-analysis of longitudinal data from 188 publications challenges these assertions that life events affect well-being and happiness (Luhmann et al., 2012).

Nevertheless, in coming to his conclusions, Kislev draws on sociologist Robert Weiss's (Weiss, 1973) definition of loneliness "as a natural response of the individual to certain situations and not as a form of weakness," and puts forward two typologies of loneliness: emotional and social. While emotional loneliness refers to feeling like there is no one close to whom one may turn, social loneliness refers to not having a wide circle of friends and acquaintances who can provide "a sense of belonging, companionship, and membership in a community" (p. 53). These two forms of loneliness can be viewed as representing a dichotomy of quality (emotional) versus quantity (social). Building on this premise, I would argue that many of those in the Love Jones Cohort who report being lonely are experiencing what I would term *situational loneliness*. Those subject to situational loneliness experience bouts of loneliness (which can be social or emotional) that ebb and flow over short periods of time, with levels of intensity that range from mild to moderate (but rarely intense); in other words, such loneliness appears to be temporary and situational rather than habitual and consistent.[4]

For many in the Cohort, the situational loneliness of the SALA lifestyle was related to practical concerns and fears about personal health. Lillian, in expanding on her comments earlier about coming home to an empty house, talked about the issue of living alone and getting ill: "I have a head cold, you've got to figure out [how to feel better and get medication]. Thank God for Instacart and some other [delivery] services now. I can outsource my groceries and that kind of stuff." For Lillian and others in the Cohort, the outsourcing of tasks a partner or housemate might otherwise take care of is a reoccurring theme of the SALA lifestyle.

For Tanya, the biggest negatives around the SALA lifestyle concerned safety and having to be self-reliant, especially in the case of a medical emergency: "If something were to happen to me, if I was to fall and slip or hurt myself, I don't have anyone there as a partner in crime to help support my needs or take care of me." Many women in the Cohort reported fears around safety, mostly related to being injured or dying without anyone realizing or being within reach to help (though it was generally unclear whether their hoped-for support was specifically envisioned as taking the form of a romantic or non-romantic companion).

Alexandra was one of those in the Cohort who took a more sanguine view of the situational loneliness she might occasionally experience, refuting the assumptions of some of those in her network: "It's not as bad as people would think. A lot of people assume that because I'm alone, that I automatically want company. That's not always the case." Layla, while making clear she appreciated the freedom that the SALA lifestyle brought her, did admit that on occasion she "would like someone to come home and talk to." Again, Layla did not distinguish between romantic and non-romantic "company" in this regard. Given that her comments allude to engaged dialogue rather than physical intimacy, it is entirely possible that for Layla – and for others in the Cohort – greater non-romantic but intimate and deep emotional interaction with family and close friends may hold a path to addressing the situational loneliness attached to the

---

[4] For a broader conversation on situational versus chronic loneliness as a risk factor for morality, independent of race, see: (Shiovitz-Ezra & Ayalon, 2010). Shiovitz-Ezra and Ayalon (2010) use three waves of the Health and Retirement Study (HRS), a nationally representative sample of Americans over the age of 50 years (1996, 1998, and 2000), to examine whether various classifications of loneliness have impact on risk for mortality. They define situational loneliness as a "transient experience, albeit painful."

SALA lifestyle. This certainly appeared to be the case for Robin, who felt that having family around was sufficient companionship to allow her to enjoy her SALA lifestyle without recourse to a partner or children: "I have a lot of family and my nieces and nephews are around when I want them to be around."

These comments again highlight the rationale underlying the value placed on friendship networks by the Cohort's women. Among the Cohort's men, who may have less access to the close emotional friendship bonds the women possess, some expressed concern about the potential loneliness arising from the lack of a romantic partner or unavailability of friends. As Brett confided: "I think just that being alone, if you have the human spirit, you yearn to be with somebody. You go through a tragic situation or some sort of troubled unfortunate occurrence. It is just better to have someone there with you. A wife. A partner." Meanwhile, while Rick was keen to emphasize the importance he attached to spending time with his friends, they may not always be on hand as he would wish them to be, potentially prompting bouts of situational loneliness: "I think sometimes when you are single and you have friends who are dating and are in exclusive relationships, it can get a little ... I hate the word 'lonely.' But if you want to share [something] with a friend but they're busy with a significant other, it can get a little bit harder." Relatedly, Joseph expressed concerns regarding a lack of close friendships as he grows older: "You break away from childhood friends. I'm in a different city, so I'm not around people I grew up with anyway ... It's hard to trust people and develop relationships."[5]

---

[5] Only two respondents mentioned sex: Joseph and Nancy. Joseph segued into the idea that only a few Cohort members mentioned. This is friends who morphed into "friends with benefits" – no-strings-attached, commitment-free sexual partnership, an arrangement that has the potential to blur the lines between platonic friends and lovers. Joseph calls this "in-house." When asked to explain the term, he responded, "You know? Having a girl, you can just be there to crash, have sex with every night, whenever you want ... Regular sex, as opposed to having to go out and worry about still trying to hunt and get." Nancy noted that her SALA status does not allow her to have regular sex and she thinks the act is "very important just for [her] mental state." Nevertheless, looking at Black college students, social psychologist Naomi Hall-Byers and colleagues (2014) studied the dating and relationship practices of Black students at a HBCU. In this context Black women outnumber Black men. This sex-ratio imbalance, coupled with a power dynamic in the favor of the man, influenced relationship making. They found Black female college students competed for the attention of Black male students and were willing to engage in certain types of casual relationships and hookups, similar to Joseph's point of "friends with benefits," all of which were seen as desirable by the Black male student but to the possible detriment of the Black female student (Hall et al., 2014; Hall-Byers, 2022). The scholars concluded, "This

Related to Rick and Joseph's concern about friends moving in different directions, Ashley elaborated on her own anxieties about changing friendship dynamics: "It's a weird kind of life transition where it's like half of your friendship circle is still on that single and hanging out thing, and then the other half is settled with kids, and you're just trying to figure out how you navigate through that … It can get lonely. It's just you." Ashley's response succinctly summarizes a key issue raised by many of the Cohort interviewees: Though they value their friendships, it can at times feel like they are at different stages of their life course compared to some of their friends. Such differences, if improperly or inexpertly navigated, can lead to Cohort members regarding these relationships as being unreliable, unstable, and/or incapable of offering a source of social support over the long term. Ultimately, as alluded to in Rick, Joseph, and Ashley's comments, this may lead to feelings of situational loneliness.[6]

6.3 Familial Expectations and Biological Pressures

Many members of the Cohort mentioned the fact that as they grow older, the expectations placed upon them by friends and family multiply, and with such expectations comes pressure: to do well at school, to choose a career, and – above all – to marry and have children. Ashely (29), for example, emphasized how she was under "a whole, whole, whole" lot of pressure from her mother and grandmother to get married and have children. In some cases, however, Cohort members admitted that such expectations and pressures were self-imposed, with London suggesting that the length of time she had spent in her current relationship was leading to an increasing level of self-imposed pressure: "I am seeing someone, and I think we're at the point where it's going to be, now what? … I want a life partner … We've been dating for like a year and a half."[7]

---

dynamic has set in motion a climate in which some women are 'settling' for undesirable partners or for types of relationships they do not want (e.g., casual and/or hook-ups)." For college-degreed Black women, Clarke (2011) found similar patterns. "Low levels of sexual activity or high levels of celibacy can be constituted both by sex without romance and romance without sex. Both are conditions familiar to those Black women who have difficulty entering committed romantic partnerships with males of their choosing" (p. 171). This suggests that some Black women choose to be in unfulfilling situations for the sake of being in a modicum of assemblance of a respectable relationship (Collins, 2005; Landor & Barr, 2018).

[6] Loneliness in relation to well-being is further discussed in Chapter 10.

[7] In this section, ages of the quoted Cohort members are stated, given the relevance to the biological pressures of being late thirties and early forties.

External pressures from family extended to the Cohort's men as well as its women. In answer to whether he felt under pressure to get married, Derwin (30) – who had a new girlfriend – exclaimed, "God yes, by everyone. By my friends, by my family. Suddenly by my girlfriend. But it's very subtle. It's there. Societally, you know." Derwin referred to age as being a central factor: "There's this silent deadline people have of 30. That it's the time to get married."

While traditionally it is assumed that it is usually women who are eager to wed as soon as possible, this was certainly not always the case among the Cohort. Kendra (30) told of how she had ended a relationship with a man she was dating who was five years older than her and expressed a readiness for marriage: "I'm single . . . I am dating . . . [Previously] I got into a relationship very prematurely . . . I would say that I'm much more ready to be a mother than to be a wife, but then it's that thing where to be a mother, I have to be [a] wife." Here, Kendra reveals her frustrations at how powerful societal expectations regarding marriage and what is "respectable" are impeding her personal desire to have children without submitting to such constraints.

The Cohort members referred to what they perceived as a particularly annoying aspect of the SALA lifestyle: the need to constantly field questions from friends, family, and colleagues regarding their SALA status. Given this irritation, it is perhaps unsurprising that some interviewees responded to queries regarding their dating status with brief, sometimes one-word answers. Having a prepacked answer to questions about their dating life (e.g. "I am dating, but it is not serious" or "I am okay with being alone") was, for many, part and parcel of the Love Jones Cohort lifestyle. SALAs, it seems, are tired of having their dating lives constantly scrutinized and questioned by family and friends.

The following are not direct quotes, but a compilation of the types of questions that the Love Jones Cohort often had to contend with as part of their SALA lifestyle: (1) "Where's your girlfriend/boyfriend? I haven't seen a girlfriend/boyfriend around you in a while." They may even go as far as to ask about a specific ex-partner who to them seemed like a good prospect. (2) "Whatever happened to so-and-so? Tell so-and-so hello." This even though the Cohort told their family members that the said person has moved on and is happy. (3) "Do you have anything to tell me?" as if the dating practices and updates of the Cohort are for public consumption of their friends and family, and at any time and in any place. Furthermore, if they did have updates, given various forms of pressure, the Cohort might be more than willing to share updates as soon as they happen. (4) "I really like this guy/girl, do you? I can see you all are happy, right?" This suggests that if the

Cohort looks happy and respectable, then family and friends will approve. This acceptance is based on the outer appearance of the relationship. The actual value, fulfillment, and happiness of the Cohort seem to be an afterthought, marginally important, or inconsequential to the perceived view of a successful relationship. (5) "Who are you dating now?" and "What's going on?" The Cohort spoke of how their peers as well as younger members of their network (nieces, nephews, and godchildren) inquire about their single status and, in some cases, try to set them up on dates.

London recounted an amusing anecdote about her godchildren playing matchmaker when she attended school functions: "Oh, my godchildren pressure me. When they were younger, they would invite me to their school functions and introduce me to their male teachers with, 'Here's my teacher, he's single.'" London was often embarrassed by her godchildren. "Oh wow. Really, kid? Like just embarrass me, call me out in front of your teacher for the hook-up. But it comes from a place of love, so it doesn't bother me." Jokingly, London retorted, "But I don't want the little crumb snatchers to get married before I do."

For the Cohort's women, biological pressures formed another key aspect of the SALA lifestyle. Tina (30), for example, observed that while she was not currently putting pressure on herself, this might change in three or four years: "I just think that there's obviously a biological reason why there's that pressure, so maybe if I froze some eggs, I would not feel that pressured, but who knows."

For those women in the Cohort who wished to have children, the fears they held regarding the ticking of their biological clock became more pronounced with age. This was a central theme in their SALA lifestyle, given that by the very nature of the fact they were single and living alone, the Cohort's women did not – for the most part – have viable partners with whom they would be willing to consider having children with. As alluded to in regard to Kendra's comments, this obstacle is predicated on the Cohort's women wishing to take more traditional – that is, "respectable" – path into parenthood.

Several Cohort members spoke of how, as Black SALA women in their late thirties and early forties, they were faced with difficult decisions about having children: whether to freeze eggs, pursue artificial insemination, have a child out of wedlock, adopt, or resolve to never have children.[8] Grace

---

[8] Even with such alternative routes, understanding structural forces and anti-Blackness is important. In collaboration with National Public Radio (NPR), journalist Michele Norris created "The Race Card Project," where she asked people around the world to

(35), for example, who proclaimed that planning out her life was important to her, intended to visit a sperm bank if she was unable to find a suitable mate with whom to have a child. Carrie (38), meanwhile, spoke of her self-conscious resistance to external and internal pressures to have children: "I don't have a lot of external pressure, and that helps me with my own internal pressure. You hear in the media; you should be concerned as a woman about your biological clock. You hear all these things, and you internalize it . . .I think, unfortunately, a lot of women make bad choices, being desperate . . . I just refuse to be that person."

Lillian (37), however, forced to confront her internal pressure to marry and have children, felt herself to be at a crossroads: "I would like to have children and a family inside of marriage . . . The pressure for me now is that I have to make a decision, relatively quickly, about freezing my eggs." Lillian grappled with what these alternatives meant in the context of her SALA lifestyle, asserting, "That's one of the 'not a benefit' of being single. I have to pay that, at least $12,000 fees [storage fee for eggs], by myself." Ultimately, she circled back to the idea of societal and biological pressure she felt under to have children, common to many of the women in the Cohort: "If it's any pressure, it's just the simple fact of my being too old to have kids."

It is important to note that not only did some members of the Cohort not wish to get married, but some did also not want to have children. Here, LaToya (37), Alyssa (48), Melinda (50), Renita (52), and Robin (49) were all explicit in saying they were not interested in having children, whether biological or adopted, with LaToya summing up the sentiment expressed: "I never had the desire and I never met anyone I really wanted to procreate with." However, among the women in the Cohort who did not want to settle for being child-free, consideration of whether to freeze their eggs was an inevitable part of their SALA lifestyle. Conversely, Simone never considered not having children: "No, because I see people with no children, and they're miserable. They show like they're having a good time, but they are miserable and annoying because they're the ones with the dogs."[9]

share – in just six words – their experiences, questions, hopes and dreams, laments, and observations about identity. In relation to these alternative routes, a 2013 special issue of The Race Card Project was published under the six-word title: "Black Babies Cost Less To Adopt." See www.npr.org/2013/06/27/195967886/six-words-black-babies-cost-less-to-adopt for more on this story, and read (Norwood, 2015) for colorism in the adoption process.

[9] Simone's statement picks up a tension that might exist between those who desire to have children and those who did not, or do not, have children. One assumption in this tension

Megan (26) and Layla (47) refused even to freezing their eggs, with the former responding, "I don't know how I'd feel about freezing my eggs and getting a sperm donor . . . I don't know why, and it kind of goes against my liberal mindset. I would prefer to just adopt. So, no, no freezing." Layla, meanwhile, asserted that given her age [47], she would not consider freezing her eggs, "because my clock has ticked."

Others, while not explicitly ruling it out as an option, shied away from making an immediate decision on the basis they were uncertain whether they would remain in the Cohort in the long term. Tivana (31), for instance, stated, "I'm trying not to think about that. It will be an option if I'm single more than two or three years [from now]." Adoriah (32), meanwhile, had previously considered freezing her eggs, but was hopeful that her current relationship was on course for marriage, meaning that "I don't feel that I need to do that because things are actually happening [toward] . . . starting a family."

Still others were deterred by the cost of freezing eggs, and the impact this might have on their SALA lifestyle, with Christine (35), observing, "If it didn't cost so much, I would consider it. There's a lot I could do with $10,000." Similarly, Celeste (35), summed up her attitude by saying, "I'd rather just get knocked up than pay $12,000."

Adoption was another legacy option that a number of the Cohort's women had considered in the context of their SALA lifestyle and the absence of a long-term partner with whom to conceive a child. Lillian, who grappled with freezing her eggs, had also contemplated adoption. Raised in foster care, Lillian gave a detailed account of her often-conflicting thought processes regarding adoption. Despite worrying that "I don't know if I'm fully equipped to adopt a child. I'm also a product of foster homes," Lillian went on to assert, "I would have the ability to adopt a brown baby." However, again harking back to the discussion of respectability politics, she expressed the reservation that "Part of the challenge I think I have is [with adoption] you don't have a father still. Every child deserves a father [in the house with them]."

---

is that all women want to have children, but as stated earlier, several women in the Cohort told us that this is not always the case. Clarke (2011) argues that "exacerbated by the contemporary era's proliferation of reproductive enhancement technologies, compulsory motherhood – the hegemonic belief that all women want to be mothers, usually referring to giving birth – maintains a hold on women even as, alternative, productive sector roles have become available to them." For more on the debate on mental, physical, and emotional health of people with pets (especially women and those who are living alone), see Cline (2010) and McNicholas et al. (2005).

Olivia (54), a member of a Greek sorority, spoke about how her girl-friends decided to adopt children as single women in their fifties. According to Olivia, they are regarded by others as selfless (translated to mean respectable), in contrast to the stigma attached to a woman who gives birth to a child out of wedlock: "Because then that's a bastard, that's a child out of wedlock, you know what I mean? But when you adopt a child, that's so altruistic, yet the circumstances are the same."

Among the Cohort's men, such concerns about the potential options available for becoming a parent in the context of a SALA lifestyle were, unsurprisingly, less pronounced. In terms of adoption as a potential parenting pathway, Jamir (42), Walter (age unspecified), and Reggie (30) all expressed a lack of interest in adopting. While Jamir seemed largely opposed to the idea ("I probably won't adopt for personal and spiritual reasons."), Walter hadn't even felt the need to give it consideration: "As a single man I have not thought about adopting a child." Though Reggie had discussed adoption with a woman he was dating, he was clear: "That was the only time I thought about adopting. Outside of that, no, because I want to see little dark babies come out [biologically born] and be able to play and enjoy themselves."

By contrast, Richard (30) and Justin (32) were more open to the idea of adoption, with the former noting that whether or not he ended up getting married, the possibility of adopting remained on the table: "My mother was a foster care worker. I saw foster kids all the time . . . Honestly, I would think that even if I did have children, and I think me and my girlfriend actually discussed this, that we would maybe have one and adopt another." Justin, one of thirteen children, expressed a strong desire to father children, whether biological or adopted: "I want them to carry on my name."[10] Nevertheless, the marked contrast between the level of concern expressed by the Cohort's men and its women regarding childbearing or adoption points to the fact that the familial, societal, and biological pressures imposed on and/or by the SALA lifestyle are gendered in nature, with women often bearing the brunt of these external (and sometimes internal) constraints.

---

[10] Comments such as these align with the findings of the 2013 Centers for Disease Control and Prevention (CDC) report by Jo Jones and William Mosher, which reports that Black fathers are very involved, if not more involved, with child rearing compared to white or Latino fathers in similar living situations, thereby challenging the notion of the persistent myth of the "absent" Black fathers (Jones & Mosher, 2013). Also see the following essay by Candice Jenkins: https://keywords.nyupress.org/african-american-studies/essay/family/

More generally, what this chapter has shown is that in considering how the Black middle class go about leading their lives, interacting with others, and approaching the possibility of parenthood, those who are SALA face a number of challenges and concerns that may not be shared by married couples or families. If a holistic understanding of the everyday lives of the Black middle class is to be achieved, therefore, due consideration must be given to SALA perspectives on, among other things, friendships, familial and romantic relationships, and parenthood.

Intergenerational Mobility and Disseminating Wealth

In what ways, if any, do the SALA lifestyle choices of the Love Jones Cohort – in particular, the fact that many of them will not have children – change the conversation on intergenerational transferences of wealth? This line of inquiry offers a pathway toward understanding how the Love Jones Cohort navigate wealth-related issues and outcomes, and what the implications of this might be both for themselves and for the Black middle class more generally. In the exploration of the previous, current, and future wealth experiences and decisions of the Cohort, light is shed on the ways in which the members of this demographic group traverse the various stages of their life course without a partner or child. Such information may challenge our preconceptions of what we think a Black middle-class household is, does, or should be, and the life pathways open to those bearing both Black middle-class and SALA status. Scholars Melvin Oliver and Thomas Shapiro (1997, 2013) make compelling arguments for adding wealth as a fourth objective indicator of middle-class status (education, income, and occupation are the other three), noting that wealth is "used to create opportunities, secure a desired stature and standard of living, or pass class status along to one's children" (Oliver & Shapiro, 1997, 2013).

While Chapter 8 focuses on how those in the Cohort accumulate wealth, particularly in terms of decision-making related to homeownership, this chapter explores the crucial issue of intergenerational mobility and the dissemination of wealth: in other words, what wealth, if any, Cohort members have had handed down to them from their parents, and how they intend to make use of and pass on their own wealth in the absence of children. It is only by interrogating these issues, and how they impact wealth transfers from one generation to the next, that we can begin to fully understand the implications of the rise of the Love Jones Cohort for the future of the Black middle class. In terms of our Cohort interviewees, it is notable that nearly two-thirds (65%) – though far from all – of the Love Jones Cohort are second-generation Black middle class.[1] Also notable is that most Cohort acknowledged that their SALA status and lifestyle – to a greater or lesser degree – shapes their views on wealth decisions. All this will be explored in greater detail in Section 7.1 and in Chapter 8.

7.1 Intergenerational Mobility

Among the social science literature, there is copious documentation of devastating wealth inequalities and racial stratification (Darity & Mullen, 2020; Oliver & Shapiro, 2013), suggesting that those in the Black community are not as securely positioned in the middle-class category as their white counterparts. As Oliver and Shapiro put it: "The Black middle class position is precarious and fragile with insubstantial wealth resources" (Oliver & Shapiro, 2013). Darity and Mullen (2020), meanwhile, state, "Wealth is the best single indicator of the cumulative impact of white racism over time." They also provide data from the 2016 Survey of Consumer Finance to illustrate this racial wealth disparity: "Median Black household net worth ($17,600) is only one-tenth of white net worth ($171,000). That means, on average, that for every dollar the middle-class white household holds in wealth – measured by assets like homes, cash savings, and retirement funds – the middle Black household possesses a mere 10 cents" (Darity & Mullen, 2020).[2] An absence of inherited wealth (particularly homeownership) represents a formidable obstacle preventing asset accumulation by Black Americans – with such assets considered a central pillar in providing stability and security to the middle class (Oliver & Shapiro, 2013). Given the cumulatively low rates of Black homeownership, Oliver and Shapiro believe that "[i]t is entirely premature to celebrate the rise of the Black middle class. The glass is both half empty and half full because the wealth data reveal the paradoxical situation in

---

[1] It was rare, if at all reported, that a parent(s) class status was not middle class, and the interviewees were also not middle class. The assumption is that class reproduction was based on parents being middle class and the interviewees also being middle class.

[2] Based on a 2021 Census report, *Wealth Inequality in the U.S. by Household Type*, grounded in 2019 Survey of Income and Program Participation (SIPP) data, and measure wealth as the value of assets owned minus the liabilities (debts) owed. The median wealth has not changed much. A Black (lone) householder continues to hold less median wealth ($14,100) relative to an Asian (lone) householder ($206,400), a white (lone, not Hispanic) householder ($187,300), and a Hispanic origin (any race) householder ($31,700). www .census.gov/library/stories/2022/08/wealth-inequality-by-household-type.html?utm_cam paign=20220801msacos1ccstors&utm_medium=email&utm_source=govdelivery

which Blacks' wealth has grown while at the same time falling further behind that of whites" (Oliver & Shapiro, 2013).

There is a well-documented association between race, wealth, and mobility, with sociologists Colleen Heflin and Mary Pattillo (2006) finding that middle-class Black Americans are highly likely to have low-income siblings and to incorporate the socioeconomic status of their extended families into their own conceptions of class standing (Heflin & Pattillo, 2006). Meanwhile, sociologists Fabian Pfeffer and Alexandra Killewald (2019) find that, in relation to household wealth, Black children with less-wealthy parents are on average much more likely than white children with similar wealth-holding parents to have downward mobility (Pfeffer & Killewald, 2019). Similarly, economist Raj Chetty and colleagues (2020) report that intergenerational mobility differs widely by race, even when Black and white boys come from same socioeconomic status and neighborhood (Chetty et al., 2020)[3].

Moreover, there is a widespread assumption that if someone grows up middle class, they will maintain that class status into adulthood, and that each generation will maintain or exceed the class achieved by their parents. Research suggests, however, that this is much less likely to be the case for the Black middle class (Akee et al., 2019; Chetty et al., 2018, 2020; Chetty & Hendren, 2018; Darity & Mullen, 2020; Heflin & Pattillo, 2006; Pfeffer & Killewald, 2019), especially Black men (Chetty et al., 2018; Chetty et al., 2020). Using income as a measure, economist Chetty and colleagues found "Black Americans have substantially lower rates of upward mobility and higher rates of downward mobility than whites, leading to large income disparities that persist across generations" (Chetty et al., 2018). In addition, Darity and Mullen (2020) argue that mobility processes contribute "directly to the maintenance of high levels of racial economic inequality across generations" (Darity & Mullen, 2020, p. 34).

In his 2017 presidential address to the National Economic Association (NEA), Professor Darrick Hamilton (Hamilton, 2020) laid out why wealth disparities are a structural issue from the perspective of stratification economics, a burgeoning subfield within the broader discipline of economics: "Stratification economists look beyond individual factors and investigate structural and contextual factors that preserve the relative status of

---

[3] For data on similar and related topics explored by Chetty, visit the following website: opportunityinsights.org.

dominant groups through *intergenerational resource transfers and exclusionary practices* to explain intergroup disparity" (p. 340).[4]

Hamilton closed his lecture by offering 10 policies that could in some ways address such structural inequalities.[5] Of particular relevance regarding intergenerational wealth for first-generation members of the Black middle class who may lack any inherited wealth from their parents (an issue highlighted by several Cohort members, as will be seen later in this section) is the idea of "baby bonds," which is essentially analogous to a social security program for young adults, providing them with the financial capital to build assets and cultivate economic security independent of the financial position and decision-making of the families into which they were born.[6] Until such policies are given serious consideration, it is inevitable that structural racism and discrimination will continue to impede intergenerational wealth for Black Americans (Kochhar & Fry, 2014; Thomas et al., 2018). Darity and Mullen note that "Blacks cannot close the racial wealth gap by independent or autonomous action" (p. 31); federal intervention is required.

All of the aforementioned provides context for the situation in which those in the Love Jones Cohort, as a subset of the Black middle class, find themselves. Such issues of structural racism were acknowledged by some in the Cohort, with Walter, for example, observing: "It means that you have, or your family has, overcome some obstacles to get you to where you are today … Obstacles such as people who really didn't want you to be where you are, and they would do things to prevent you from making that kind of progress."

Figure 7.1 shows how the Love Jones Cohort view their class status relative to their parent(s). Scholars describe class reproduction as transferring class status from one generation to the next. In this regard, fully 65% of the Love Jones Cohort expressed that they had the same class status as their parents. In terms of the SALA categories investigated, the figures for class reproduction break down as follows: 72% for over-40s compared to

---

[4] For more elaboration, see Darity et al. (2015) and Hamilton (2020) for a detailed discussion of stratification economics (Darity et al., 2015; Hamilton, 2020).

[5] For the full list, see Hamilton (2020). Two related policies are *reparations* for slavery, Jim Crow, exclusion from the New Deal and related postwar policies, and *baby bonds*.

[6] Darrick Hamilton is keenly targeted at addressing wealth inequality, and as such, the one-time payment when the child reaches adulthood would be restricted toward some asset-enhancing activity, such as a down payment on a home, finance to start a business or attend higher education, or a rollover toward retirement savings. Moreover, the accounts would be progressively endowed based on the child recipient's family financial position.

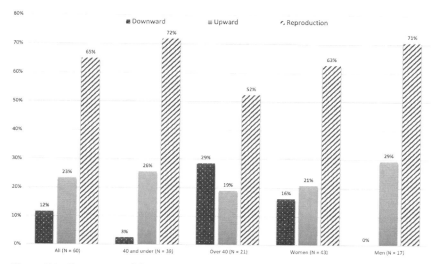

Figure 7.1. Percentage of the Love Jones Cohort, by age and gender, who report their class status as the same or different from their parents

52% for under-40s; and 71% for men compared to 63% for women. Meanwhile, just under a quarter (23%) of the entire Cohort consider themselves to hold a higher class status than their parents, with this figure rising to 26% for those under 40 (compared to 19% for those over 40) and to 29% for the men in the Cohort (compared to 21% for the women). Conversely, just 12% of the overall Cohort reported having a lower class status than their parents. Here, however, greater variation was seen between groups: whereas only 3% of under-40 Cohort members reported a downward movement in class status, this rose considerably to 29% for the over-40s. Moreover, while 16% of women reported a fall in class status, not a single man did likewise.

Celeste and Kendra both expressed that while their parents had passed down knowledge and a middle-class perspective on wealth creation, this had not been accompanied by any substantial material wealth. Celeste observed, "This generation, and in my generation, had parents that maybe pushed us out of the working class. We have these concepts of owning and having things and assets, but we miss generational wealth." Reflective of her SALA lifestyle, Celeste drew heavily on her friendship networks for useful wealth-building information and resources, describing hypothetical interactions with her friends: "Have you taken this class? Have you talked about this? Have you done this? How much are you saving? What percentage are you saving?" Kendra, meanwhile, felt, "With millennials, since we don't necessarily have the type of financial advantage as our parents had, we still have the foundations of our upbringing and middle class but not necessarily the financial component but it's just a way of life."[7]

7.2 Financial Support to Family Members

Members of middle-class Black families are significantly more likely than the white middle class to financially support their parents and extended family and networks (Chiteji & Hamilton, 2002). This additional burden of providing social and financial assistance to less-advantaged family members and the larger Black community has both short- and long-term implications for wealth accumulation and dissemination (Pattillo-McCoy, 2000). Though, as shown in Figure 7.1, the majority of the Cohort is second-generation middle class, a significant minority are among the first generation in their families to attain middle-class status, which potentially brings with it even greater responsibilities in terms of taking care of the needs of the immediate and extended family (Chiteji & Hamilton, 2002; Heflin & Pattillo, 2006).

Alexis, for example, spoke with pride of how she was the "first in my family to go to school. I'm the first in my family to move away. I'm the first in my family to accomplish quite a bit." She revealed that her brother, who is four years older than her, was a benefactor of her stocks, explaining that "[e]ven though I'm 31 years old, I'm very big on how do I make sure that I put things in place just to make sure, as I'm learning myself, how to also help my family to make better decisions." Nevertheless, Alexis's attitude toward assisting her family had changed over time, and she now felt the need to set clear boundaries: "Honestly, even helping my family has changed quite a bit. I'm not the ATM for them, and I've had to make those decisions because I have to build for myself."

Alexis's story is reflective of the wealth of literature suggesting that Black women in particular face a unique set of challenges associated with upward social mobility, including experiencing pressure to provide financial capital to family and friends, combined with feeling unable to say no (Higginbotham, 2001; Sacks et al., 2020; Woods-Giscombé, 2010).[8]

---

[7] For more on generational analysis and Black Millennials, see Allen et al. (2020).

[8] In a 2012 article that I wrote with economist Jessica Gordon Nembhard (Nembhard & Marsh, 2012), we suggested several policy recommendations for low-wealth women of color: (1) promote, enact, and enforce livable wages in the public and private sectors; and increase disposable income; (2) require jobs to include comprehensive benefits – sick leave and flex time, health insurance, retirement accounts – so that everyday emergencies and

A 2012 *The Washington Post* article even went as far as suggesting that a Black woman's personal checkbook is often the de facto bank account for needy family members (Thompson, 2012). Another article in the same paper quantifies *The Washington Post*/Kaiser Family Foundation collaborative survey of 800 Black women in the following terms: "Several women interviewed said they put their own plans on hold so they could help others. The Post-Kaiser poll found that 60 percent of Black women have loaned money to friends or family, with the rate rising to 73 percent among those who earn $65,000 or more" (Mui & Jenkins, 2012).

An anecdote recounted by Glenda, who was adamant in asserting, "My parents are definitely not middle class," is illustrative of the above. Glenda described how her father lost his pension due to a heated argument at work that turned physical. As a potential consequence, Glenda's father asked her to pay his rent. In Glenda's case, however, she was able to say no – or rather, she felt she had no choice but to do so: "I didn't have it. I had a little bit of money in my savings account and my rent money, and that's all I had." Even so, the "maybe 800 bucks" Glenda had in her savings account, she felt might be perceived by her father as constituting a significant amount of money. Glenda opined that taking financial care of her family "[m]akes [building wealth] more complicated. I don't give as much to my family now, but I still give too much. I hate to admit it, but my savings account is pretty low right now because I've given away so much money." In terms of disseminating their wealth to the next generation, a view echoed by members of the Cohort ultimately felt that they had insufficient assets to make the expense of drawing up a will or living trust worthwhile.

For some, having SALA status – and therefore having no partner or children to support or pass down wealth to – also has a direct impact on notions of responsibility to family and wider networks. Rick was one of those who felt his SALA lifestyle was more conducive to providing assistance to his family: "Sometimes just because you're a single person, you might be able to do more than when you have other responsibilities. Or

---

catastrophic shocks do not reduce assets or put a woman in debt; (3) regulate, even prohibit, predatory lending, irresponsible lending agencies, and high interest rates; increase the number of and access to credit unions and other community development financial institutions that provide affordable and quality financial services and credit, and keep capital circulating in communities; (4) increase women's access to and participation in joint ownership and cooperative ownership of businesses and housing; and (5) provide asset accumulation incentives and support through tax credits and other incentives for owning some kind of savings account, homes, businesses, and/or stocks and bonds. For the exhaustive list of policy suggestion, see Nembhard and Marsh (2012).

you are in a situation where you are married, dating, cohabitating with someone, and their responsibilities affect yours', so you're not able to give what you want to give."

7.3 Estate Planning

Those in the Love Jones Cohort are aware of the advantages bestowed by the transfer of class status and wealth (or not) from their parents to themselves. How, then, do they regard making this transfer to the next generation in the absence of a partner or children? This question is particularly pertinent given the demographic shift in the Black middle class with a rise in the number of Black singles, living alone (as suggested by my quantitative work). Most crucially, in terms of the existing social science literature, it begs the related question of how the Black middle class will continue to reproduce itself into the coming generations. As will be seen later in this section, while many (particularly the younger) members of the Cohort have given little thought to disseminating their wealth in the long term, others are coming up with innovative ways to transfer their wealth from one generation to the next. Given their SALA status, this does not take the form of a straight-line intergenerational transference of wealth, but rather is what I would term a segmented intergenerational transference of wealth.[9] The Love Jones Cohort are transferring their wealth to nieces and nephews, godchildren (which speaks to the value they place on their friendships), and the social organizations they are affiliated with.

Before turning to whom Cohort members anticipate leaving their assets, however, it is necessary to explore the legal mechanisms in place for enabling intergenerational wealth transfers. In terms of formalizing the wishes of those leaving behind an inheritance, a legal document is required, such as a living trust or will.[10] A 2016 Gallup Poll comparing the

---

[9] The terms "straight line" and "segmented" are loosely based on sociologist Karyn Lacy's work on strategic assimilation and the Black middle class staying connected to the wider Black community, and literature on immigrant assimilation. In this latter body of literature, the terms represent two major forms of assimilation: straight-line assimilation is where immigrants attempt to fully incorporate themselves into the mainstream (R. E. Park et al., 1925), while segmented assimilation suggests that immigrants integrate with certain portions of society (Portes & Rumbaut, 2001; Portes & Zhou, 1993; Rumbaut & Portes, 2001). For a more detailed discussion, see Portes and Zhou (1993).

[10] The difference between a will and a living trust is that whereas the will goes into effect only after death, the latter takes effect as soon as it is created.

percentages of those possessing a will by age[11], income, education, and race (broken down by white and non-white) threw up the alarming statistic that only 28% of non-white adults compared to 51% of white Americans have a will (Jones, 2016).[12]

Elsewhere, gerontologists Catheryn Koss and Tamara Baker (2018) sought out to test whether the disparities in advance care planning between older Black and white adults can be explained by differences in estate planning (Koss & Baker, 2018). Using data from the Health and Retirement Study,[13] they found five interesting results. First, roughly a third of Black participants had advance directives. Second, slightly over a quarter (27%) of Black participants had a will or living trust. Third, compared to married older adults, those who were divorced or never married were less likely to have wills or trusts. Fourth, when controlling for estate planning, the odds of having an advance directive were equal for white and Black participants. Fifth, substantial race disparities in estate planning remained even after controlling for financial variables – home ownership, wealth, and income (Koss & Baker, 2018). The study suggests that Black Americans face cumulative disadvantages that not only span their life course but also factor into their final days.

Figure 7.2 shows that across the entire Cohort, just over a quarter (26%) have legal documents, such as a will or living trust, to manage their assets if something were to happen to them. Two noteworthy trends are observable. First, 42% of over-40 Cohort members have an asset management document in place compared to a mere 15% of those 40 and under. Second, there is no gender difference, with an identical 26% of men and 26% of women having a prepared legal document. In addition, 5% of Cohort members claimed to have an "unofficial" document to address asset management should something happen to them, though it was unclear what exactly this meant in practice.[14]

On being asked whether they had engaged in estate planning, responses from Cohort members ranged from an emphatic "yes" to a defiant "no" to evasive rambling that could be seen as rhetorical incoherence – defined as

---

[11] The author is clear that there is a relationship between age, income, and having a will.

[12] Visit the website for more information: https://news.gallup.com/poll/191651/majority-not.aspx

[13] The study involved 6,946 participants, all of whom were 50 or over and just under 2,000 of whom were Black.

[14] The percentages total to 100. The categories are mutually exclusive. Unofficial documentation may include a written agreement between family members who may (or may not) hold in a court of law or a stipulated benefactor on a retirement account.

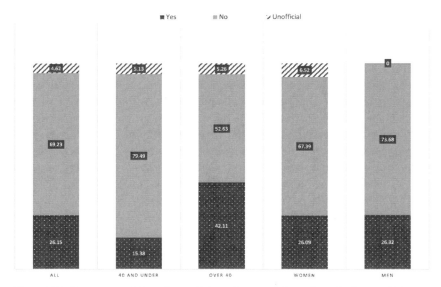

Figure 7.2. Percentage of Love Jones Cohort, by age and gender, who have a living trust, will, or other unofficial documentation to disseminate their wealth

"grammatical mistakes, lengthy pauses, repetition, etc.," which can be seen to increase "when people discuss sensitive subjects" (Bonilla-Silva, 2006).

As shown by economist William Darity and colleagues (Darity Jr. et al., 2018), there is a common misnomer that "greater financial literacy will close the racial wealth gap" (see Myth 5 in Appendix C). Given this, it is easy to understand why some of the Cohort may have interpreted the question about estate management as an attack on their level of financial literacy, and so gave rhetorically incoherent responses in order to avoid saying no and thereby reveal their self-perceived ignorance. Previous research on perceptions of "middle classness" among Black Americans reveals that within the group, a certain degree of knowledge regarding asset management, and the norms and values associated with it, is probably expected. This potential expectation forms an element of the respectability politics that has long been a defining element of the Black middle class (Drake & Cayton, 1945; Du Bois, 1899; Frazier, 1957) and is currently being challenged by contemporary scholars, especially Black female academics (Collins, 2004; Cooper, 2018). Among the Cohort, Celeste was one of those who admitted that she did not have a living trust or will, though she quickly went on to qualify this by saying, "Up until now, I think I just hadn't thought about it. Now that I've been in my career for ten years, and

I recently had this conversation with a girlfriend about this exact thing, leaving our money to someone because neither one of us have children. I've recently been contemplating the fact that I need to make a living will."

More generally, three main themes impacting whether or not a Cohort had a will or living trust emerged during the interviews: (1) circumstances or interactions; (2) knowledge or lack thereof; and (3) aging and adult responsibilities.

Regarding *circumstances or interactions*, several of those Cohort members who had had a living trust or will drawn up had been spurred into action by particular life events or interactions. Renita, for example, recounted how an encounter with a naval officer was instrumental in her seeking to formalize the distribution of her assets in the event of unforeseen circumstances: "At one time in my career, and I came across a few people that had a lot of property and money and stuff, and one of the gentlemen, he was a retired Naval officer. He gave me some good reasons why [to get an asset management document] . . . because when you leave things up to everybody else, people make decisions that you may not have wanted."

Bianca's decision to get a living trust came after she went into the hospital for surgery, which prompted her to reflect on how, despite her SALA status, it still made sense to secure the future dissemination of her assets: "I hadn't thought about it since I wasn't married and didn't have children. But when I went into the hospital, it's one of those questions before you have surgery, even though it was relatively minor, they thought it was a good thing to think about."

Lillian, meanwhile, spoke candidly about how personal bereavement at a young age had prompted her to get a living trust: "I lost my mother when I was 18, and I handled all of her affairs by myself at 18. I learned that lesson very early on, and she did not have a living will, she did not have things set up. It's just the smartest way to manage your money before the government takes what your family should rightfully have."

Many of those who were more evasive about whether they had made a will or living trust offered responses along the lines of saying they were thinking about it or that it was a "work in progress." Rick, for example, while acknowledging that the death of a friend had forced him to give the matter consideration, made the excuse that he simply hadn't got around to it, having not made it a priority due to his age: "Not as of yet, but I should. For me, it's just time, even though I encourage my mom to do it, and encourage my grandfather to do it because he has some property. I guess for me, you're single, you're young [aged 33 at the time of the interview], and you're not really thinking about it. But honestly, I do know it's time to think about it. I recently had a friend that passed away. And it makes you think about those things." Meanwhile, Shannon claimed to be in the process of securing her wealth through a living trust, in part because her brother was in a debilitating car accident: "I'm working on that. I am in a process of working on that." Likewise, Simone asserted, "I'm working on it, seriously working on it. I want to make sure that things are the way I want them to be, so it's black and white."

In terms of how *knowledge or lack thereof* influences Cohort members' decision-making, several Cohort members had put off consideration of making a will or living trust due to what they perceived as their own lack of experience, understanding, or resources in the area. Dawn, for example, emphasized she didn't feel she had been given the knowledge tools to make an informed decision, nor did she feel it was currently worthwhile given her level of wealth: "I don't think we were taught that. I'm starting to learn those things. And it takes money, and I have not been able to build wealth. So I don't have extra money to do anything extra." Joseph, meanwhile, also pointed to a lack of guidance: "Honestly, when it comes to doing stuff like having things on paper and going and setting up those documents, I haven't had a lot of experience. I haven't really had people to show me this is how you do it, and this is the importance of doing it."[15]

At the other end of the spectrum, however, Reggie had drawn on the knowledge granted him by his background in finance, which had convinced him of the wisdom of drawing up a will, regardless of the fact that he anticipated a change in his SALA status in the near future: "I went to school for finance, and I understand how important it is for everything to be documented. Knowing exactly who is the sole beneficiary if something happens ... Nobody ever plans on anything happening to them but

---

[15] It is worth noting that Simone's rationale for considering a will or living trust seemed partially based more on the treatment of Black people and the distrust with various racist financial institutions among others. Such mistrust is ingrained in Black culture. There is a wariness toward signing official documents for some Black people. The worst loss is the loss of life. Health care is a clear and blatant example of mistreatment. In her 2018 book, Tina Sacks discussed the treatment of the Black middle class in the health-care system. To build her case for the current health-care treatment of the Black middle class, Sacks provide historical context of the mistreatment of the larger Black community. She highlighted two egregious cases: the Tuskegee Syphilis Experiment (an unethical study to examine untreated syphilis in Black men) and the Mississippi Appendectomy (a term used to denote the eugenic practice of overuse of hysterectomy among African American women). For more information on these cases, read Washington (2006) and Sacks (2018).

hopefully in the next couple of years, I'll start a family and all that stuff. Of course, my will will change."

In terms of *aging and adult responsibilities*, several of the younger members of the Cohort cited their age and the lack of responsibility that accompanied their SALA lifestyle as the reason they had not drawn up (or even considered) a living trust or will. As previously mentioned in relation to Figure 7.2, Cohort members aged over 40 were almost three times as likely (42%) to have a living trust or will compared to their younger counterparts (15%). Kevin (25) was one of those in the younger age bracket who, despite having assets, had not given much thought to a will or living trust: "I guess it may just be a product of my youth. I wouldn't think about putting together a will or trust or something like that for people to inherit what I have. Just the fact that I am young. I don't expect to die any time soon."

Similarly, neither Jerome (30) nor Justin (32) felt that the question of whether they had drawn up a living trust or will, or who they intended to leave their assets to, was of great importance given their age. Jerome asserted, "If I'm thinking about distributing wealth, that means I'm dead or something, so I haven't thought about that much. They say you're more aggressive when you're younger as far as with stocks and with other investments. You get more cautious as you get older." Justin, meanwhile, pointed to his SALA status as a reason for not having to concern himself with the issue: "I don't really think about it much. I don't really have anyone to answer to, as far as a wife, I don't have any kids. If I have it [assets], I'll give it to whoever needs it."

7.4 Wealth-Dissemination Choices

Figure 7.3 documents to whom Cohort members plan to disseminate their wealth. As can be seen, the most popular answer by some distance (57%) is "parents," which is reflective of the fact that many in the Cohort initially answered the question from the perspective of their present circumstances rather than thinking to the future. Celeste's answer, which was preceded by the longest pause of her entire interview, is illustrative of this: "Right now, I have my parents listed, which probably isn't the best thing because they'll hopefully go before me. Me and a friend were just talking about this. I don't have siblings, so I don't have anyone to leave it to right at this moment."[16] Walter, meanwhile, appeared to have something of an epiphany during the

---

[16] There was an interesting issue that emerged while the Cohort discussed beneficiaries. More than half the Love Jones Cohort (57%) said they expected their assets would go to

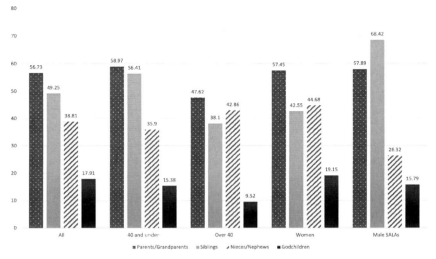

Figure 7.3. Percentage of the Love Jones Cohort, by age and gender, who will leave their assets to parents/grandparents, siblings, nieces/nephews, and/or godchildren

course of his interview. Having initially stated that his parents would inherit his assets, he was then asked if he had any godchildren, nieces, or nephews, and whether he would consider letting them inherit. Walter, upon pondering the question, answered, "I just did," before collapsing into laughter.

In fact, the choice of parents was so prevalent that we had to revise the interview protocol, proactively asking the Cohort to think ahead to their later life and how this might impact their decision-making. As touched on in Section 7.2, there are a number of possible reasons why a large number of Cohort seemed reluctant to look meaningfully beyond their current situation. For some, it may be a defense mechanism against seeing their single status as permanent: They do not want to think about making long-term decisions as a single person, as they hope to get married and so anticipate making such wealth-dissemination decisions with their partner. For others, it may simply be that, given they are relatively young and do not have a partner or children, there is simply no point in devoting time to such questions. In effect, their SALA status exempts them from having to think long term. When members of the Cohort were probed further about the future and long-term asset dissemination, however, they did come up

their parents. They talk about their transfer of wealth in present terms. The discussion did not start in the future tense.

with various possible nonparent recipients: siblings (49%), nieces and nephews (39%), and godchildren (18%).[17]

Meisha explained that she had discussed her dissemination wishes with her mother, who knew that all of Meisha's assets were intended for her niece, who has a developmental disorder. However, Meisha admitted that if she were to have her own children, this would alter things – though never to the exclusion of her niece: "It will go to my child, children, and, of course, my niece. I want to make sure she's always taken care of because the whole [developmental disorder] issue bothers me. So, my niece will always be included in this [asset planning]."

Gwen explained that she and her siblings were single and child-free, and that she would have to consider where her wealth would go if her parents and siblings died before she did. In doing so, she admitted that she had not thought about the lack of ability to transfer to the next generation prior to this interview. Meanwhile, Marquez, as an only child, expressed that he would be happy to leave his assets – which at the time of the interview included an individual retirement account (IRA) – to his friend's children.

Bianca was clear that if anything were to happen to her, her assets would go to "[m]y parents and my nieces and nephews. They're all listed as the beneficiaries on my 401k." Bianca also brought her godchildren into the discussion, professing to consider them part of her own family: "Because I don't have any children and, I consider them [her godchildren] sort of being my children."

The views expressed by Marquez, Bianca, and others like them in the Love Jones Cohort point to a more open understanding of family that is not strictly confined to a partner and biological children. Instead, they are happy to consider nieces and nephews, godchildren, and friend's children as potential heirs to their assets. As mentioned previously, this is not a straight-line intergenerational transference of wealth from parent to children, but what can be termed a segmented intergenerational transference of wealth. In other words, the Love Jones Cohort are finding innovative ways to transfer their assets to family members, friends, and other segments of the Black community. It may be argued that in the minds of many in the Cohort, these groups are central to how family should be defined and what it should encompass.

---

[17] The totals do not equal 100%, as the categories are not mutually exclusive. Furthermore, the godchildren category also includes informal godchildren, such as the children of friends.

In 1968, Andrew Billingsley pioneered a new approach to studying Black families – one that affirms cultural "difference" and praises the strengths of Black families, rather than focusing on "problem" families (i.e., female-headed) (Billingsley, 1968). In 2022, sociologist Christina Cross and colleagues argue that what is missing in this literature "is a full integration of how the foundational pillars of white supremacy, namely structural racism and heteropatriarchy, impact both family formation and child outcomes, especially among diversely configured Black families" (Cross et al., 2022). Billingsley and other researchers (Hatchett & Jackson, 1993) have argued that taking a dichotomous approach to characterizing families – middle-class married couples versus poor single-headed households – underestimates variations among Black families. Billingsley (1968) identifies three categories of Black families: primary families (two-parent), extended families (other relatives, in-laws), and augmented families (non-related individuals). As indicated previously, the desire among many of the Cohort to pass their assets on to nieces/nephews or even godchildren/friends' children points to the value they place on their extended and augmented families. In terms of the latter family type, its importance to the Cohort is further reinforced by the centrality of friendship networks to their lifestyle and well-being.[18]

In terms of passing on assets to the wider Black community, a number of Cohort members stated they would segment their assets between family, social clubs, and institutions of higher learning they were affiliated with. Notably, however, none of the men expressed an intention to bequeath their assets to nonfamilial social institutions and organizations; by contrast, 10% of the Cohort's women said they would bequest a portion of their assets to charity and/or social organizations. Of this latter group, half planned to donate to unspecified charities; a quarter planned to donate to churches; and a quarter planned to donate to scholarship funds or Greek organizations. London, for example, asserted, "[I]f my mother dies, precedes me in death, I will actually leave some of my assets to my alma mater where I went to school . . . I'll probably request that they use the money to endow a scholarship to assist other African American females into those institutions." Joanna, meanwhile, said, "So I'm giving to church. I'm giving to other non-profits or if there are other things that I'm interested in." These findings align with Bella DePaulo's (2018) conclusion in a *The Washington Post* blog post: "A comparison of the charitable donations of

---

[18] This aspect will be explored further in the "Coping Mechanisms" section of Chapter 10 (Section 10.6).

today's 25- to 47-year-olds to the same age group 40 years ago showed that contemporary couples are giving less. So are single men. Single women, though, are holding their own." Supporting this assertion, Professor of Philanthropic Studies Debra Mesch and colleagues (Mesch et al., 2019) found that single Black women (32%) are more likely to give to charity than single Black men (22%).

7.5 The Impact of SALA Status on Wealth-Dissemination Decision-Making

Several members of the Cohort felt that being single made their dissemination decisions easier, as they did not have to consider another person's wants, issues, or concerns. In discussing asset dissemination, Ashley, Joanna, Grace, and Rick all expressed the freedom their SALA status granted them in similar ways. Ashley explained, "Say I'm not single. Now I'm thinking about this whole other person, and then that person's family, and all of those things. It would be much more complicated." Joanna was assertive in laying claim to the freedom her single status afforded her ("I decide what I want to do, if it's political, if it's social, I decide, and I don't have to answer to anyone."), while Grace gave the blunt response, "I can be selfish."

In his reply, Rick also seemed to have internalized the stereotypical notion that singleness can be equated with selfishness – something a number of scholars have challenged (DePaulo, 2006, 2011; Kislev, 2019; Klinenberg, 2013) – while at the same time acknowledging that despite this perceived "selfishness," being single allowed him the freedom to distribute his wealth in more altruistic ways: "I think when you're single – and some people may disagree – there is a level of selfishness . . . Because you have to take care of you." However, he could "give a donation to UNICEF or United Way."

Despite the fact that singles may have greater freedom when it comes to deciding how to disseminate their wealth, they still feel a responsibility or a perfunctory obligation for providing resources to their extended family. Thus, while singles may decide to make donations to charities or institutions, the amount they have at their disposal will to some degree be determined by the financial support they feel obliged to provide to their extended family (Chiteji & Hamilton, 2002; Mui & Jenkins, 2012; Sarkisian & Gerstel, 2016; Thompson, 2012).

In looking ahead to the possibility of moving out of SALA status and the impact this might have on assets previously accumulated while single, several members of the Cohort discussed the possibility of prenuptial agreements. Renita asserted that even if she were to marry, she would still be influenced by a SALA mindset: "We would definitely have to do a prenup, at my age [52] and what I have ... I still would be thinking more of the mindset of probably 'mine.'" Rick, meanwhile, took a more passive approach. "You're doing you, I'm doing me, and there are things that we'll do together." In some cases, prenuptial agreements were clearly articulated as being desirable. In other cases, a potential comingling of assets or a desire to protect assets from a partner were discussed in more nuanced ways. A few members of the Cohort, in talking about building a life with someone else, described how they would put down financial parameters, such as keeping their financial accounts, insurance policies, and assets separate.

Racial wealth disparities are ubiquitous, consistent, persistent, and stubborn in America. The Black middle class are not immune to these racial wealth inequities. Given this, it is important to understand both whether and to what degree those in the Love Jones Cohort are receiving wealth through intergenerational means, and how – given their single status – they intend to disseminate their assets, which may involve helping extended or augmented family members acquire middle-class status. In terms of asset accumulation, a home is likely to be the largest asset a member of the Love Jones Cohort will acquire in their lifetime. However, given that many in the Cohort greatly value the freedom granted them by their SALA status, it is also possible they may feel a reluctance to be tied down by a mortgage. Thus, we now turn to focus on how those in the Love Jones Cohort are accumulating wealth, with a particular focus on their attitudes to homebuying and related challenges.

8

Homeownership and the Accumulation
of Wealth

8.1 The Racial Wealth Gap

Before proceeding to examine in detail the Love Jones Cohort's attitudes to wealth accumulation and homebuying, it is important to note that, regardless of their middle-class status, those in the Cohort are operating in an environment of considerable structural racism when it comes to acquiring assets. While many scholars have addressed, and continue to address, the systemic and racist underpinnings of wealth in America, much of the mainstream political and media discourse continues to perpetuate the pernicious idea that poverty among Black people is the fault of poor character and an individual problem. Contrary to this, sociologist Tyson Brown (T. H. Brown, 2016), in examining racial/ethnic inequalities in wealth trajectories in middle and late life, finds evidence suggesting a tendency for wealth inequality to increase over the life course. Drawing on Brown's work, Boen et al. argue,

Racial wealth inequality reflects a form of cumulative disadvantage (Brown, 2016): Black–white wealth inequality emerges early in the life course due to racial differences in familial wealth, widens across the life span as whites experience more rapid rates of wealth accumulation than Blacks, and persists across generations and historical time as families unequally pass along wealth to their descendants. (Boen et al., 2020, p. 156)

Turning to Black singles, specifically women – who, as previously pointed out, make up the bulk of our Cohort interviewees – a 2017 research brief based on the Panel Study of Income Dynamics (PSID) revealed that "Black women do not experience gains in wealth that typically are expected with aging or increased educational attainment. Young, single Black women with a college degree face particularly dramatic stumbling blocks in accumulating wealth." Single Black women *with* a bachelor's degree hold

$5,000 in median wealth, while a single Black woman without a bachelor's degree holds $500 in median wealth (Zaw et al., 2017). Moreover, "Among college-educated single women, Black women have the highest level of student debt and struggle to pay off the debt in early adulthood despite working full-time" and "Older (over age 60), single Black women with a college degree have a mere $11,000 in wealth, in stark contrast to the $384,400 in median wealth among their single white women counterparts" (Zaw et al., 2017).[1] As this suggests, Black female SALAs in particular face harsh challenges when it comes to wealth.[2]

Table 8.1 lists 10 of the most persistent myths surrounding racial wealth inequality, drawn from the 2018 report "What We Get Wrong About Closing the Racial Wealth Gap." As the authors of the report state:

> We contend that a number of ideas frequently touted as "solutions" will not make headway in reducing Black–white wealth disparities. These conventional ideas include greater educational attainment, harder work, better financial decisions, and other changes in habits and practices on the part of Blacks. While these steps are not necessarily undesirable, they are wholly inadequate to bridge the racial chasm in wealth.

Appendix C provides a brief discussion of each myth, all of which provide some context for the wealth-building social environment that the

Table 8.1. Ten of the most persistent myths surrounding the racial wealth gap[2]

Myth	Brief synopsis
1	Greater educational attainment or more work effort on the part of Black people will close the racial wealth gap.
2	The racial homeownership gap is the "driver" of the racial wealth gap.
3	Buying and banking Black will close the racial wealth gap.
4	Black people saving more will close the racial wealth gap.
5	Greater financial literacy will close the racial wealth gap.
6	Entrepreneurship will close the racial wealth gap.
7	Emulating successful minorities will close the racial wealth gap.
8	Improved "soft skills" and "personal responsibility" will close the racial wealth gap.
9	The growing numbers of Black celebrities prove the racial wealth gap is closing.
10	Black family disorganization is a cause of the racial wealth gap.

[1] See the report for more alarming statistics: https://assetfunders.org/resource/women-race-wealth/

[2] Darity et al. (2018).

Love Jones Cohort operate in. However, it is Myth 10 ("Black family disorganization is a cause of the racial wealth gap") that is crucially relevant to this chapter – and, indeed, this book – given that some pro-marriage advocates argue that SALAs are negatively impacting (economically and socially) the Black race by not getting married. As previously discussed, despite social scientists having long defined the Black middle class in family terms (as married couples with children), my research shows that a growing percentage of the Black middle class are single people living alone (Dickson & Marsh, 2008; Marsh et al., 2007; Marsh & von Lockette, 2011; Marsh & Peña, 2020), who, regardless of whether they later choose to get married, continue to accumulate wealth in order to maintain their middle-class status.

In a 2014 article entitled "Marriage As Black Citizenship," law professor Robin Lenhardt (2014) argues, "Forces within and without African America remain deeply invested in promoting marriage as a key strategy for eliminating black disadvantage ... Conservatives, capitalizing on a growing national debate about inequality, increasingly tout marriage's capacity to build wealth for the fragile black families ... ignoring real questions about the availability and suitability of partners" (p. 1355). Citing work by Dorothy Brown on racial differences in social security survivor benefits and Thomas Shapiro on wealth disparities and holdings, Lenhardt asserts that "getting married had no statistically significant impact on African-Americans" and that "marriage among African-Americans typically combines two comparatively low-level wealth portfolios, it does not significantly elevate the family's wealth." Lenhardt concludes by asserting, "Demographic realities and the increasingly socio-economic fragility of Black loving relationships necessitate a greater focus on nonmarital families – their status, specific needs, and capacities" (p. 1356). Building on this, I argue that more research needs to be done on Black couples who are not equally yoked financially, and where marriage or cohabitation might leave them. Such research has clear implications for those within the Cohort who anticipate finding a partner and those who decide to remain single.

In general, Black Americans lack net worth – assets minus liabilities. Darity and Mullen (2020) report that, as of 2016, the median Black household net worth ($17,600) is only one-tenth of white net worth ($171,000). Moreover, aside from differences in homeownership rates, considerable racial gaps were observed in terms of home equity. A 2014 research report by Rebecca Tippett and colleagues highlights two related trends in relation to home equity and race. First, they found, "While all racial and ethnic groups lost home equity as a result of the Great Recession, people of color suffered significantly more losses than whites." Second, they found, "Homeownership is still the key driver of wealth. Among homeowners, home equity still makes up the bulk of their personal wealth. For whites, home equity accounts for 58 percent of their net worth . . . For African Americans, home equity accounts for nearly all of their personal net worth (92%)" (Krivo & Kaufman, 2004; Tippett et al., 2014).

Studies continue to document that prospective Black homeowners are discriminated against in the housing market (Quillian et al., 2020), with the long-term consequences of such discrimination including less accumulation of equity over time, and the possibility for being underwater or holding an upside-down mortgage – where the mortgage is higher than the home value (Faber & Ellen, 2016).

The Urban Institute reports that prior to the financial crisis of 2007–2008, the rate of Black homeownership peaked at almost 50%. However, "From 2000 to 2015, that gain was more than erased as forces within and beyond the housing market aligned to reduce the Black home-ownership rate to 41.2 percent" (Choi et al., 2018).[3] More generally, Black households tend to be harder hit before, during, and after times of recession. Addo and Darity (2021), in finding that the racial wealth gap was sizeable pre, during, and post the Great Recession (roughly following July 2009 through 2019), observe that Black (and Latinx) households recovered "slower and experience lower relative gains" than non-Black households (Addo & Darity, 2021). In addition, younger members of the Black middle class face further challenges, with a 2018 Urban Institute study of millennial homeownership showing that "[m]illennials are less likely to be homeowners than baby boomers and Gen Xers." The study identifies the homeownership rate for millennials to be 8% lower than for baby boomers and Gen Xers (Choi et al., 2018; p. v). All these challenges are relevant when it comes to wealth accumulation among the Black middle class, including the Love Jones Cohort, whose situation is further nuanced by their SALA status.

8.2 Homeownership and Assets among the Love Jones Cohort

Figure 8.1 reveals that 43% of the Cohort owned or were buying homes, which is comparable to the national average. In the first quarter of 2020,

---

[3] www.urban.org/urban-wire/state-millennial-homeownership.

the Black homeownership rate in the US was 44% (U.S. Census Bureau, 2020). In terms of other assets, three-quarters (75%) of Cohort members had retirement accounts, which differs markedly from the national picture, where reportedly 62% of American Black working-age households do not own assets in the form of a retirement account (Guzman & Vulimiri, 2015; Rhee, 2013)[4]. Moreover, a third (33%) of the Cohort held stocks and bonds. It is notable that across all three of these categories, a higher percentage of women than men reported holding assets: for homeownership this was 44% compared to 41%; for retirement accounts this was 79% compared to 65%; and for stocks and bonds, it was 37% compared to 18%. In terms of age, over-40 Cohort members were slightly more likely to own a home (48% compared to 41%) and a retirement account (81% compared to 72%) compared to those 40 and under. The reverse was true in terms of stocks and bonds (33% for under 40s compared to 29% for those 40 and under), perhaps indicating a greater appetite for risk among younger Cohort members.

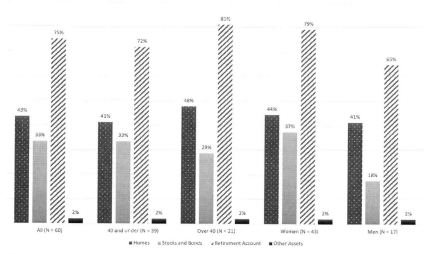

Figure 8.1. Percentage of the Love Jones Cohort, by age and gender, who own homes, stock and bonds, retirement accounts, or other assets[5]

---

[4] A 2021 Census report finds that, independent of race and based on SIPP 2019 data, the two assets that accounted for 65% of households' wealth is home equity and retirement accounts. www.census.gov/library/stories/2022/08/wealth-inequality-by-household-type .html?utm_campaign=20220801msacos1ccstors&utm_medium=email&utm_source=gov delivery

[5] The percentages do not equal to 100% because the categories are not mutually exclusive.

Issues of homeownership versus renting, and the implications this has for the freedom many in the Cohort see as being a key element of the SALA lifestyle, were raised by numerous interviewees. Such concerns were often riven with contradictions. While some of the Cohort – particularly its younger members – are appreciative of the freedom their SALA status gives them in being able to take risks or prioritize immediate comfort without worrying about the consequences this might have for partners or dependents, most are also acutely aware of the need to plan for the long term, especially in the absence of a familial safety net.

Christine, for instance, while keen to emphasize the advantages of being SALA when it came to taking advantage of work opportunities and increasing her income ("I have the time in my day or in my life to pursue other career opportunities and spend time doing that, as opposed to devoting it to a relationship.") went on to express, "I'd feel more comfortable if I had a second income, a partner, so to speak in terms of purchasing a home and things like that." Meanwhile, Bianca, as a renter, chaffed against middle-class expectations regarding homeownership, perceiving it as a threat to the freedom her SALA status afforded her: "I don't really buy into the idea that buying property is the American Dream. Being single, I like being able to kind of pick up and follow the opportunities."

In general, younger adults are living with their parents longer, or with roommates (boarders) in order to pool their resources and make ends meet. Many are hesitant to put their trust in the housing market, nor do they want the economic and geographic burden of homeownership (K. O. Lee & Painter, 2013). Journalist Ethan Watters (2004), in proposing his Urban Tribe theory, suggests that rather than getting bogged down geographically with a home and a family, younger people do want to be able to move around the USA, even globally, should the perfect job or opportunity present itself (Watters, 2004).

Alexis and Kevin, aged 31 and 25 respectively, were among those in the Cohort who subscribed to this mentality. Alexis pointed to the freedom to take risks her SALA status conferred on her: "Right now because I'm single, I'm able to take assignments for my job. Even in stocks, you can take a little bit more risk because you have a little bit more leeway versus being married and having children." Similarly, Kevin observed that being unbounded by responsibility to others gave him greater control in terms of his finances and wealth accumulation: "I feel that when you're single, you have more opportunity. From a business standpoint, you don't have as many blocks as far as relationships, including another person in your financial decisions. I feel it's a lot easier to think about jumping out there and making investments."

Paige (33), in observing that her parents are probably lower middle class ("We were never hungry, and we always had shelter and food, but they definitely didn't make and don't make nearly what I do."), went on to discuss how she considers herself as being not only middle class, but "Even upper middle-class." This self-classification was based on the long litany of assets she owned in addition to her home, which she reeled off in a matter-of-fact fashion: "retirement account, stocks, mutual funds. I have another property, and I also have a business." Among the members of the Cohort who weren't homeowners, some were quick to highlight the non-property assets they owned. Jamir, for instance, revealed, "I have precious metals. I have gold and silver." Bianca, meanwhile, spoke of having "other assets, including a 401K."

Grace (35), while acknowledging that her preference was to take advantage of her SALA status to seek comfort in the here and now, sounded a note of caution in terms of her longer-term attitude to wealth accumulation: "To me, tomorrow is not guaranteed, so I'd rather be able to be comfortable now and then also, at the same time, putting away something for the future. No, I'm not one of the types of people where I'm like, 'Oh, yeah, I'm going to put all this [money] in this particular stock.' No, because if it caves, I'm going to be really pissed off, and I don't want to do that."

The need to plan for the future in terms of wealth accumulation, and in doing so mitigate the potential risks of not having a safety net should their SALA status be retained into older age, was something that concerned Celeste (35), Wendy (52), and others in the Cohort. Celeste, for example, admitted that she and one of her married girlfriends discussed ad nauseam the need to plan: "I think about things like the housing bust. [I question if] am I saving enough? Am I putting enough away? When my safety net and my parents are gone, I'm not gonna have anybody to call if something happens. And I need to make sure that I have six to twelve months [savings] in advance."

Wendy, as one of the older members of the Cohort, put less stock in the freedom that renting might have afforded her, and was adamant that doubts about her SALA status no longer impeded her attitude to wealth-building: "Oh no, I got over that a long time ago. It made better business sense to buy instead of rent. [I was] just throwing money away. I did have some misgivings, being single. I just had to come to a point where I don't need to wait for a significant other to do something, to do these types of things."

Simone outlined how her SALA status, gender, and cultural upbringing in the Caribbean had helped form her approach to wealth creation – one that would seem contrary to the mainstream wisdom in America that the best route to gaining wealth among the Black middle class is through married family formations: "In the Caribbean culture ... They teach the girls to be strong, independent, to stand on their own two feet, then have your own stuff ... [My mother told me to] Be strong, get your own property, get your own assets. Then when you're done, travel the world and see things. Then you can start your family." Following her mother's advice, Simone bought property in both the DMV and in the Caribbean.

8.3 Homebuying as an Investment

For most people, the Love Jones Cohort included, the purchase of a home is the biggest investment they will ever make. While social considerations were important to the Cohort's homebuying decisions (as will be explored further in Chapter 9), many were driven at least in part by the investment potential of the property in question. The Cohort saw it as a means of increasing their wealth over the long term; for properties with potential appreciation and resale value, they were often willing to spend more than they initially wanted.[6] Here, it is of note that 77% of those in the Love Jones Cohort who were homeowners reported having equity in their homes.

Paige was one of those who asserted that she had purchased her home as an investment opportunity: "My realtor said it would be a good investment for what I was looking to do. I was actually interested in [the] Northwest [community], over by Howard [University] because I knew the area. He was right, so I picked there." Lafayette, meanwhile, spoke of his clear-eyed investment strategy in buying a large home on a suburban cul-de-sac, something that at the time his friends questioned: "It's funny because all my friends' bought townhouses around that time. They all thought they'd be there a couple years and buy a bigger house. Seventeen years later, they're still there ... Because I live in a cul-de-sac, I can resell to a single

---

[6] The Washington, DC, metropolitan area is one of the most expensive real estate markets in the United States. According to a real estate listing service, Bright Multiple Listing Service (MLS), the median home price as of April 2019 in the Washington, DC, metro area was $475,000. Furthermore, according to a 2020 *Washington Post* article, there was a new milestone in DC: "the median sales price for a single-family home in the city rose above $1 million for the first time, to $1.1 million in October, according to Bright MLS." Report by Michele Lerner, December 2, 2020: Median sales price of houses in DC now exceeds $1million.

person, a couple, or a family. A four-bedroom house. More space than what I need? Yeah. But I was thinking about long term."

Some Cohort members discussed how they had conducted considerable research before choosing a neighborhood, with their final choice influenced by plans for economic development in the area. Nancy spoke of how she had specifically looked for planned growth in neighborhoods, and as a result set out to find a condo in what is known as the Arts District – an eclectic artist's community in Hyattsville, Maryland: "The price point at the time was really good. Value and appreciation, that definitely was the impetus." Meanwhile, Brett observed of his home, "I like the fact that it's across the street from Walter Reed [Army Medical Center], which is now closed.[7] It's going to become a Wegmans or Whole Foods. My property value will be increased even further for what I'm paying."

While the Cohort employed considerable financial wisdom on seeking out property to purchase, the outcome was not as they expected. Although our data was collected in 2015, several years after the housing crash of 2007–2009, its effects still resonated with several Cohort members. Despite having lost some equity, Simone was driven by her Caribbean background to stay the course rather than selling her house and cutting her losses: "In my culture, when you buy a property, you don't sell. You pay it up, you own it, move on to the next property. That's how we build wealth; build wealth through real estate. You keep it in the family. Some said, 'Oh, you should sell or walk away.' I just rode it out."

8.4 Discrimination against Single Homebuyers

Having looked at the Cohort's homebuying choices from an economic perspective, it is necessary to ask the question of whether they are discriminated against or suffer a penalty due to their SALA status. A 2020 study signaled that single women are at a disadvantage when buying and selling their homes (Goldsmith-Pinkham & Shue, 2020), though it failed to provide a racial analysis. Singles may experience overt discrimination in the housing market because of their single status: In one study, a cadre of scholars found that both actual estate agents and some study participants who were serving as hypothetical rental agents openly admitted they would

---

[7] "The Walter Reed Army Medical Center closed in 2011. By Act of Congress, the hospital was merged with the National Naval Medical Center in Bethesda, Maryland, and was redesignated "The Walter Reed National Military Medical Center." https://walterreed .tricare.mil/About-Us/Facilities/Our-Rich-History

rather rent an apartment to a married couple over a single person. Moreover, the study participants saw nothing inherently biased about their choices (Morris et al., 2007).

Among those in the Love Jones Cohort who touched on possible discrimination in the homebuying process, Deborah was most vocal. She felt the banks treated her differently because she was single, and that she had found buying her home "[v]ery difficult. Because it's just you, it's just your own solo income. The banks scrutinize every single thing. It's a little bit more difficult than if you had a partner."

As a prospective homeowner, Megan's comments echoed Deborah's in terms of the difficulties of buying on a single income. However, Megan did not perceive this obstacle as constituting discrimination due to her single status. Rather, she simply interpreted having a partner as making home-buying easier from a practical perspective: "Being single does affect that because I think if I was in a relationship or married, I would be able to buy a house that was worth more and probably in a nicer neighborhood with nicer amenities . . . One of my sorority sisters, she's engaged and getting married in a few months, and the properties that her and her fiancé can look at, and just the wealth that they have together, is a lot more than I have by myself."

Carrie expressed a similar point of view, expressing frustration that her single income was insufficient to buy a property where she would ideally like, but failing to fully connect it with her SALA status: "I don't know if it's so much the single status. I think in our society today, most people have two incomes. When you have one income, it is hard, especially when you live in the D.C. area. [It is] so expensive. I want to live in a really nice lifestyle. I want to continue to grow too. I find that sometimes it is a little bit of a struggle of where is a good place to kind of live."

Dual-income homebuying was a reoccurring theme among the Cohort and central to Brett's perspective on asset accumulation: "I believe that it has the potential to impact my being able to obtain additional assets, because there's no two incomes there. I believe if you have two incomes in a home – one mortgage – that gives you the ability, hypothetically, or hopefully gives you the ability to actually save more and gives you the ability to invest more in properties and other assets." Brett was unable to secure a home in the open housing market, so ultimately he had to settle on a private sale, buying a house from his brother, who had married and built a home elsewhere: "I bought the house from him after looking all over D.C. during the mortgage boom. It was hard. I lost a lot of bids for homes, properties."

For Deborah, Megan, Carrie, and Brett, and others like them in the Cohort, it can be that their SALA status means they face social and structural economic challenges to homebuying that non-singles may not. This potentially puts significant obstacles in their path to accumulating the assets they may need to maintain middle-class status. Even so, few of them seem to perceive this as overt discrimination; rather, they see the advantages bestowed on couples in homebuying as being the natural order of things. Moreover, they often might appear to buy into the view propagated by respectability politics that a married family unit is inevitably better than being single, overlooking the fact that while a partner may make it easier to secure a home loan and sustain a middle-class lifestyle, it is also possible that they may come laden with debt and serve as a potential liability to wealth accumulation.

8.5 Debt and Taxes

The issue of debt – particularly student debt – loomed large in the accounts given by several members of the Love Jones Cohort, often influencing the decisions they made regarding their future. Scholars Jason Houle and Fenaba Addo (2019), in using the method of debt trajectories – measuring a variable over age or time – to test the idea that student debt is racialized and disproportionally burdens Black youth, find that "compositionally, racial inequalities in student debt account for a substantial minority of the Black–white wealth gap in early adulthood and that the contribution of student debt to racial inequalities in wealth increase across the early adult years" (p. 571). They conclude, "racial inequalities in student debt may contribute to the fragility of the next generation of the Black middle class. That is, although Blacks benefit socially and economically from post-secondary education, in an era of high debt and rising costs, they fall further behind whites in its pursuit" (Houle & Addo, 2019, p. 573).

Derwin, for example, who had recently entered his thirties, was very focused on dealing with his previously accumulated student debts. Moreover, he unquestioningly viewed moving in with a partner or wife – and thereby renouncing his SALA status – as having a positive effect on reducing his level of debt, mirroring views of earlier scholarship on the Black middle class: "I'm more focused on paying off student loans, making sure I don't have any debts, making sure my credit score is high, which was not a concern that I had in my 20s … At some point I'll be in a dual-income household, so saving would be easier because many bills would be cut in half."

London, meanwhile, in discussing potential motherhood in the context of a SALA lifestyle, spoke of how her student debt directly impacted the choice she made: "That whole freezing egg thing wasn't a big thing in my early 30s. I would have done it then. I thought about it last year. I went to see about it, and the doctor was like, 'Well, you could do it, but the chance of everything working out, it's not worth it.' I was like, hmm, I can work to pay off student loans, or I can take a shot at freezing some eggs that might not work." Ultimately, London chose not to freeze her eggs.

As legal scholar Dorothy Brown (2021) shows, there is racism in America's tax laws (Brown, 2021). This, combined with the fact that the tax laws favor some married couples, can have a significant financial impact on those in the Love Jones Cohort. This points to the notion – discussed earlier and backed up by comments from several of the Cohort – that Black families feel an obligation to provide support to other family members and close friends. For these and other reasons, Brown recommends that marital status should have no influence on taxes and argues returning to individual filings (Brown, 2021).[8] Black feminist and social scientist Jessica Moorman (2020), meanwhile, finds that "single status inequities in work (Kennelly, 1999) and the tax code (Traister, 2016) are attached to real social harms for Black women" (Moorman, 2020). To address these inequalities, Moorman suggests, "Laws overhauling the tax code so that single and married adults are taxed in comparable ways and policies banning single status discrimination in the private sector are needed. Perhaps it is time for single Black women and other single adults to organize and caucus for their own political interests" (p. 445).

In a 2013 article for *The Atlantic*, Lisa Arnold and Christina Campbell compared four hypothetical Virginia women in order to estimate the cost of being single (Arnold & Campbell, 2013). Two of the women were assumed to be single and two married, with hypothetical salary levels set at \$40,000 and \$80,000. Based on this, they found that "[o]ver a lifetime, unmarried people can pay upwards of \$1 million more than their married counterparts for health care, taxes, and more" (Arnold & Campbell, 2013). Irritation at paying an unfair financial penalty due to their SALA status was something Nancy, Lillian, Gwen, and other Cohort members expressed. Nancy, for example, observed, "Lately, it [her single status] has hindered me. There are new tax laws put in place ... I am

---

[8] www.bloomberg.com/news/features/2021-03-10/america-s-tax-code-leaves-black-people-behind-dorothy-brown

outside of the tax bracket that I was in before, so my tax rate has increased."

Lillian, meanwhile, who both owned a business and was in the process of purchasing a home at the time of the interview, discussed the connection between her single status and her assets: "I don't have any write-offs. It's just me. I don't have any kids, so I get penalized probably the most, especially at my age [37] and being by myself." In terms of the implications for maintaining SALA status, Gwen was explicit that the unfairness of the tax system was a strong driver in pushing her toward getting married: "I want to pursue that because of the tax shelter. When you're single and if you have no children, you're heavily taxed. I think I'm more interested, I'm more keen on [getting married] because I know that I'm being taxed heavily because of my status."

8.6 Growing Older and the Possibility of Marriage

Views on wealth accumulation and how it related to SALA status varied according to age among the Cohort. Some of the younger Cohort members – those under 40 – discussed how their views on wealth and spending had changed as they grew older, and/or how they anticipated their understanding of wealth development would evolve if/when they exited their SALA status (i.e., got married). Peter (31) felt that his age and SALA status had thus far prevented him from acquiring the knowledge base he needed to invest: "I would hope that as I age, I would know more about things like stocks and bonds and where to invest and where not to." Meanwhile, Reggie (30) expressed that while his SALA status had given him the freedom to spend extravagantly when he was younger, he now took a more mature view of how best to invest his financial resources: "When I was younger, I would buy Jordan's [tennis shoes] and shoes and all this crazy stuff, not even thinking about how much money I'm spending . . . Now that I'm older, I'd rather go get some nice loafers . . . or something like that and be comfortable, and put my money elsewhere, where it could better benefit me."

Tanya, as one of the older Cohort members at 44, echoed Reggie's view that priorities change with age, particularly in the context of a SALA lifestyle. In outlining her shift away from a more materialistic focus and urge to maintain her status, Tanya used the example of her condominium: "It's technically too big for me, and I wouldn't mind downsizing, even though people would look at it and be like, 'Why would you give up this space?' Space is fine, but I realize the older I get, the less I really need . . .

when it comes to my wealth or how I look at money or choose to spend money, I don't feel the need to have to go out and keep getting stuff to make myself feel better or to live up to a certain status."

A number of Cohort members discussed how they felt a greater burden of responsibility in terms of their wealth and spending decisions as they got older, and that this was directly related to the anticipation (among the men) or hope (among the women) that in the near future they would no longer be SALA. Among the men, Justin (32) stated, "I feel like as I age, I want more family and that's going to take responsibility. So, I am a little more cognizant about how I spend." Joseph (31), meanwhile, was clear that he would make different decisions upon any change to his single status: "I would think of how much wealth I would need to support a family, like a wife and kids. I might start trying to put back [save] for them to go to college or I would look into buying a house. Bigger area, bigger space. I would investigate different ways to bring in residual income, so that we have more disposable income."

Justin and Joseph's comments indicate a perception that, while they remain among the Love Jones Cohort, there is no great onus on them to be cognizant about their wealth and spending decisions, but that once they incorporate a partner and children into their lifestyles, they see their consumption patterns as changing. Here, Justin and Joseph's attitude relates back to a previous point made in the book: that while many of the Cohort's men *assume* an appropriate opportunity will eventually present itself to change their SALA status, for those among the Cohort's women who wish to marry, they merely *hope* such an opportunity will present itself. For example, Megan (26), who grew up poor and was hoping to buy a house, stated in relation to her future wealth-building: "I plan to be making more with my job, a career ladder, I'm pretty much guaranteed a raise almost every year, as long as I perform okay, but I do hope to get married in the future, so I know that will add to my wealth as well." Megan's assumption that marriage represents a wealth-building strategy is fraught with pitfalls, as will be explored further in Chapter 9.

In articulating her vision for the future, London (40) revealed the complications that arise in hoping but not assuming a change in SALA status will come, particularly when it comes to wealth-building and home-ownership choices. London, who at the time of the interview asserted that due to her SALA status "I don't have a home because I choose not to have a home at this point," outlined her Plan B: "My plan is, between now and 45, to pay off my consumer debt and purchase a home on a 15-year fixed [mortgage], so by the time I'm 60 – before I'm retirement age – my house would be paid for." However, she then pivoted to reveal – accompanied with much laughter – that her Plan A involved marriage: "I'm hoping that I might find a husband between now and then. We'll get a house together, but if we don't, the plan B is alright."[9] Elaborating on how this uncertainty over her future SALA status influenced her wealth-related decision-making, London noted, "I am more cautious in making financial decisions 'cause I don't have that spouse to balance it out."

Overall, our Love Jones Cohort interviewees were cognizant of how their SALA status – in conjunction with family background, gender, age, a desire (or otherwise) for marriage, and responsibility to both family (friends) and the larger Black community – can shape thinking about potential wealth-building opportunities. It is also clear that, when it comes to wealth accumulation, while the freedom that comes with SALA status can be an advantage in some cases, buying a home on a single income can impose a significant structural economic obstacle. In terms of homebuying, Pattillo (2013) notes that many in the Black middle class come from poor families, have poor relatives, and are living in neighborhoods between the white middle class and the Black poor, which affects the value of their home (Pattillo, 2013). This opens the Black middle class and their networks up to economic vulnerability. Chapter 9 builds on what we have learned about the Love Jones Cohort's homebuying choices to look in greater detail at where they choose to buy or rent, how they interact with their neighbors, and how this is influenced by factors such as an area's racial make-up and perceived security, as well as the Cohort members' SALA status.

---

[9] Anna duCille, an English professor, discussed how some Black women were challenging the idea of the value of marriage and its subjugation against Black women. "Even many diehard women's rights activists, from writers and public intellectuals like Frances Ellen Watkins Harper and Pauline Hopkins, to the antilynching crusader Ida B. Wells-Barnett and the writer and educator Anna Julia Cooper, argued for the reimagination of Black marriage as a partnership between equals, jointly committed to uplifting the race, and warned women of the dangers of accepting less." duCille interpreted Harper in *The Two Offers* (1859) – credited as the first published short story by an African American woman in the US – by suggesting, "Harper's message is clear: a single life of service to mankind (or to the race) is better than marriage to a man for whom a wife is a possession to be used, abused, and discarded like any other object owned" (duCille, 2018, p. 45).

Neighborhood Decisions and Interactions

This chapter examines how the lifestyles of the Love Jones Cohort shape their decision-making when it comes to choosing a neighborhood and, beyond that, how they interact with their neighbors. Given that "married with children" has traditionally been considered the standard middle-class household formation, the choices made by Cohort members as partner- and child-free individuals are of great relevance in terms of understanding the present situation and future direction of the Black middle class. Aside from affordability, the Love Jones Cohort takes into account a number of factors when selecting a neighborhood, including racial composition, safety, amenities, sense of community, and neighborhood demographics. Although a quarter of our Cohort explicitly stated that their SALA status was an important factor in choosing their neighborhood – for a plethora of reasons including economics, safety, or finding a life partner – two-thirds of the Cohort felt it was not something directly impacting their decision-making. Joseph's response sums up the view of many in the Cohort: "I'm guessing you mean did I want to live around a lot of other single people? I didn't think of that as a primary motivator when I was putting my list together." Nevertheless, as will be seen in this chapter, even if they were not consciously making their neighborhood choices based on their SALA status, in many instances it seems their single lifestyles – as well as their socioeconomic position within the Black middle class – play a key role in how they view residential options.

9.1 Racial Composition

Before moving onto the observations and opinions of the Love Jones Cohort, it is first necessary to provide context by addressing the issue of racial residential segregation – a factor that the Cohort, as a subset of the

Black middle class, is inevitably affected by. Motivations behind moving to a particular neighborhood encompass factors ranging from lifestyle to architecture to racial affinity. "Choice," however, has limitations, with residential segregation resulting from racism, one such limitation that has been extensively studied by social scientist. The three leading perspectives in the literature attribute racial residential segregation to (1) economics, (2) discrimination, or (3) preferences. A fourth explanation that is gaining momentum is a life-course perspective. In terms of *economics*, income and wealth disparities impair the ability of the Black middle class to purchase homes in certain areas; as we have seen, members of the Black middle class often do not inherit wealth from the previous generation with which to purchase their homes (Darity & Mullen, 2020; Oliver & Shapiro, 2013). When the Black middle class become homeowners, they live in less affluent and desirable areas than the white middle class, and in proximity to poor Black residents (Alba et al., 2000; Pattillo, 2005; Pattillo-McCoy, 2000).[1] As Mary Pattillo observes in a 2005 article: "Research findings clearly show that middle-class Blacks in the United States have more favorable residential outcomes than poor Blacks but still live in poorer neighborhoods than the majority of whites on all measures."

Discrimination against potential Black homebuyers in the housing market has been widely documented (Howell & Korver-Glenn, 2018; Korver-Glenn, 2018; Massey et al., 2016; Massey & Denton, 1993). The discrimination perspective highlights a range of public policies and private practices that perpetuate racial residential segregation and deter Black home-seekers from moving into predominantly white neighborhoods (Krysan & Crowder, 2017; Myrdal et al., 1944; Rothstein, 2017).[2]

---

[1] The theory of out-migration from urban areas to the suburbs is a specific kind of economic perspective on residential segregation. This theory explains how individuals' economic gains shape their ability to purchase into a more economically and socially attractive housing market. Wilson (1987, 2012) theorizes that an exodus of the Black middle class from central cities – that is, heavily populated cities, often predominantly Black, at the core of a large metropolitan area – has occurred in the last several decades (Wilson, 1987, 2012a, 2012b). This out-migration or "Black flight" leaves behind neighborhoods comprised of poor Black residents (Johnson & Roseman, 1990; Quillian, 2002; Roseman & Lee, 1998; Wilson, 1987, 2012).

[2] At the federal level, beginning in the 1930s and continuing through the 1970s, the Federal Housing Administration adopted federal-driven racist practices to maintain and reinforce racial residential segregation. For example, "red-lining" was a discriminatory rating system used to evaluate the risks associated with loans made to borrowers in specific urban neighborhoods and caused banks and private lenders to deny loans based on racial criteria (Massey & Denton, 1993). At the private industry level, discriminatory practices include racial steering and blockbusting. Other discriminatory practices over the years have included

A large body of literature suggests that people's own residential *preferences* perpetuate racial segregation. Studies find that white Americans are generally unwilling to consider living in certain areas or are willfully unaware of certain areas due to their racial blind spots (Krysan & Bader, 2007, 2009; Krysan & Crowder, 2017). This shapes their house-hunting choices, as well as their inclination to move out of a particular neighborhood once it becomes racially mixed (Krysan & Bader, 2009; Krysan & Crowder, 2017; Quillian, 2002; W. J. Wilson & Taub, 2011).

Meanwhile, the emerging work on *life course* and segregation (Britton & Goldsmith, 2013; K. Crowder & Krysan, 2016; South et al., 2016) indicates that where people live during adolescence plays a significant role in determining where they live as an adult, and ultimately their life chances.

While just over half the Cohort interviewees said race was not a factor in selecting their neighborhoods, among the other half Lillian, Nancy, Joseph, and others were explicit in expressing a preference for living in a neighborhood with some sense of a Black presence. Lillian, for example, though welcoming a degree of diversity, was clear that she did not want to feel isolated due to her race: "I like diversity. There is some diversity here, if you look around us right now, probably every continent is represented right now but it is important to me to see reflections of myself, at least on some level." Nancy expressed a similar opinion: "I do prefer a diverse neighborhood. There have to be Black people in the neighborhood. It's really just a mindset honestly... I don't want to sound racist; I can't do too much of any one kind. It's just me. I do like a little bit of a rainbow." Joseph also spoke in terms of diversity: "Yeah, I did want to be in a Black area or where ethnic people live. My neighborhood is diverse, a lot of Hispanics, Asians, Africans, a good mixture of people. I just feel comfortable in that environment."

The anxieties associated with feeling isolated, marginalized, or excluded as a racial minority within a predominantly white community or environment is one possible reason why many of the Cohort are seeking neighborhoods with a diverse ethnic make-up and/or a Black presence. In their study of Black men on college campuses, William Smith and collaborators (2007) found that as a result of various factors – such as anti-Black male stereotyping and marginality, hyper-surveillance, control, and racial

real estate agents providing minorities with insufficient information and assistance, and/or steering them toward specific neighborhoods; lenders refusing to offer mortgage credit or offering with exorbitant interest rates (e.g., subprime loan); and neighbors being openly and violently hostile to minorities who move into white neighborhoods.

microaggressions – "students reported psychological stress responses symptomatic of racial battle fatigue," defined by the scholars as "a theoretical framework for examining social psychological stress responses (e.g., frustration; anger; exhaustion; physical avoidance; psychological or emotional withdrawal; escapism; acceptance of racist attributions; resistance; verbally, nonverbally, or physically fighting back; and coping strategies) associated with being an African American male on historically White campuses" (Smith et al., 2007, p. 552). This same framework potentially offers insights into the Love Jones Cohort, who, given their middle-class status, often find themselves navigating in predominantly white spaces. Lafayette, for example, said he was "drawn to this area initially by the abundance of professional Black people. Where I grew up, I went to a small private school. I was the only one, just me." Among the Cohort interviewees, Kendra and Jerome were perhaps the most unequivocal about not wanting to live in a majority white area. Kendra was adamant that "I did not and I don't want to live in a majority white neighborhood; just don't. I feel very strongly about that," while Jerome bluntly asserted that "I wanted to be around Black people, some people my age and color."

There were two members of the Cohort, however, who offered a contrary view in terms of racial preference, explicitly stating that they did *not* want to live in a predominantly Black neighborhood. One of these was Grace, who explained that she did not want to live in Maryland because "[t]here's too many of us [Black residents] in Maryland. Race mattered about Maryland. It didn't matter about where I lived at in Virginia; . . . I like Virginia because of [its] diversity. I'm used to being around a lot of different ethnic groups." It is noteworthy, if contradictory, that in this exchange, Grace uses the first-person plural "us" – including herself in the group of people she does not want to live exclusively among. London, while initially claiming that race "wasn't a factor at all for me. It was the least important," then went on to say, "And, honestly, I did not want to be in a predominantly African American neighborhood. I either wanted to be in something extremely diverse or I wanted to be in something that was predominantly white. For me, growing up, my worst experiences were in Black environments. And then coming here [DMV], I looked around predominantly Black environments. I just didn't see anything that was worth the money." In both cases, Grace and London's preference for a diverse or predominantly non-Black environment seems driven by past experiences and upbringing.

In 2010, I collaborated on a study with sociologist John Iceland. Using census data from 2000 and a common statistical demographic measure to calculate the residential segregation between two groups – the dissimilarity index[3] – we sought out to investigate, among other comparisons, the level of segregation of Black SALA households from white SALA households and from both Black and white married-couple household (Marsh & Iceland, 2010). In doing so, we found that Black SALA households are less segregated from Black married-couple households (0.33), more segregated from white SALA households (0.63), and most segregated from white married-couple households (0.73).[4] From our study, it can be suggested that socioeconomic opportunities related to a college degree and the economic freedom of being child-free may be what allow SALA Black households to integrate residentially with married-couple households to a greater degree than previously believed. However, we also found that racial residential segregation between Black and white households remained high regardless of household composition and economic factors. Specifically, Black SALA households are less segregated from Black married-couple households than from all white households, suggesting the role of race and racism is, indeed, more important than household composition in shaping residential patterns in U.S. metropolitan areas (Marsh & Iceland, 2010).

9.2 Safety

Fifteen percent of the Love Jones Cohort said they factored safety into their decisions on where to live, whether physical or psychological. Serenity, who had purchased her house because of its garage, was among those who discussed physical safety. She noted that as a nurse working 12-hour shifts, pulling into her garage gave her a feeling of security: "I feel pretty safe. That's a big factor for me. I just was like, 'Okay, I'm a single female. I got to

---

[3] When the index is converted to a percentage, it varies from zero (no separation or complete integration) to 100 (complete separation). A score of 60 or above is considered a high level of residential segregation.

[4] There is asymmetry in the patterns of segregation of white SALA and Black SALA households. White SALA households are as similarly segregated from Black SALA households as from all Black households. In contrast, Black SALA households are less segregated from white SALA households (0.63) than from all white households (0.60). This could, in part, reflect socioeconomic differences across various groups. It could be that Black SALA households are less segregated from white SALA households than from white married-couple households because of smaller income differences among the two SALA groups. In contrast, white SALA households, which tend to have higher incomes, may be more similar to other kinds of Black households with multiple earners than to Black SALA households.

be living somewhere safe.'" Similarly, Patricia professed, "My choice of where to live was based on what I could afford and what was going to be comfortable for me. I wanted to make sure that my second house had a garage for security purposes, so that it wasn't obvious when I was home and when I wasn't home." Meanwhile, Deborah chose her neighborhood "[b]ecause I wanted to live in a neighborhood ... where I felt safe, where I can come here at any time. You're by yourself and there's no one to come and rescue you. So [safety] was important for me."

Serenity, Patricia, and Deborah all allude to the fact that their SALA status combined with their gender was a key motivating factor in prioritizing safety in their housing and neighborhood choice. While the Cohort's women placed greater emphasis on physical safety, the men were more likely to reference the material safety of their possessions. Joseph, for example, explained, "I work on computers, so that's a big thing. I want to make sure that my equipment's safe. My unit is good. It has a locked door in front ... So, safety is something I could check off."

Antonio, meanwhile, linked the physical security of his belongings with the psychological safety of living close to where he grew up as a child (which ties in with the life-course perspective mentioned earlier): "I wanted to be in a neighborhood where it's quiet. When I come home, I feel at peace. I can go ahead and leave my windows open and know that nobody's coming in to try to steal something from me."

Maurice stated quite simply that his reason for choosing his upper-middle-class Black neighborhood was "[j]ust for the factor of safety."[5] It is

---

[5] Maurice's comments can also conjure up notions of "John Henryism" – a strong behavioral predisposition to cope actively with psychosocial and environmental stressors (Hudson et al., 2016; S. A. James, 1994; S. A. James et al., 1983). In short, "Known for his strength in steel-driving, John Henry challenged a railroad owner to a competition of man versus a newly invented steam-powered drill in order to protect the jobs of Black American men that would surely be replaced by this machine. Shortly after defeating the steam-powered drill, Henry died of exhaustion" (Felix et al., 2019) and some say with the sledgehammer still in his hand (Hudson et al., 2016). The fable represents a powerful allegory that "high-effort coping to confront obstacles to upward mobility could accelerate the aging process and result in poor health outcomes" (Felix et al., 2019; p. 13). Drawing from Black respectability politics, vigilant coping can refer to some Black people believing that based on past experiences, they must shield themselves from daily slights, prejudice, and overt discrimination by proactively and actively managing their impression to the outside world and by paying particularly careful attention to their physical appearance and clothing, as well as the way they speak. Others – like Maurice – may simply choose to avoid social situations and places where they anticipate experiencing discrimination (LaVeist et al., 2014; H. Lee & Hicken, 2016). Health, mental well-being, and coping strategies are discussed in Chapter 10. Maurice's comments can also stir up notions of *Whistling Vivaldi*, a reference to the book by social psychologist Claude Steele. In the

unclear what form of safety Maurice is referencing. He could be alluding to physiological, psychological, and/or economical safety. He could be signaling that his community is a middle-class Black oasis that offers him a haven from the daily proclivities of being a Black person (and male) in America. Maurice might be seeking refuge and protection through his neighborhood choices, from racial microaggressions he might be experiencing in other environments.

9.3 Transportation and Amenities

Public transportation, amenities, and their relative location were recurrent themes in where Cohort members decided to live. As busy professionals, many valued living close to work in order to decrease commute time, with Renita asserting this had been the overriding factor in her decision-making process: "I was just looking for something that was close in proximity to my job. I can't tell you anything about my neighborhood or anything. I sleep there. That's about it." Ashley was also emphatic in this regard: "When I was living with my parents in Arlington, I was commuting an hour to work, and it was awful. Awful! When I started looking [house hunting], that was the number one thing. I was like, I have to be able to get to work in thirty minutes or less." Megan, meanwhile, emphasized the importance she placed on access to a well-functioning public transport system: "When I was choosing grad school, I decided I needed to live in a city with a great public transit system. I moved to where I live in Silver Spring [a suburban city located in Montgomery County, Maryland, just north of Washington, DC] because of the proximity to the metro. And it was nice and safe!"

Aside from commuting considerations, Celeste and London, among other Cohort members, were guided by the social requirements of their SALA status, consciously selecting locations in the suburbs that offered them easy access to a broader variety of nightlife and entertainment options. Both Celeste, who lived between Washington, DC, and Baltimore, and London, who lived between Washington, DC, and Annapolis, reported that their choice of location was driven by having two options for socializing with friends, thereby providing them with a wider

book, Steele recounts a story of a Black male friend. To defuse the fears of white people, the friend whistled melodies from the Italian composer Antonio Vivaldi. This was to signal that he was a "good" Black person and that certain stereotypes attached to his group do not apply to him. Such daily and command performances by members of the Love Jones Cohort might be exhausting; therefore, they seek solace by choosing to live in neighborhoods that protect both their physical and psychological well-being.

variety of things to do. Moreover, Celeste spoke of the development happening in the neighborhood she selected: "We have a new gym; we have a new movie theater. They've been building it up. I like the access. I can get to anywhere I need to. There's public transportation or at least it's not far."

Cohort members spotlighted the importance of local entertainment and health facilities – amenities that complement the SALA lifestyle – in their neighborhood choice, speaking of how these amenities provided them with various activities to engage in. Here, it is worth noting that approximately 12% of the Cohort told us their single status impacted their neighborhood selection process in terms of wanting to live somewhere that would increase their chances of finding companionship (romantic). As might be expected, they had looked for a home in an area with an active social life in the hopes of meeting someone. As Derwin explained, "Actually, being single made me move here because it was in the city. It was near bars; it was near things to do. If I was already hooked up, I probably would've chosen somewhere more boring."

More generally, exercise facilities were consistently mentioned as a key amenity. As an activity that can easily be conducted either alone, among friends, or with romantic partners, working out is an activity very conducive to the Love Jones Cohort lifestyle. In relation to this, Alicia Smith-Tran (2021), investigating Black women recreational distance runners, has examined how "Black middle-class Americans band together to experience liberation and joy in physical activities where they historically and contemporarily have been excluded, both formally and informally."

Alyssa attributed her love of Bikram Yoga (the more recently rebranded hot yoga) as being what brought her to her neighborhood. She had selected her apartment complex because it provided security, amenities, and was close to where she practiced yoga: "It offers everything – concierge, security, swimming pool, garage, parking. High-rise living in the city. I love it." Alexis echoed these sentiments, explicitly linking the amenities offered at her apartment/condo complex to her SALA lifestyle: "It's built like a hotel, so you have 24-hour concierge service. You have security. You have a pool, a lounge, yoga studio, gym. It has all those commodities that I think fit that young professional lifestyle."

9.4 Family and Friends

Wendy, Nancy, Tanya, Alexandra, Celeste, among others, cited proximity to family and/or friends as informing their neighborhood choice. Wendy, whose decision to purchase a home with her sister had both a social and an economic dimension, was among those in the Cohort who were open to pooling resources with siblings and other non-romantic housemates for the sake of asset building and homeownership: "I owned a home in western Virginia for about ten years. I lived alone – me and my dog. And then my sister's job dried up where she was living, and I just told her to come on, let's get back together and that was what led us to come up here."

Nancy, meanwhile, explained how, given her SALA status, being among her close network of friends had been important in choosing where to live: "At the time, my friends, some lived in DC. We chose to live near each other, so we could all just be within a few minutes if something happened. We all lived in this same radius of about 10 miles." Tanya considered both her family and friends in her decision-making process on where to live. Tanya wanted to be close to her mother, who was in a health-care facility.

Alexandra wanted to be close to her job, as well as her girlfriends (as they represent what sociologist Andrew Billingsley would call her augmented family). In fact, her friend lived in the apartment that Alexandra moved into: "It was closer to my job. One of my girlfriends lived in the apartment and she told me about it and so I looked into it and it was just closer to where I worked at the time which meant spending money on Metro was going to be easier and time so now I would have a much shorter commute which means I could sleep a little bit later." Alexandra also wanted to be close to her sorority: "Plus being active in my sorority most of our meetings took place in that general central DC area so it would be easier to get to them as well."

A similar point is echoed in Celeste's decision on selecting a neighborhood. Celeste "had met that one girl who lives right in my community," who also worked with her. Celeste also realized "there was another girlfriend I knew from California who lived maybe down the street, around the corner." Celeste knew several people in the community she decided to move into, and she liked "that it was a ... small community with other communities around it. That was important for me and the fact that it was near the freeway so I could get to my other friends because I don't have family out here ... based on the fact that I'm single. I wanted to be near my friends, near people that I knew."

9.5 The Impact of SALA Status on Neighborly Interactions

As we have seen in the previous section, some members of the Love Jones Cohort want to live in integrated neighborhoods, while others prefer predominantly Black neighborhoods. More generally, a number of

Cohort members stated they were keen to feel a sense of community within their chosen neighborhood. As such, it is important to explore their neighborly interactions, and in particular how these might be impacted by their SALA status. The Love Jones Cohort, despite not having partners or children, are middle class, and so have the economic wherewithal to buy homes in suburban areas – residential spaces that many may view as traditionally being the preserve of married couples with children. Thus, one question explored in this section is whether there is any perceived tension between the Love Jones Cohort and married couples in their community.[6]

Almost half of the Love Jones Cohort lived in non-Black, family-oriented neighborhoods. Of those in the Cohort who discussed their neighborly interactions, their level of interaction with neighbors ranged from no interaction with neighbors ("mind your own business") to frequent interaction, with roughly half (52%) saying they never or rarely interacted with their neighbors, and the other half (48%) saying they often or sometimes interacted with their neighbors.

Jamir and Reggie were among those who enjoyed more substantive interactions with their neighbors. Jamir proclaimed, "It's very interactive. Just everybody pretty much interacts with each other around here." Reggie expressed similar views: "I speak to my neighbors all the time. I mainly live around females. There's four different females in the little corner where my

---

[6] Spatial/social buffering theory suggests that the Black middle class retain ties to the Black poor, making it difficult to disconnect the Black poor from the Black middle class (Charles, 2003). By way of illustration, consider Baldwin Hills, California. Baldwin Hills is a predominantly Black area in Los Angeles County and also has many of the tracts with the highest percentage of Blacks. This area encompasses both multimillion-dollar homes and a housing project that was known during the 1980s and 1990s as "the jungle" (indicating its reputation as a dangerous area). In the 2001 film *Training Day*, this housing project was used as the location for a scene in which a detective engages in a midday gun battle. That same year, the director of the film *Love and Basketball* used a multimillion-dollar home in the same area to represent the residence of a former star professional basketball player. These divergent cinematic representations of Baldwin Hills illustrate the propinquity of the Black middle class and the Black poor. Baldwin Hills is a dramatic example of a widespread phenomenon: The Black middle class are not far removed physically from the Black poor, and they serve as social buffers between the white middle class and the Black poor. Such spatial buffers potentially align with Darity's notion of structural forces causing class tensions and economic inequalities between Black and white middle classes. These buffers might also extend Wilson's notions of possible class tensions between Black America's haves and have-nots. In this case, the haves are presumably to be those who are married couples, and the have-nots are purported to be those in the Love Jones Cohort.

apartment is. They're all pretty cool and I speak to them on a daily basis, when I see them."

At the other end of the spectrum, Renita asserted in no uncertain terms that she had no interaction at all with her neighbors: "I don't know my neighbors. I don't know anything about any of them. I don't even know who they are." Tanya, meanwhile, despite having met her neighbors, engaged in little, if any, interaction: "I know just this little group up by me, and that's it. I see everyone else. We've had a street party. Everybody on the street gathered, we met each other, but as far as interacting, not really." Simone mentioned that though she had many single neighbors, she only interacted with them "[s]poradically, just hello, good afternoon, that's it." She attributed this to her upbringing and cultural conditioning: "Back home, I didn't really interact with my neighbors like that. I mind my business, keep it moving."

This idea of minding one's own business was also mentioned by other members of the Cohort, perhaps reflecting a desire to clearly delineate between their private and public lives, and so avoid the stress of nonessential neighborly interactions. The impression given by Joseph was of a higher priority being given to other uses of people's time in the public sphere: "We don't really talk to each other a whole lot. Everybody's just kind of minding their own business, doing what they do, going where they need to go. People be out, they'll be visible, but people just don't interact like that."

A pet owner among the Love Jones Cohort, Alexis mentioned slightly more regular interaction with neighbors but conceded that it was a byproduct of having to walk her dog. "I have a dog who's like my child, and this is a big dog community. They know his name before they know my name. Like, 'Oh, you're Encino's mom!' It's like, 'Yeah, hey!' That's my social life right there, walking my dog."

9.6 Gender and Race

Issues of gender and race were highlighted by some Cohort members as limiting neighborly interactions due to perceived societal proscriptions. Lafayette was among the men in the Cohort who mentioned gender as impacting the level of neighborly interaction he felt able to engage in as a SALA man, explaining, "Single female? The neighborhood wants to probably help out, make sure to keep an eye on her. Single male? I think people for the most part, they don't get too close, for whatever reason." This perceived stigma attached to single men, who may be seen as posing a physical or sexual threat, was also touched upon by Derwin, who lives adjacent to college housing. Moreover, Derwin went on to spotlight how preconceptions around gender intersect with racial considerations: "I try to be friendly to the Black folks that have lived there for a while, because I'm not from [the area]. I interact with them on the same level. 'What's good,' 'What's going on,' 'How's it going,' in the same manner I interact with the young white male students. Typically, not the young white girls because I do not want to frighten them."

Here, Derwin alludes to his anxiety at being around white female neighbors, and the risk he faces – like other single Black men (as well as women and children) – of being accused by a "Karen"[7] of not belonging in the neighborhood and having the police called on him. Thus, Derwin is forced to find the appropriate balance between not too much engagement (which may be interpreted as having sexual overtones) and disengagement (which may be interpreted as a signal he does not belong). For Black people living in predominantly white neighborhoods, having to engage in this performative dance can – as elaborated in Tina Sacks's 2018 book *Invisible Visits* that focuses on Black women navigating the American healthcare system – be psychologically exhausting over time (Sacks, 2018).

9.7 Interactions with Married Couples with Children

Turning to another aspect of living a SALA lifestyle among married family units, Joanna gave not having children as a possible explanation for her limited interactions with neighbors: "You know a handful of people, but you don't really. You don't have the block parties, you don't have things like that, what we used to have that really built community. Maybe if I had kids it would be different because then they would interact with the other kids. But it's just me, so I'm in and out." What is perhaps unclear is whether Joanna feels excluded from interacting with those of her neighbors who are parents, or whether, as someone with SALA status, she feels little impetus to engage with those who have children.

While research suggests child-free people are viewed in a negative light by wider society due to their lack of offspring (Ashburn-Nardo, 2017; Daum, 2015; Letherby, 2002; Morison et al., 2016; Park, 2002), none of

---

[7] "Karen" embodies the racial microaggressions that Black people continue to face. Given that this chapter deals with neighborhoods, I want to highlight cases where Black bodies were assumed to be in the wrong physical space or in the wrong racial body and harassed by white women, commonly referred to as a collective Karen.

the Cohort were explicit in saying that their neighbors regarded them in a negative light for being child-free. Olivia, in fact, spoke how she engaged with and was made to feel welcome by a neighbor across the street: "[T]he two youngest [children] who were both in high school ... They were very welcoming to me when I came to the neighborhood. I would wake up on snow days and find the boys had cleared my driveway, my car, my wheelchair ramp. When I come and go, I feel like I'm a part of the family structure because it's like an announcement to the whole neighborhood I'm home or I'm leaving. 'Hi, [Ms. O]!' 'Bye, [Ms. O]!' It's a nice neighborhood."

Moreover, while some Cohort members did touch on the marital status or family type of their neighbors, usually noting couples with children (about 40% of the Cohort noted this family type), none spoke of potential tensions within the Black middle class between those who are married and those who are SALA. Given this, it can be argued that there does not appear to be any great divide between the married and the non-married within the larger Black middle class, at least from the perspective of the Love Jones Cohort.

Generally, those in the Love Jones Cohort appeared largely unconcerned with how their neighbors regarded them. Nevertheless, as alluded to in this and previous chapters, Cohort members are subject to psychological pressures related to race, class, gender, and their single status. In Chapter 10, therefore, we turn to the health and well-being of the Love Jones Cohort, asking what coping strategies they employ to deal with issues such as loneliness, stress, and, in some cases, the perceived stigma attached to being single and child-free.

Health, Mental Well-Being, and
Coping Strategies

As part of the Black middle class, the Love Jones Cohort faces distinct health risks associated with being a racial minority with access to socio-economic resources. Prior research has demonstrated that, compared to their white equivalents, Black Americans enjoy fewer benefits from their middle-class status. Moreover, they may even be threatened with additional risks not faced by their lower-class counterparts. As such, middle-class Blacks may find themselves in precarious situations that are potentially detrimental to their health and well-being. Despite this, our understanding of how being Black, middle class, and SALA impacts the health and well-being of the Love Jones Cohort as a demographic group remains limited, with, qualitatively speaking, not much known about how SALA status shapes mental and physical well-being. The public health literature and research on well-being suggests that being Black and middle class in America does not equate to overall positive health outcomes, due largely to prolonged exposure to racism. In this chapter, we consider how this societal context impacts the members of the Love Jones Cohort, whether their well-being is further complicated by their SALA status, and what coping mechanisms they employ to deal with the challenges they face.

While most of the Cohort indicated they were in good health, they reported experiencing "situational depression or anxiety," which was often tied to stressful life circumstances, with work and finances emerging as a common stressor plaguing the lives of SALAs. Cohort members spoke of feeling stressed, overworked, and frustrated at their financial situations and/or jobs. Moreover, many Cohort members, while also highlighting the positive aspects of their SALA lifestyles, admitted it did at times lead to the situational loneliness discussed earlier in the book, often with negative impacts on their mental health. Despite this, a good number of Cohort members reported that their families – despite occasional negative feelings of obligation and responsibility toward them – served as sources of support, guidance, and love. Many also emphasized the importance of close friendships and augmented families in maintaining well-being and providing a coping mechanism during times of high stress and anxiety.

10.1 Health and Well-Being Disparities in the Black Middle Class

Before turning to the perspectives offered by our Cohort interviewees, it is necessary to set out the context for the health and well-being disparities currently in evidence among the Black middle class in America, and how this may form a key element in the ways Cohort members experience stress, anxiety, and negative mental-health outcomes. Evidence from a host of studies indicate that Black Americans have higher mortality rates than white Americans (Kung et al., 2008; D. R. Williams & Mohammed, 2009) for most of the 15 leading causes of death (which include heart disease, cancer, strokes, diabetes, hypertension, and homicide). Not only do these inequalities persist across all levels of socioeconomic status (Braveman et al., 2010; D. R. Williams et al., 2016), there is even evidence of greater disparities among high socioeconomic status individuals (Farmer & Ferraro, 2005; Wilson et al., 2017), with some studies suggesting that racial disparities in health increase in magnitude as socioeconomic status increases (Bell et al., 2018). Thus, members of the Black middle class may face an increased risk of health issues compared to their white and lower-class counterparts.

These patterns have sparked a vast body of research investigating the effects of race and class status on health. Compared to their white equivalents, Black Americans tend to have lower incomes, lower levels of education, and are more likely to be poor (Williams et al., 1997). As such, early research on Black–white health disparities tended to focus on socioeconomic differences between the groups. This conflation of race and class has led some scholars to assume that differences in health outcomes for Blacks and whites will disappear once class status is accounted for (Farmer & Ferraro, 2005; Williams et al., 1997). However, most studies demonstrate that Black–white differences persist even after controlling for economic factors (Farmer & Ferraro, 2005; Williams et al., 1997). This underscores the fact that racial disparities are driven by more than just variation in resources. The lower-class status of Black people reflects not just individual-level disadvantage, but the structural and historical marginalization of Black Americans as a group (Williams & Mohammed, 2009). Residential segregation, for example, has played a major role in restricting access to resources, while at the same time increasing exposure to toxins (Crowder & Downey, 2010; Downey et al., 2008, 2017; Pais et al., 2014).

There is also evidence that poor health and well-being is inextricably linked to the systemic and interpersonal racism Black Americans are disproportionately exposed to compared to other racial and ethnic groups (Brown et al., 2000; Williams & Mohammed, 2009). Although this body of research is growing, studies have only recently begun to examine the health of groups such as the Black middle class that simultaneously occupy advantaged and disadvantaged social positions (P. B. Jackson & Cummings, 2011; P. B. Jackson & Williams, 2006). Given the substantial evidence indicating that greater socioeconomic resources result in better health outcomes (Kawachi et al., 2010), the assumption that middle-class status is beneficial to Black Americans' health has been, and often still is, common in the literature. Empirical evidence has not, however, been consistent with this expectation.

For instance, studies have demonstrated a number of unexpected health patterns among the Black middle class. Jackson and Williams (2006) identify several of these, with one being that college-educated Black women do not have comparable rates of infant mortality and other pregnancy outcomes relative to their white counterparts (Colen et al., 2006; Hogue & Bremner, 2005; Murray & Bernfield, 2010; Schoendorf et al., 1992). In fact, the Black–white infant mortality ratio actually rises as level of education increases, such that Black women with over 16 years of education suffer higher infant mortality rates than white women with a lower-than-high-school-diploma level of education (P. B. Jackson & Williams, 2006; Schoendorf et al., 1992). These results directly contradict the expectation that higher class status leads to better health. Black men also experience health paradoxes.

While many studies have found that socioeconomic status is inversely related to suicide rates for white men, the opposite is true for Black males (P. B. Jackson & Williams, 2006). Additionally, homicide rates for Black men do not follow expected trends. Despite research showing that socio-economic status is inversely associated with homicide rates among all racial and ethnic groups, the homicide rate of Black males in the highest education category exceeds that of white males in the lowest (Jackson & Williams, 2006; Williams & Mohammed, 2009). More recently, sociologist Kanetha Wilson and colleagues (2017) revealed racial disparities in obesity and self-rated health among adults with household incomes over $175,000 (Wilson et al., 2017). Moreover, public health scholar Caryn Bell and colleagues (2018) found that Black–white disparities in obesity are widest among adults who completed a four-year college degree (Bell et al., 2018).

The lack of protection that higher class status offers Black Americans health-wise has led scholars to investigate the lived experiences of the Black middle class in hopes of discovering why, despite adequate resources, they continue to have poorer health relative to their counterparts in the white middle class. The findings of such research suggest that although Black people might achieve middle-class status based on education and income, their health is not positively impacted by this step up the class ladder. This is due to a variety of reasons, including a lower than expected return on their efforts to achieve middle-class status, stress due to discrimination, and structural issues such as residential segregation. Given these findings, there is a theoretical explanation that drives our work on the Love Jones Cohort.

For over three decades, researchers exploring the complex relationships between the social world and group-level differences in health have turned to the stress process model as their guiding framework. Originally coined by sociologist Lenard Pearlin and collaborators (1981), and drawing on the literatures on stress, coping, and social support, the stress process model attempts to explain how differential exposure to stressors associated with one's social location gets "under the skin,"[1] thereby shaping health outcomes. Originally based on three major components – sources of stress, mediators of stress, and manifestations of stress (Pearlin et al., 1981) – the model has more recently been elaborated in order to better explain racial/ethnic and socioeconomic differences in health (Turner & Turner, 2013; R. J. Turner et al., 2010). Linking each of these components, the stress process model provides a clear means for understanding the mechanisms driving persistent disparities in health and well-being.

Analysis of the Black middle class has often focused on their experiences within communities or specific institutions such as educational domains or the workplace. However, the effects of racial inequality reach much further, patterning individuals' experiences of and group differences in health and well-being. It has long been established that an individual's race and class status can significantly impact on their health, with a wealth of literature revealing variations in health status among those in disadvantaged positions, particularly minority racial groups and people of lower-class status.

---

[1] In public health, the term "under the skin" is an idea based on "the concept of allostatic load attempts to bridge the gaps between the physiological, biological, and social sciences. Both allostatic load and related concepts such as inflammation and metabolic syndrome facilitate the exploration of mechanisms whereby different environmental challenges and stressors" (Green & Darity, 2010).

The stress hypothesis has received growing acceptance as the prominent framework for understanding these group differences (Aneshensel, 2009; Thoits, 1983; Turner & Avison, 2003). Simply put, stress theory asserts that differentiated exposure to stress, as determined by advantaged and disadvantaged social characteristics, leads to differentiated health outcomes. This stress process model can also be mediated and/or moderated by the presence or absence of psychosocial factors such as social support, self-esteem, and mastery (Pearlin et al., 1981; J. Taylor & Turner, 2002; Thoits, 1999; J. C. Turner, 2010).

Investigations of racial discrimination in the lives of Black people have revealed that it acts as a distinct form of stress with serious implications for health (Turner & Avison, 2003; Williams et al., 1997). Public health scholars David Williams and Selina Mohammed (2009) identify three principal ways in which stress affects the health of this segment of the population: (1) Exposure to stress can give rise to negative emotional states that in turn lead to psychological distress, ultimately compromising health; (2) experiences of stress can lead to negative coping mechanisms such as smoking, overindulgence of alcohol, overeating, neglecting sleep, failing to exercise, and not taking prescribed medicine; (3) psychological and behavioral responses to acute and chronic stressors can lead to structural and functional changes in multiple physiological systems (for example, neuroendocrine, autonomic, and immune systems). Taken together, these mechanisms place the Black community at a major disadvantage for health and well-being.

Despite a number of studies investigating health effects on those with a disadvantaged racial status, only more recently has the focus shifted to include groups like the Black middle class, which simultaneously occupy advantaged and disadvantaged social positions (P. B. Jackson & Cummings, 2011; P. B. Jackson & Williams, 2006). The assumption has been that middle-class status, regardless of racial background, is protective, with previous research demonstrating an association between higher educational attainment and improved health status (Kawachi et al., 2010). Similarly, countless studies have shown a relationship between higher income and superior health. However, as scholar Jay Pearson (2008) notes, the protective effects of higher status have primarily been tested on white people. Therefore, we should not assume they exist – at least in the same way – for Black people. Though health disparities research has found higher social status to be protective against morbidity for Black people, this does not extend to mortality. This suggests that while Black people with higher education and income can access medical and preventative care, they can do little to reduce the incidence of death or lengthen healthy life span (Geronimus et al., 2001; Pearson, 2008).

Thus, investigating the health of the Black middle class, as well as the impact that stress has in a variety of social domains, promises to provide fruitful and important insights into the effects of social stratification. As will be argued, the health of the Love Jones Cohort is guided by the stress process model.

10.2 Well-Being and Mental Health among the Love Jones Cohort

The Love Jones Cohort are single and living alone in the Black middle class. As outlined in the previous section, the data on the Black middle class suggest that their class status does not offer them as much protection from negative health and well-being outcomes as might be assumed. Nevertheless, in honing in on their single status, there is research that suggests that being SALA may serve as a protective measure to mental well-being in certain regards. One of the central premises of sociologist Elyakim Kislev's (2019) cross-sectional work points to the idea that those who have been living alone might be better equipped to handle their single status later in life than people who suddenly find themselves returning to single status after marriage. Kislev's (2022a, 2022b) more recent work uses the Panel Analysis of Intimate Relationships and Family Dynamics (pairfam) to explore and challenge the assumptions of marriage and happiness. Elsewhere, however, there is scant work exploring mental health and well-being among Black middle class SALAs, and how they navigate these intersecting identities.

Figure 10.1 shows the Cohort equally split as to whether their SALA status had a positive or negative influence on their well-being, with 47% reporting that their SALA status had a negative influence on their well-being, the same percentage reporting a positive influence, and the remaining 6% reported both a positive and negative influence. This equal split was reflected among both the over-40 (50% positive/negative) and 40 and under (45% positive/negative). Looking at gender, however, there was a discernable difference in attitudes between the Cohort's men and women: While 55% of the women reported their SALA status as having a negative influence on their well-being, only 42% of the men did so. Conversely, only 41% of women reported a positive influence, compared to 50% of men.

In terms of mental-health status, of those members of the Love Jones Cohort who answered the question concerning whether they experienced

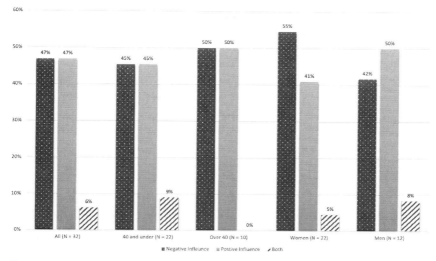

Figure 10.1. Percentage of the Love Jones Cohort, by age and gender, who report their SALA status as having negative, positive, or both negative and positive influence on their well-being

depression or anxiety, 27% claimed some level of depression, 30% some level of anxiety, and 14% some level of both depression and anxiety (with most of the individuals in this latter category being women). In terms of those who had at some point been clinically diagnosed with depression and/or anxiety by a doctor or licensed clinician, the percentage was 37%, indicating that a significant portion of the sample had – either currently or in the past – experienced issues with depression or anxiety even if some no longer felt they were facing such challenges.

Christine, London, Natalie, and Olivia were some of the Cohort members who expressed feelings of distress that were tied to a particular context or circumstances. Christine, who is a therapist and described herself as someone who thinks about everything really hard, asserted, "Are there times that I feel down? Yes. Are there times where I feel anxious about something in that situation? Yes." Christine explained that she had not been clinically diagnosed with anxiety or depression. Rather, what she is describing is what may be termed *situational depression* and *situational anxiety*. Christine's response was consistent with past studies distinguishing between more general symptoms of psychological distress and diagnosed psychiatric disorders such as severe depression (Horwitz & Wakefield, 2007; Payton, 2009). While distress is attributed to living in stressful circumstances, a psychiatric disorder represents internal dysfunction arising from interacting factors such as genetics, medical illness, and environmental stressors (Barnes & Bates, 2017).

This pattern of attributing psychological distress to situational depression or anxiety was apparent among a number of Cohort members, especially women. While London, for example, felt that in general her mental well-being was stable, she pointed to the biological mechanisms of her menstrual cycle as provoking a temporary disruption of her emotional health and well-being: "From the standpoint of my hormones when my cycle starts, I get really depressed they go coo coo and crazy. It was situational depression."

Natalie, while initially claiming she did not suffer from depression or anxiety, went on to explain how stressful events and challenging life circumstances related to her physical health had triggered symptoms of depression: "I have [a musculoskeletal disorder] though, and apparently depression is part of that, so they usually treat you with like an antidepressant. That never worked for me because I'm not depressed. The [medication] made me feel like I was swelling from the inside out and was going to burst out of my skin. I was quickly gaining weight. It felt like a pound a day. I was like I can't take this and I'm not. I think it made me depressed."

Olivia described how broader societal situations had impacted her mental well-being: "I've never been diagnosed with clinical depression, but I know that I've been depressed. I was depressed after 9/11 when the media kept showing people jumping off of roofs, and it was just a very dark time. It was very oppressive, and it made me decide that I have to limit how much negativity I can have in my life. I actually stopped watching news."

The Cohort's men also discussed experiences of depression in relation to particular life events. Antonio explained, "I did go through depression when I was younger, I'll say, middle school. I went through that phase where I went through a suicidal experience." Antonio did not have a formal diagnosis and claimed that depression is not something he struggles with now, despite having had to face the challenge of moving from West Africa to America. In fact, Antonio elaborated that his SALA status constitutes a source of happiness, as he is able to take care of himself and do whatever he wants when he wants. This independence is what many interviewees reflected on when explaining why they were happy in their SALA status.

Some interviewees, such as Gwen and Walter, did discuss more serious mental-health challenges, although most noted such issues were in the past. For example, Gwen said, "I had depression at one phase in my life where I actually needed to take something, but an ongoing issue? No. It was just a period of stress that I was going through." Gwen did not elaborate on what that stressful moment was in her life but stated that she was not actively seeing a mental-health professional. Walter, meanwhile, revealed, "I was diagnosed as bipolar. I had an episode maybe about a decade ago but ever since I came out of that, I haven't had any other issues with it."

Research has shown a generally low prevalence of reported psychiatric disorders among Black Americans relative to their white counterparts and other groups, but that when Black people do experience major psychiatric problems, their symptoms tend to be chronic and severe. Additionally, they are less likely to seek professional treatment. However, given that many of the Cohort reported being able to overcome such challenges, it may be the case that their middle-class status does, in fact, provide some support in resolving their mental-health issues more effectively.

10.3 Family Tensions and Situational Loneliness

Those in the Cohort cited a number of factors as having a negative impact on their mental and emotional well-being, some of which were related to or directly arising from their SALA status. One such factor was strains in familial relationships, which may have a particularly potent impact on those in the Cohort who, in the absence of a partner or children, attach considerable importance to their family (and friendship) networks. Joanna, for example, described the emotional burden of dealing with her mother, who was "stressing me out. She is having some mental health challenges. I'm very concerned about her, as she's aging."

Other members of the Cohort described their SALA status as causing them to feel distant from their families. Madison, for example, explained, "The family that I have that's closest to me, I can't really relate to them. We relate, but I'm single, they're not. Certain things that I experience, sometimes I wonder whether or not they get it. That contributes to me feeling alone. I'll go to the family event and everyone is involved and consumed with their kids and their husband, and here I am [alone]."

More generally, various Cohort members referred to *situational loneliness* – which we have already touched upon in Chapter 6 – as playing a problematic role in their single status. As Christine observed, "I think that [single status] definitely affects my mental health sometimes." Melinda, meanwhile, remarked, "Sometimes you get lonely. I'm an emotional eater so sometimes I eat when I'm lonely and not when I am hungry."[2]

Tanya noted that her SALA status brought with it both happiness and difficult moment provoked by loneliness: "I would say 70 percent of the time I am happy, and I would say 30 percent you can get lonely." She then went on to express a desire for companionship as a remedy for her loneliness but was open as to whether this would take a romantic or non-romantic form: "There are good days there are bad days. No one wants to grow old and be alone. I'm hoping at some point there will be companionship. I have to wait and see what presents itself to me whether it would be in a marriage or just for kicking it, hanging out, whatever us old folk will be calling it when it happens."

Paige and Brett, among other members of the Cohort, took a more negative view of the impact their SALA status had on their mental well-being, explicitly linking their lack of a romantic partner with the loneliness they experienced. Despite being clear that she was unwilling to rush into a relationship just for the sake of changing her SALA status, Paige confessed, "Loneliness. Honestly, that's what it means. It's kind of bleak, but I don't want to lose hope because I don't want to have this aura of negative energy surrounding me. [There are] opportunities to certainly move somebody in and potentially take care of someone or co-exist." Meanwhile, Brett's anxieties had been heightened by personal experience of the vulnerabilities he perceived in being single: "I had back surgery in October. I was unable to care for myself in any respects. That kind of was an eye-opening experience."

Sociologist Eric Klinenberg's (2016) article on loneliness discusses how scholars need to think more critically about potential risk factors associated with living alone and, once (and if) these are identified, consider appropriate interventions. With a demographic shift toward singlehood, social institutions will need to be more proactive in putting protective measures in place to allay the fears expressed by members of the Cohort.

10.4 Financial and Work-Related Worries

Despite their middle-class status supposedly putting them on a stronger footing than their lower-class counterparts, a number of the Cohort cited finance-related worries as provoking significant stress and anxiety. In this

---

[2] For work on depression and marital status, especially during COVID-19, see Hearne (2021).

regard, the Cohort's women are perhaps at a greater risk, with a 2012 *The Washington Post* report concluding that "Black women have more trouble paying their bills or getting a loan than white women . . . Nearly half of the women surveyed said they help out elderly relatives, and more than a third regularly assist friends or family with childcare – outpacing white women in both cases. This means the ongoing distress felt by Black women can quickly ripple through their social networks." Simone's story was reflective of this scenario. Recounting how she had to deal with her mother's expectations that women must be financially independent, while at the same time raising her younger brother, she admitted, "I get anxiety when my money isn't right. I get depressed when I just have $5,000 in my bank account. I'd be like, 'Where's my money? I just have $5,000. Where did it go?' It went to bills and stuff. 'Man, I just need to get it together, as in a reset.'"

While Alexandra did not consider herself as having "any regular issues" with depression or anxiety, she pointed to her financial situation as a major source of stress with the potential to undermine her mental health: "Three years ago when I lost my job, I went through a bout of depression as far as trying to figure out what's going to happen when money runs out. I guess there was some anxiety there, too, because I was going on a lot of interviews and getting a lot of no [responses] until I finally got a yes. That was just very stressful."

Work also emerged as a key area of concern for members of the Cohort, with 64% of members expressing that they had experienced work-related feelings of anxiety. While, of course, jobs can be a source of stress for many people, given that SALAs are by definition the sole breadwinners in their household, this serves to coat on an additional layer of anxiety. Furthermore, the fact that they do not have responsibilities to a partner and children can cause them to spend more hours at the office, with their workplaces misguidedly assuming they have more time to commit to work because they do not have outside responsibilities (Casper & DePaulo, 2012). Additionally, institutional and interpersonal racism – something the Cohort's middle-class status by no means shields them from – means many Black Americans face barriers in the workplace, such as a Black tax (Black Americans having to work twice as hard to be viewed as equal, mentioned in Chapter 3), coupled with the everyday stresses of work. All of these can take a toll on the health of the Cohort. For example, although Jerome – who, earlier mentioned, was emphatic about living around Black people – did not directly mention the stress of being a Black person in America when professing that the everyday grind of the workplace as provoking constant low-level stress ("Deadlines. Burdens of trying to keep up with the job. Trying to get a better job. The minutiae of working in a stressful job."), I argue it can be implied.

Though many in the Cohort framed the stress of their job as being par for the course, for others the stress of overwork, coupled with their SALA status, threatened to take a more serious toll on their mental well-being. Natalie, in reflecting on her work–life balance, confessed, "As a consultant, I'm always on. I get my email on my phone, I have my laptop, just always on, commuting to work." As such, she found balancing her household, personal goals, and professional goals "really hard and something always slips." Moreover, she worried about the impact on her health and the potential consequences of getting sick, which she felt would be exacerbated by the fact she was single: "Making sure you don't get sick in between all of that because if you get sick a lot of things are slipping and then you have to pick them all back up because there's nobody else there to do them." Natalie summed matters up by highlighting the emotional burden of responsibility she feels weighed down by attempting to keep her head above water financially: "It's just a lot of responsibility that kind of weighs on you and then trying to make sure you're financially stable because in all that stress and always being on, you can make bad financial decisions because you're trying to do what's easiest and what's easiest is most convenient." In terms of work–family balance, the feeling of "always being on" referenced by Natalie was also touched on by other interviewees. Shannon, for example, described, "Overworking myself, for sure. Sometimes I do put a lot on my plate. It does, it wears me down."

Kevin reported feeling overwhelmed and frustrated but for slightly different reasons, primarily because his work was not what he had expected or hoped for. Kevin related his story of graduating from college as an engineer and then being out of work for a year: "It's kind of messed up. To think that a degree could open any door for you, and for me, that wasn't the case." Kevin's disappointment at not being able to find a job despite his degree and best efforts ultimately contributed to a decline in his mental health. Unfortunately, his situation is consistent with research demonstrating that, relative to whites, Blacks receive lower returns for higher educational attainment, a situation reflected at all education levels. Sociologist Devah Pager conducted a landmark study on male jobseekers by race (Black and white men) with similar educational attainment. Pager found that white men who were potential applicants *with a felony conviction* were more likely to receive callbacks for an interview and offer than Black men *without a criminal record* (Pager, 2003).

10.5 Single Stigmatization

On top of the various well-being issues outlined previously, those in the Love Jones Cohort might have to contend with "singlism," defined by social psychologist Bella DePaulo (2006) as "[p]eople who stereotype, stigmatize, marginalize, or discriminate against people who are single." Aside from the tax structure, DePaulo mentions various practices that disadvantage those in the Love Jones Cohort and in some cases might impact their health. For example, singles cannot add any other adult to their workers' health-care plan; gyms may offer free memberships to partners but not friends; and meal delivery services usually only offer plans for two or more people.[3] In addition to these discriminatory policies and practices, the societal expectations of those with SALA status can impose psychological strain. Here, the perceived stigma of being single may intersect with issues of gender, class, race, sexuality, and age, as will be seen among members of the Cohort, in this section.

Various Cohort members reported feeling stigmatized due to their SALA status, both as a result of external societal pressures and their own internalized feelings toward singleness. Opinions on who faced greater stigma within the Cohort and the reasons behind this varied considerably. Some felt geographic area played a role, with everyone who referred to this factor claiming stigmatization was stronger in the American South. Some felt older singles were more stigmatized, while others said younger ones were. In particular, feelings ran high in relation to whether stigma was more strongly directed toward women or men. Related to this, Cohort members cited racial as well as sexual orientation issues.

Some researchers have suggested that while young unmarried people are considered perfectly acceptable, those over 40 are often viewed as past their prime, even pitiful in their quest to find love (Byrne & Carr, 2005; DePaulo & Morris, 2005; Krueger et al., 1995; Morris et al., 2008). Brett, a 44-year-old banker, was one of the members in the Cohort who believed stigma against singles becomes more pronounced with age. He illustrated his perspective by recounting an interaction he had at a business dinner with a young white male plastic surgeon, who told him, "Okay, you're not married, you're a nice guy, Black. I worked with several surgeons, Black, female surgeons, who want to be married. You seem to me to fit that bill." Brett surmised the surgeon was suggesting, "You can't play forever," and so

[3] www.wealthenhancement.com/blog/cost-of-being-single

responded, "I'm not playing. I haven't met any of the women that you're talking about." Brett articulated that as people grow older, "People are really going to say, 'What's wrong with you?' Unless you were married."

Rick (33) echoed Brett's sentiments, and in doing so touched on the stereotype of singles as being selfish: "When you're 50 and single, and not ever been married before, I think the stigma is that you're probably extremely, extremely selfish because, 'Oh you've never been married. You've gotten that old, what's wrong with you?'"

Tanya (44) linked the stigma of being older and single with divorce, suggesting that people are more accepting of folks who are 40 and above if they were already married and already had children. Tanya thinks people are less accepting if someone is single and never been married or has no children. Then, for Tanya, the stigma holds.

Contrary to the aforementioned viewpoints, Sheri (33) thought that younger SALAs were more likely to be stigmatized than the older ones: "At 50, they feel like maybe the pool is small, so there's a reason why you're probably going to be single, because you don't have a lot to choose from. When you're 30, they feel like you have a lot of people to choose from, so maybe there's something wrong with you." Renita, who at 52 fell into the older age bracket, expressed the related point that with age comes a greater ability to deal with internal and external pressures to conform to societal norms: "When you get to 50, honey, there's a lot of things you don't really care about; what people say, or think is one of them. When you're 30 you want to be in with the in crowd and do what's popular."

Tanya, meanwhile, felt that though stigma against singles existed, the rise of single-family units as a demographic and changes in societal attitudes toward marriage were leading to greater acceptance across both younger and older age groups: "There's so many of us that are in our 40s and 50s that are in this era that aren't married, no kids. I think it's more commonplace. There are definitely going to be a group of individuals who still think 'Okay there's something wrong with that.' For 30-year-olds … I just feel the value of [the] institution of marriage, I don't think it's important anymore. The value of it has diminished." Carrie also equated demographic changes in singlehood to greater (though incomplete) acceptance of SALA status: "I think the stigma is lessening but I think there is still some."

Megan (26) raised the issue of how age and gender intersect when it comes to stigma, arguing that while women are particularly affected by the stigma of being single, this diminishes over time: "There's still this stigma of being the single woman and people being like, 'You're gonna end up a spinster and a cat lady.' . . . People question your worth as a woman if you don't have a partner. I think once you're 50, though, people probably don't really care; as you get older, you care less and less about other people's life situations."

Alexis (31) highlighted that being stigmatized for being single can lead to self-esteem issues, particularly for older Black women: "I think at 50, if you're single and you've never been married or been in a relationship, there are probably a lot of self-esteem issues because people probably put a lot of labels [on you], unfortunately." Here, Alexis pointed to how the situation was exacerbated by gender and racial stereotypes: "If it's a man, it's like he's just a playa . . . If you're a woman, it's as if something's wrong with you. Especially if you're a career-driven, educated woman. You're an angry Black woman."

Several of the Cohort's women concurred with the view that women suffer greater stigma than men, highlighting the gender disparity in societal framings of singledom. Kendra, for example, observed, "For men it's like, even the terminology, the way you use like bachelor pad and the perception of a woman living alone specifically as you get older it's like, an old spinster, an old maid." Lillian echoed this view, in terms that reflected her annoyance at the perceived injustice of the situation: "For a man, oh, he's just having fun. But a woman? Nobody wants you. You must be a crazy old maid. All that stuff. But for a guy, no, he's just doing a George Clooney." Kelsey, however, offered a contrasting opinion, claiming that educated, middle-class women such as those in the Cohort were subject to less stigma than their male counterparts: "I think Black people, I think all people, give Black women more of a pass if they're single and have a certain level of education because they feel like the men aren't there or maybe they're not open."

Among the men, though Jerome conceded that "[w]omen always get the short end of the stick," others were less willing to concede the point. Brett was unwilling to be drawn on whether gender was also a factor in single stigmatization: "I do think that society, people, often do look at factors like that if you're 50, start looking at you sideways to some degree. I can't say it's more for a woman or more for a man." Rick, meanwhile, complained that single men are often labeled in derogatory terms: "I guess for lack of better words, you're a 'Ho' you're just out there, you're bitter, you're jaded, you're scared. I'd say scared is a part of it. You're just playing the field, you're not mature, and that's not always it."

An interesting and telling point is that while men may feel the sting of being stigmatized for being single, it is easier for them to change their status when it suits them – that is, simply deciding to renounce their SALA status and get married. Some among the Cohort's women viewed this gender difference in ways that cast negative light on the men, with Shannon, for example, stating, "It's a lot easier for men. Men can date down; they can date up. Most likely, they prefer to date someone who is younger than them. They have no discretion." Robin, meanwhile, suggested some Black men opt to marry for somewhat cynical reasons once they become successful in the corporate arena: "because in the corporate world it's known that a man needs to have a wife to go to corporate events and be included with all the other corporate people."

The issue of a person's sexuality being questioned due to their SALA status was raised by several Cohort members, reflecting a tendency among wider society to equate singleness with homosexuality – in other words, that individuals may be single because they are gay but do not want to come out of the closet. Renita, for example, observed, "[F]or women, you do get a little more flack [if] you've never been married. People want to know are you a lesbian?" Adoriah, meanwhile, felt that such preconceptions about sexuality – and an assumption that being gay could be equated with something being "wrong" – could equally be applied to single men: "I'm 32 and I think, definitely, from this point on, if you are a single woman … but, I think there is a stigma, basically, 'What's wrong with you?' if you're not married, don't have a boyfriend, don't have kids … Also, if you're a guy, if you're single, people kind of question what's wrong with him, 'Is he gay?'" Kelsey admitted that she herself, along with her girlfriends, was guilty of such stereotyping: "Me and my friends even talk about this: when we meet men and they're like over 40, they haven't been married, they don't have kids, and they don't look like they've had a long [term] relationship, you start to wonder are they in the closet or what's wrong."

While many of the Cohort acknowledged that a degree of stigma existed in relation to being single – differing only in terms of which age group or gender was most impacted – for Shannon, she felt such notions should have no bearing on people's perceptions of themselves and their relationships. Shannon, for example, considered the impact of stigmatization on the mental health of older SALAs as negligible compared to the physical and psychological effects of aging: "Honestly, when you're 50, you're so caught up on someone taking care of you, that you don't even deal with any of that [stigmatization]." Despite initially claiming there was no significant stigma attached to being single, however, Shannon then appeared to backpedal, adding, "Not if you're a Black female, unfortunately." Asked to expand on her rationale for saying "unfortunately," she explained, "I just think that there's this false perception of Black women wanting to be independent. It irks me because it's not realistic."

10.6 Coping Mechanisms

In terms of dealing with well-being issues associated with being SALA, from situational loneliness to dealing with the stress of stigmatization, those among the Cohort discussed a variety of coping mechanisms and strategies. Most prominent among these, as has already been touched on previously in the book, was augmented family networks – that is, the support provided by close family members and wider friendship groups during periods of distress. In the absence of a partner to lean on, such networks are key to the emotional and mental well-being of those with SALA status, the Cohort included. I might also flip the script. In the absence of a network of friends to lean on, a partner is key to the emotional and mental well-being of married people.

Regarding mental health, 52% of Cohort members noted the importance of family, with most citing positive relationships. Adoriah (32) contextualized this point by talking about her relationship with her parents: "They are my best friends … We have a really good relationship so that brings about a lot of peace too in my life and mental health." She also discussed the central role of her close friendship group, saying she knew "who my real friends are and who I can communicate openly and honestly with, and it's mutual, and having at least one confidant you can tell them something that you know you won't hear it repeated unless you say it yourself."

Alexandra (33), meanwhile, stressed the importance of having her roommate around to turn to when she is going through a bad breakup or going through a career crisis, though she seemed hesitant to explicitly couch her issues in mental-health terms: "Well my roommate was there when I lost my job but we don't really talk about mental health per se, but she knows that if I was going through something that I would come talk to her, like if I had a bad breakup or something."

Engaging in exercise as a means of maintaining both physical and mental well-being was mentioned by several Cohort members, with Kevin (25) claiming, "When you're single you concentrate a little more on your physical fitness. You run; you try to keep a gym membership together. You're out more. I feel like in a lot of ways it's a positive because I've seen so many buddies fall to the wayside once they get a girl." Shannon

(50) was of a similar opinion, arguing that her SALA status allowed her greater freedom to look after her physical – and by extension, her mental – health: "If anything, I have more time to address my physical health . . . I feel a little overworked or anxious about anything, then I go running. It's definitely a release." Madison (35) noted that being single not only gave her more time for self-care[4] but also provided her with greater impetus: "I notice when I was in relationships, I put on a lot of weight. Just got comfortable because I was with that person. Being single. I don't do it just to be marketable. I just have more time for myself to figure out what's important to me. It's easier for me to stay in better health and shape."

The idea that mental-health issues should be dealt with by seeing a professional was met with a mixed reception among the Cohort. I argue that this is perhaps unsurprising given what I perceive as high levels of religiosity in Black America and social conservatism in the Black church. Reflecting this, Nancy (43, *estimated*) explained how she utilized her faith to deal with "natural anxiety," saying, "That's when I start praying more, reading more of my Bible, really trying to zen myself out, so I'm not thinking." Of those currently speaking to someone about mental health–related issues, only 30% identified this person as being a professional, with the remainder turning to friends, family, or clergy in their attempts to deal with emotional distress.

Despite this, some members of the Cohort were open and positive about seeing a therapist or other mental-health professional. Melinda (50), for example, stated, "Oh yeah. I'm used to seeing my therapist. I haven't been there in a while. She's a social worker. She's amazing." London (40) asserted that seeing a therapist was a perfectly rational response to experiencing mental distress: "I don't have a problem with going to see a therapist. I think your brain is your most powerful organ and if something's wrong, you need to get help for it. If your heart's hurting I'm not going to tell you to pray about it, [I am] going to tell you go to the cardiologist."

---

[4] In a 1988 essay, Audre Lorde wrote the idea of, "Caring for myself is not self-indulgence, it is self-preservation, and that is an act of political warfare" (Lorde, 1988, p. 130). Or as Activist Brittany Packnett Cunningham would say it, "I am an Activist and Joy is my Resistance." Black joy stems from such a notion of self-care (Brooks, 2020; Golden & Utah, 2015; Lu & Steele, 2019). For more on this topic, see Taylor (2021) on self-love; Adkins-Jackson et al. (2019); Neil and Mbilishaka (2019); Evans et al. (2017); Evans (2021); Berger (2018); and Strings, S. (2019). Sabrina Strings is the cofounder of *Race and Yoga* journal – a publication that employs an intersectional approach to race and yoga.

Though several members of the Cohort mentioned visiting a mental-health professional at some point over their lifetime, in most cases, however, they were no longer speaking with them. Tanya (44) described her experience of seeing a therapist in ambivalent terms: "I went to a therapist a couple years ago. Finding a therapist is like finding a hairdresser or a boyfriend. It's hard to find one that actually clicks. She was okay. I saw her for a little while, but I felt like I didn't get a lot out of it." Megan (26), meanwhile, was more positive about her childhood experience of speaking to the school counselor: "Back in [middle school], my father passed away when I was [young] and I just kind of never dealt with that, and it kinda came back up, in middle school. So, I spoke to the school counselor about it for maybe a few months, and that actually really helped."

Nevertheless, the majority of the Cohort claimed never to have spoken to a professional, with some reacting negatively to the very idea of doing so. Renita (52), for example, exclaimed, "No. Jesus. I mean, seriously." Others focused on more practical concerns preventing them from seeing a therapist, with Tina (30), for example, noting, "No, it's just not covered in my insurance." Some Cohort members said they were not currently seeking professional help because they did not see the value in it.

Antonio (28) was candid in speaking about how he had battled suicidal thoughts when he was younger: "If people ask me or I have a conversation, I will tell them about my past ... It's a part of growing up and learning. If you don't talk about your past and know where you've been and where you're going, people don't know how to help you when you're in need of help." Relatively few of the Cohort, however, shared Antonio's mindset of being open and unashamed about discussing past mental-health episodes, pointing to a potential vulnerability when it comes to dealing with more serious mental-health issues.

Given, as I argue, that the trend is toward SALAs constituting a growing proportion of the Black middle class, consideration must be given to the well-being needs of this demographic subset, rather than assuming what works for married family units works for single-person family units. This is a particularly pressing concern given the unique challenges being single and living alone potentially possesses, from situational loneliness to stigmatization by those from other societal groups (as well as from within the Cohort itself) needs to be addressed and dismantled. Moreover, how issues of well-being intersect with issues of gender, age, and race among the Cohort merits further exploration.

Conclusion

This book has explored a number of interrelated theoretical questions, including whether our views of what constitutes the Black middle class needs to be redefined, and how traditional notions of family are challenged by the rise of the Love Jones Cohort. Throughout, the underlying impetus has been to interrogate the unique lifestyle of the Love Jones Cohort, and thereby understand how their intersecting identities of race, class, gender, and singleness shape their life decisions.

There are four main implications arising from this study. First, not only have Black singles long constituted a significant proportion of the population, but this trend will likely become even more pronounced for the foreseeable future. As such, they should be regarded as trailblazers for the singlehood movement and how to do singlehood efficiently. Second, membership in the Love Jones Cohort can be due to choice, circumstances, or in many cases a combination of the two. Thus, to make judgments of SALA status based solely on individual behavior and without looking to structural context is shortsighted. Third, the Love Jones Cohort should play a central role in how the Black middle class is defined, with any such redefinition acknowledging that one-person households (and their assets) count as a family for such purposes. Fourth, although some members of the Love Jones Cohort face mental health and well-being challenges, they have developed a variety of coping mechanisms appropriate to their SALA lifestyles. These coping mechanisms should be taken seriously, with institutional measures considered that focus specifically on the needs of those who are SALA.

BLACK SINGLES IN THE SINGLEHOOD MOVEMENT

As this book has demonstrated, an amalgamation of structural forces and individual behaviors underlie the rise in Black singles more generally, and the Love Jones Cohort specifically – particularly Black women falling within this demographic. The theoretical implications call for collective action among those interested in the topic. It is important that a multilevel approach to singlehood in Black America is continually considered, encompassing both individual agentic choice *and* structural factors (Clarke, 2011). Likewise, whether or not one formally adopts an intersectional lens in examining singlehood, it is important to acknowledge that for many people, their singleness is informed by intersecting and marginalizing identities (Moorman, 2020; Pepping et al., 2018). Often, such characteristics are viewed as constituting some form of deficit, especially among single women (Moore & Radtke, 2015; Simpson, 2016), or are regarded as being part of a transitory phase of life, associated with such negative traits as being passive or lazy (Lahad, 2012). These presumptions obstruct a more holistic understanding of how these intersecting identities shape the lifestyles and decision-making processes of the Love Jones Cohort.

This book has pointed to how the Love Jones Cohort may be regarded as innovators, offering pathways for other non-Black singles to navigate their solo lifestyles and the singlehood movement. Put another way, the members of the Love Jones Cohort are showing the rest of the world how singlehood can be done. Despite this, the current face of the singlehood movement is not reflective of Black singles or the Love Jones Cohort. We must question why that is.

LINKING THE LOVE JONES COHORT TO STRUCTURAL ISSUES

A bevy of factors has led to the emergence of the Love Jones Cohort. While some may resort to the reductive and judgmental explanation that there is simply something wrong with those in the Love Jones Cohort – that they are just too picky, difficult, career driven, or selfish for a meaningful relationship – a more critical account requires one to adopt a broader view that addresses a variety of structural and systemic issues.

When considering intimate relationships, it is prudent to include historical, institutional, and structural factors in the conversation, including knowledge of the racism, gendered racism, and respectability politics undergirding the notion of marriage. Many scholars continue to question the utility of marriage, especially for Black women (Clarke, 2011; Collins, 2004; Henderson, 2020; Hunter, 2017; Lenhardt, 2014; Romano, 2018). Scholar Aneeka Henderson (2020) "proposes theories that reorient our conception of racial justice" as it relates to marriage. Henderson coins the term "marriageocracy" in order to unmask "the liberal fantasy that marriage, much like the American Dream, is a fair and equitable accessible competition and exposes it as a cultural logical pervading self-help relationship books, political policy, and broader cultural discourse about marriage, while upholding bootstraps courtship politics and rendering institutional structures – such as unemployment, health care, and education – entirely inconsequential" (pp. 8–9). Such a perspective speaks very much to the institutional environment faced by those in the Love Jones Cohort.

Communication professor Jessica Moorman's (2020) research finds that Black women are engaging in "strategic singlehood" – the "intentional practice of enacting or maintaining one's single status for the purposes of growth, safety, or exploration." As Moorman asserts, this strategy "refutes demographic and structural explanations for Black women's single status . . . as well as popular understandings of Black women's lives . . . both of which overlook the role of agency in Black women's decision-making regarding their single status" (p. 443). Regarding the Love Jones Cohort, I find that some members are engaged in a particular form of strategic singlehood that I term *pragmatic singlehood*. Some chose singlehood, and for others singleness chose them.

REDEFINITION OF THE BLACK MIDDLE CLASS AND FAMILY

This book has shown that there is a growing number of Black Americans who are not only single and living alone (SALA), but solidly part of the Black middle class: the Love Jones Cohort (Dickson & Marsh, 2008; Marsh et al., 2007; Marsh & von Lockette, 2011; Marsh & Peña, 2020). According to the 2019 updated U.S. Census Bureau definitions, those who are SALA are still considered to be merely household units, not family units. I argue that this narrow definition of family should be challenged, and that SALA households should instead be regarded as constituting a family of one.

More generally, it is necessary to question the term "family" and how it is employed. It can be viewed as exclusionary on various fronts, with, for example, the LGBTQIA+ community having both embraced and contested the term (Collective, 1977; M. Moore, 2011; K. Y. Taylor, 2017; "The Combahee River Collective Statement," 2018).[1] Moreover, scholars have

---

[1] The Combahee River Collective was founded by Black women in 1974 to address the unique issues facing Black women at the intersection of race, class, gender, and sexual oppression. The collective notes, "[W]e struggle together with Black men against racism, while we also struggle with Black men about sexism" (Taylor, 2017).

pointed to racial and cultural variances in notions of who and what constitutes family, in doing so praising the strengths of various Black family formations, especially augmented families, which incorporate non-related individuals (Billingsley, 1968). As such, Black America, scholars, and social institutions should rethink how we engage with the term "family" (Moultrie, 2021).

As has been highlighted, there are a number of social, political, and financial benefits that result from being called a family, from cell phone family plans to favorable income tax arrangements (Brown, 2021; DePaulo, 2006). With this in mind, I argue that those who are SALA should be considered a family (of one) in order to receive such benefits. In addition, the book has shown the centrality of friendship networks to those in the Love Jones Cohort. Given this, we need to embrace and institutionalize augmented families, thereby allowing those in the Cohort to establish family units with friends (and themselves) in a legal manner – an approach I term "The SALA Family Plan." This would further allow augmented Love Jones Cohort families to access benefits ranging from preferential cell phone plans to more substantive benefits in the realm of asset and wealth management.

Some have challenged my research as bringing down the Black race by not promoting the Black family. To this I respond that, as a sociologist and demographer, I am simply reporting on existing trends. In terms of my analysis of these trends, I would argue that I *am* promoting the beauty and heterogeneity of the Black family, as it actually exists – something that should be made central to relevant discussions, rather than pathologized. In reality, loving, non-romantic, nonsexual relationships between friends can involve ties that are as strong, if not stronger, than those binding a heteronormative marriage.

In essence, using intersectionality as a critical praxis, I am advocating a broadening of how we conceive of the term "family," ensuring it is inclusive of those who are SALA. All of this leads back to discussions of invisibility. Similar to Kimberlé Crenshaw's assertion that the categories of "racism" and "sexism" render Black women invisible (Crenshaw, 1990), I argue that the solo and singlehood movements render Black SALAs invisible, and that terms like "Black middle class" and "family" leave those in the Love Jones Cohort fighting for greater visibility.

Many of the Cohort members interviewed for this book have told us that, despite the structural forces they face, they are buying homes and purchasing other assets, while often providing support to their extended family and close friends. Given this, it is worth asking if *The SALA Family*

Plan can help mitigate the impact of Cohort members having to provide financially for their family and friends. If those they are providing for can be designated family members in terms of the parameters outlined by *The SALA Family Plan*, how might this impact the accumulation (and dissemination) of assets by Cohort members? I would argue that such a move could be a potential game changer, and that as such *The SALA Family Plan* has profound implications for Black institutions, all social institutions, wealth management campaigns, and policy makers alike.

COPING MECHANISMS

In a nationally representative study using data from both the General Social Survey and the National Survey of Families and Households, Sarkisian and Gerstel (2016) found that single people had more frequent contact with their friends, family, and neighbors and were more likely to both provide and receive support from people in their social networks (Sarkisian & Gerstel, 2016). Singles have also been found to be more socially integrated into their communities (Klinenberg, 2013, 2016). As we have seen from the narratives of our interviewees, however, those in the Love Jones Cohort experience varying degrees of overall well-being. This is indicative of the fact that socioeconomic status does not in itself protect the Black middle class from negative well-being outcomes, and that SALA status in many ways complicates such issues. More recently, the challenges of living alone have been further exacerbated by the 2019 Coronavirus pandemic, with the social and physically distancing this has entailed leading to higher levels of isolation.

Regardless of their preferred level of interaction with neighbors – which can range from none at all to completely involved – Cohort members are choosing where to live based in part on their SALA status, with safety (physical and psychological) cited as being a particular concern of those living alone. Thus, it may be inferred that their choice of neighborhood and/or housing options acts as a coping mechanism to protect their physical and psychological well-being. A theoretical implication arising from the Cohort's choices in this regard is the need for a more nuanced analysis of urban/suburban spaces, one that rejects any simple dichotomy between the two: Urban spaces should not be regarded as the exclusive hub of single professionals, nor should suburban areas be considered a haven reserved for married or partnered families. In practical terms, this entails a greater focus on singles in the residential segregation literature, as well as discussions on residential choices and locations more generally.

Though those in the Love Jones Cohort are, by definition, single and living alone, this does not necessarily mean they lack the social relationships essential for mental well-being. Furthermore, while many Cohort members reported feeling lonely from time to time – what I term *situational loneliness* – many also reported that being SALA was beneficial to their physical health and ultimately to their mental health.

CONCLUDING THOUGHTS

In outlining a collective social identity for the Love Jones Cohort, this book hopes to challenge established notions of what constitutes the Black middle class and family in three distinct ways: first, by providing additional, but necessary, complexity to an already complicated and contentious issue; second, by challenging the notion that marriage is a panacea for socio-economic ills, as well as a necessary vehicle for entry into the Black middle class; and third – drawing from the famous quotation from Reverend Martin Luther King Jr. that "[t]he arc of history is long, but it bends toward justice" – by advocating acceptance of the Love Jones Cohort as a demographic group, thereby bending the arc of how a family is defined toward a more open and inclusive conception.

Afterword

In January 2011, the inaugural show of *Piers Morgan Tonight* aired on CNN. On the third day of the new show, the guest was Professor Condoleezza Rice, the 66th United States Secretary of State serving from 2005 to 2009. She was the first Black female Secretary of State and the second never-married secretary (the first was James Buchanan, who served from 1845 to 1849). While this may not have been common knowledge to some people prior to May 16, 2014, that might have changed by the next morning. For the *Jeopardy!* viewers watching the last day of the Battle of the Decade with a million dollars on the line, the Final Jeopardy category was "Secretaries of State," and the question was, "Serving 160 years apart, these 2 Secretaries of State are the only ones who never married." The answer: "Who are James Buchanan and Condoleezza Rice?"[1] While some might be amused by such trivia, others could be annoyed that of all the accomplishments of Professor Rice, her never-married status is what is highlighted on a *Jeopardy!* question.

Successful SALA members of the Black middle class (usually women) are incessantly confronted with the question: *Why are you not married and why do you not have children?* This effectively imposes a deficit framework on the Love Jones Cohort, implying that no level of success is adequate unless a person is married with children. When the Love Jones Cohort is asked such a question, a nonconfrontational way to force the one asking

---

[1] www.youtube.com/watch?v=BnzRIr-F9bQ. It is worth noting that upon the death of long-time host of *Jeopardy!*, Alex Trebek, the game show clamored to find a new host. However, they snubbed CNN legal analyst Laura Coates and a Black woman – a replacement that Trebek himself endorsed prior to his death. www.cnn.com/2022/01/20/entertainment/laura-coates-jeopardy-host-scli-intl/index.html.

the question to examine themselves and their motives is to respond with "what do you mean by that?"

It is my hope that, in learning more about the Love Jones Cohort, others will be prompted to ask questions of themselves, specifically, is my understanding of the Black middle class based on implicit or explicit notions of respectability politics? Am I cognizant of how demographic changes and structural limits shape (and reshape) the Black middle class and how we define family? And am I bound by a stereotypical view of what the quintessential Black middle-class family should look like?

Going one step further, I would urge anyone tempted to ask a member of the Cohort (particularly its female members) "Why are you not married and why do you not have children?" to instead ask themselves the following six counter-questions:

First, is it *elitist* to ask the Love Jones Cohort why are you single and child-free? If your question is based on the premise that having a spouse and children is the ultimate measure of success, then my answer is yes.

Second, is it *demeaning* to ask the Love Jones Cohort why are you single and child-free? If, in asking your question, the onus is placed solely at the "boots" of the Cohort, without considering structural forces and/or agentic individual choice and preferences, then my answer is yes.

Third, is it *insensitive* to ask the Love Jones Cohort why are you single and child-free? If, in asking your question, all other life accomplishments are ignored and/or it is assumed their status is purely due to choice rather than out of necessity or circumstance, then my answer is yes.

Fourth, is it *discriminatory* to ask the Love Jones Cohort why are you single and child-free? If comparable questions are not asked of married couples – such as "Why are you married with children?" – and/or your question assumes that the dating practices and sex lives of the Cohort should be open to public consumption while discussion of the marital bed is taboo, then my answer is yes.

Fifth, is it *problematic* to be uninformed on how structural forces shape individual behavior before asking the Love Jones Cohort why are you single and child-free? If your question is based on the assumption that singleness is solely due to some form of personality deficit (rather than individual choice), without any regard for structural impediments, then my answer is yes.

Sixth, is it *provoking* a tension within the Black middle class to ask the Love Jones Cohort why are you single and child-free? If the assumption underlying your question is that only a certain household type is acceptable when it comes to membership of the Black middle class or being a valued member of society more generally, then my answer is a resounding yes.

APPENDIX A

Percentage of Blacks and Whites between the Ages of 25 and 65 Who Never Married, 1880–2019

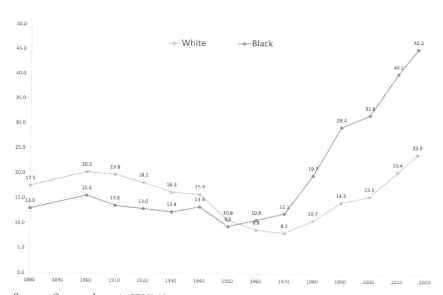

Source: Census data via IPUMS.org

APPENDIX B

Calculating the Black Middle-Class Index (BMCi), by Kris Marsh, William A. Darity Jr., Philip N. Cohen, Lynne M. Casper, and Danielle Salters

To be classified as middle class or beyond, any individual in the household must satisfy criteria for four of the indicators of the BMCi: education, homeownership, per person income, and occupational prestige. We do not have income, education, or occupational prestige upper limits on the BMCi. When we use the term "middle class," we are referring to all relatively affluent households as well as those that are extremely affluent. The BMCi is scored 0, 1, 2, 3, or 4. The maximum score is four and is the score required for classification as middle class.[1] Our stricter definition that includes homeownership overcomes the wealth vulnerability of middle class blacks that some scholars do not address.

Educational attainment. The educational attainment variable measures the highest level of schooling completed within each household. The highest value for this measure is "4+ years of college completed." If any individual in the household meets this criterion, the household is assigned a point on the BMCi. In 2000, a quarter of Black households with householders 25–54 year old's and 24 percent of Black households with householders 25–44 year old met the educational requirement for this index.

Wealth. We use homeownership as a proxy for wealth. Homeownership is one of the more significant dimensions of wealth for most persons (or households) who have positive net worth (Oliver & Shapiro, 1995). Householders who own (or are buying) a home receive one point on the BMCi. Among Black householders in the 25–54 year old range, about half own (or are buying) their homes, a figure that has been fairly constant

---

[1] We acknowledge that this is more stringent than that used by many researchers, but this classification provides us stronger evidence that a new type of Black middle class is emerging – the "Love Jones Cohort." This classification scheme is similar to Ashwini Deshpande's (2000) caste inequality index.

since 1980. For householders 25–44 year old, the rate of homeownership was slightly lower at 42 percent in 2000. The inclusion of homeownership as a variable in the BMCi led to a number of households from the Love Jones Cohort being excluded that might otherwise have the appearance of being middle class.

Per person income. When scholars examine the Black middle class, they often compare families of different sizes without making adjustments for this difference. To ensure that households of different sizes can be compared accurately, we use a per person income indicator for each household type. To calculate per person income, we use a computation technique suggested in Citro and Michael (1995). de Ruijter, Treas, and Cohen (2005, p. 312) describe this computation as follows:

Scale value = $(A+PK)^F$

"[w]here A is the number of adults in the households, K is the number of children (each treated as a proportion P of an adult), and F is the scale economy factor." P equals .7:1 or the proportion of a child to an adult. F equals 0.65 or the economies to scale.

Scale value = $(A+.70K)^{.65}$

To illustrate how this computation works, consider that households of three different types – a married-couple householder living with two children, a never-married householder living with one child, and a never-married householder living alone – all have a total household income of $50,000. The scale values for these three households are 2.215, 1.766, and 1, respectively. When each household income ($50,000) is divided by the scale value, the per person incomes are $22,568.81 for the married-couple householder with children, $35,414.26 for the never-married householder living with a child, and $50,000 for the never-married householder living alone. The latter would be the most affluent of the three.

Occupational prestige. OCCSCORE is an occupational score index that measures occupational reward; the index is available across decennial census datasets from 1850 to 2000 and is based on 1950 occupational classifications (Ruggles et al. 2004). The values are presented in 1950 dollars scaled downward by units of one hundred. For example, if median total income for economists was $20,000 in 1950, the value equals 20 for economists in all decennial census datasets.[2] As a point of reference, the

---

[2] OCCSCORE provides a consistent measure with which to compare labor market outcomes from 1850 to 2000. However, OCCSCORE has four major shortcomings. First, it does not account for changes in occupational hierarchy across time. Second, the index does not account for variation in income within occupations. Third, the index does not

highest average OCCSCORE for any racial/ethnic group in 1990 was 37.03 (the score for people of Russian ancestry). The average OCCSCORE for all men in 1990 was 29.61; for Black men it was 25.77 (Darity, Dietrich & Guilkey, 2003).[3]

For the BMCi, we interpret OCCSCORE as a measure of occupational prestige. Assuming that household members share class status, we take the person in each household with the highest OCCSCORE value and compare his or her score to the median for the highest ranking individuals in all Black households. This gives us a median score of 25 for 2000 and 1990 and 24 for 1980. A household whose OCCSCORE exceeds these medians receives a score of one on the BMCi.

account for cost of living differences. Finally, although the IPUMs staff took great care when constructing OCCSCORE, re-categorizing occupations into the 1950 classification is problematic. Occupations evolve over time, and the Census has periodically changed the occupational classification system (Ruggles et al., 2004).

[3] This truncated list provides an idea of occupational prestige based on 1950 occupations: physicians, surgeons, and dentists equal 70–highest; lawyers and judges equal 60–69; airplane pilots, navigators, and architects equal 50–59; actuaries, bankers, stockbrokers, college and university administrators and professors, school teachers, and government officials all equal 40–49; actors and directors, athletes, auctioneers, machinists, and miners equal 30–39; truck and tractor drivers equal 20–29; agricultural laborers, farm workers, baggage porters and bellhops, child care workers, gardeners, vendors, domestic servants, and nurses equal 0–19 (Darity, Dietrich & Guikley, 2001).

APPENDIX C

Brief Explanations of the Ten of the Most Persistent Myths Surrounding the Racial Wealth Gap, by William Darity Jr., Darrick Hamilton, Mark Paul, Alan Aja, Anne Price, Antonio Moore, and Caterina Chiopris

In 2018, William Darity Jr. et al., in making a case for federal policies to address reparations for American Descendants of Slaves (ADOS) identified and exposed the myths in, "What We Get Wrong About Closing the Racial Wealth Gap."

As a scholar of the Black middle class, I remain committed to and intrigued with the wealth decisions and processes of SALAs and the Black middle class and how trends among these demographic groups have both direct and indirect bearing on the identity, stability, and fragility of the Black middle class now and in the future, but my intellectual interest will not allow me to even suggest that the onus of the wealth gap in America should be placed at the feet of Blacks in general and more specifically the Black middle class.

The report addresses some of the structural forces in place that support the racial wealth gap in America and notes that exploring the mechanisms used to maintain the disparities will help inform our understanding of individual behavior. The authors state:

In this report, we address ten commonly held myths about the racial wealth gap in the United States. We contend that a number of ideas frequently touted as "solutions" will not make headway in reducing Black–white wealth disparities. These conventional ideas include greater educational attainment, harder work, better financial decisions, and other changes in habits and practices on the part of Blacks. While these steps are not necessarily undesirable, they are wholly inadequate to bridge the racial chasm in wealth.

STRUCTURES OF AND MYTHS BEHIND THE RACIAL WEALTH GAP

Myth 1: Greater educational attainment or more work effort on the part of Black people will close the racial wealth gap. Given the lack of funding, substandard resources, and overcrowding in a large percentage of predominantly African American high schools, the exorbitant cost and prolonged debt of higher education; race-based wage differentials; disparities in home lending practices; and the historic lack of intergenerational wealth needed to launch and sustain extended family, the myth that greater educational attainment and more work effort will close the gap is clearly fantasy.

Myth 2: The racial homeownership gap is the "driver" of the racial wealth gap. Redlining and/or simply refusing to make mortgages available to qualified Black people is a long-sustained practice among banks. Predatory lending targeting African Americans has resulted in many Black homeowners owing more than their home is worth. Even Black homeowners who own their homes and have equity encounter racial disparity in home values simply because the home is in a Black neighborhood. To address racialized economic disparities in all aspects of life, in June 2019, for the first time since Reconstruction, Congress began to consider a bill to create a commission to develop proposals to address the lingering effects of slavery and consider a "national apology" for the harm it has caused. If the goal truly is to eliminate the racial wealth gap, policymakers should be concerned with providing, at the very least, an initial, significant financial endowment to Black young adults to invest in an asset like a new home, as well as an aggressive campaign against housing and lending discrimination, which limits the asset appreciation of the housing stock and financial products available to Black people.

To provide some context, on June 19, 2019, the House Judiciary Subcommittee held a hearing on H.R. 40, Legislation to Study Slavery Reparations. The purpose of the hearing was to "to examine, through open and constructive discourse, the legacy of the trans-Atlantic slave trade, its continuing impact on the community and the path to restorative justice." Witnesses included: Ta-Nehisi Coates, Distinguished Writer in Residence, Arthur L. Carter Journalism Institute of New York University; Danny Glover, Actor and UNICEF Goodwill Ambassador for the U.N. Decade for People of African Descent; Katrina Browne, Documentarian: Traces of the Trade; Rev. Eugene Taylor Sutton, Episcopal Bishop of Maryland; Dr. Julianne Malveaux, economist and political commentator and professor Eric J. Miller, Loyola Marymount University.

Myth 3: Buying and banking Black will close the racial wealth gap. Darity et al. cites several researchers in explaining why this myth is particularly specious, but close the discussion with this caveat: "We must make it clear that we have no objection to banking Black or buying Black. In the interest of Black solidarity, the idea has great merit. But the failure to bank Black or buy Black does not explain why we have a racial wealth gap of this magnitude, nor will banking Black or buying Black do much to reduce the gap."

Myth 4: Black people saving more will close the racial wealth gap. There is no evidence that Black Americans have a lower savings rate than white Americans, once household income is taken into account (Hamilton & Chiteji, 2013). In fact, Maury Gittleman and Edward Wolff (2004) tracked the financial position of Black and white families and found that, once income is controlled, Black families actually have a slightly higher savings rate than their white counterparts.

Myth 5: Greater financial literacy will close the racial wealth gap. Darity et al. note that "Greater financial literacy can be valuable if an individual or household has finances to manage. Financial literacy without finance is meaningless. There is no magical way to transform no wealth into great wealth simply by learning more about how to manage one's monetary resources. While wealth begets wealth, typically no wealth begets no wealth, regardless of how astute a money manager the person may be."

Myth 6: Entrepreneurship will close the racial wealth gap. When we compile the data, even those members of marginalized communities who manage to enter into entrepreneurship largely fail due to factors ranging from under-capitalization and limited market access to outright theft and destruction. Black business has been annihilated, literally, nearly as often as it has sprouted. For example, the Tulsa Massacre of 1921 razed one of the nation's historically prosperous Black communities dubbed, at the time, the "Black Wall Street" (Fain, 2017). A robust Black entrepreneurship will require an environment where the racial wealth disparity already has been confronted and altered. Greater Black wealth and financial capital is the vital prerequisite for greater Black entrepreneurship, rather than vice versa.

Myth 7: Emulating successful minorities will close the racial wealth gap. The argument that intergroup disparities in wealth are borne out of group-based cultural/behavioral deficiencies is misleading and misdirected. Instead, we should focus on the long exposure of low-wealth racial/ethnic groups to theft of wealth and blockades on wealth accumulation. To suggest that by emulating other supposedly successful "minority" groups, Blacks, racialized Latinos, and Native Americans could close the racial wealth gap perpetuates the false narrative that their lack of assets is due to a lack of hard work, effort, or ambition rather than systematic inequities in the access to assets.

Myth 8: Improved "soft skills" and "personal responsibility" will close the racial wealth gap. The "soft skills" trope repeats the conventional idea that individuals should simply "act right," "pull up their pants," and apply the same personal responsibility values that the purportedly successful immigrant groups possess. Some individuals can indeed beat the odds and get ahead, but the larger structural conditions, including well-documented wage and unemployment gaps, prove that for Black people, doing "the right thing" is not enough to close the racial wealth gap. What is needed is an active program of wealth redistribution and the removal of structural and discriminatory obstacles that stand in the way of bridging the wealth divide.

Myth 9: The growing numbers of Black celebrities prove the racial wealth gap is closing. At the same time, the absolute number of Black CEOs of Fortune 500 companies has dwindled from eight in 2015 to four in 2017. Rather than contributing to closing the racial wealth gap, Black celebrity has been used to mask Black poverty; in 2017 the median Black family had a net worth of about $17,600. To push toward closing the racial wealth gap, the veil of Black celebrity must be pulled back enabling all Americans to understand there is no racial meritocracy in wealth, despite what is displayed on television.

Myth 10: Black family disorganization is a cause of the racial wealth gap. Darity et al. note that the increasing rate of single parent households and the prevalence of Black single motherhood is often seen as a driver of racial wealth inequities. These explanations tend to confuse consequence and cause and are largely driven by claims that if Blacks change their behavior, they would see marked increases in wealth accumulation. This is a dangerous narrative steeped in racist stereotypes. Single motherhood is a reflection of inequality, not a cause. white women still have considerably more wealth than Black women, regardless of whether they are raising children. In fact, single white women with kids have the same amount of wealth as single Black women without kids. Recent research also reveals that the median single parent white family has more than twice the wealth of the median Black or Latino family with two parents. [Thus] economic benefits that are typically associated with marriage will not close the racial wealth gap (Traub et al., 2017).

References

Addo, F. R., & Darity Jr., W. A. (2021). Disparate Recoveries: Wealth, Race, and the Working Class after the Great Recession. *Annals of the American Academy of Political and Social Science*, *695*(1), 173–192. https://doi.org/10.1177/00027162211028822

Adeyinka-Skold, S. (2020). Barriers in Women's Romantic Partner Search in the Digital Age. In R. Kalish (Ed.), *Young Adult Sexuality in the Digital Age*. IGI Global, pp. 113–137. https://doi.org/10.4018/978-1-7998-3187-7.ch007

Adkins-Jackson, P. B., Turner-Musa, J., & Chester, C. (2019). The Path to Better Health for Black Women: Predicting Self-Care and Exploring Its Mediating Effects on Stress and Health. *Inquiry: The Journal of Health Care Organization, Provision, and Financing*, *56*, 0046958019870968. https://doi.org/10.1177/0046958019870968

Akee, R., Jones, M. R., & Porter, S. R. (2019). Race Matters: Income Shares, Income Inequality, and Income Mobility for All U.S. Races. *Demography*, *56*(3), 999–1021. https://doi.org/10.1007/s13524-019-00773-7

Alba, R. D., Logan, J. R., & Stults, B. J. (2000). How Segregated Are Middle-Class African Americans? *Social Problems*, *47*(4), 543–558. https://doi.org/10.2307/3097134

Allen, S. E., Davis, I. F., McDonald, M., & Robinson, C. C. (2020). The Case of Black Millennials. *Sociological Perspectives*, *63*(3), 478–485. https://doi.org/10.1177/0731121420915202

Arnold, L., and Campbell, C. (2013, January 14). The High Price of Being Single in America. *The Atlantic*. www.theatlantic.com/sexes/archive/2013/01/the-high-price-of-being-single-in-america/267043/

Anacker, K. B., Carr, J. H., & Pradhan, A. (2012). Analyzing Foreclosures among High-Income Black/African American and Hispanic/Latino Borrowers in Prince George's County, Maryland. *Housing and Society*, *39*(1), 1–28. https://doi.org/10.1080/08882746.2012.11430598

Aneshensel, C. S. (2009). Toward Explaining Mental Health Disparities. *Journal of Health and Social Behavior*, *50*(4), 377–394. https://doi.org/10.1177/002214650905000401

Ashburn-Nardo, L. (2017). Parenthood as a Moral Imperative? Moral Outrage and the Stigmatization of Voluntarily Childfree Women and Men. *Sex Roles*, *76*(5), 393–401. https://doi.org/10.1007/s11199-016-0606-1

Attewell, P., Domina, T., Lavin, D., & Levey, T. G. (2004). The Black Middle Class: Progress, Prospects, and Puzzles. *Journal of African American Studies*, 8(1), 6–19. https://doi.org/10.1007/S12111-004-1001-5

Awosan, C. I., & Hardy, K. V. (2017). Coupling Processes and Experiences of Never Married Heterosexual Black Men and Women: A Phenomenological Study. *Journal of Marital and Family Therapy*, 43(3), 463–481. https://doi.org/10.1111/jmft.12215

Awosan, C. I., & Opara, I. (2016). Socioemotional Factor: A Missing Gap in Theorizing and Studying Black Heterosexual Coupling Processes and Relationships. *Journal of Black Sexuality and Relationships*, 3(2), 25–51. https://doi.org/10.1353/bsr.2016.0027

Bailey, M. (2021). *Misogynoir Transformed: Black Women's Digital Resistance.*. New York University Press. https://doi.org/10.18574/9781479803392

Bailey, M., & Trudy. (2018). On Misogynoir: Citation, Erasure, and Plagiarism. *Feminist Media Studies*, 18(4), 762–768. www.tandfonline.com/doi/abs/10.1080/14680777.2018.1447395

Banks, I. (2000). *Hair Matters: Beauty, Power, and Black Women's Consciousness*. New York University Press.

Banks, P. A. (2009). *Represent: Art and Identity among the Black Upper-Middle Class*. Routledge.

(2010). Black Cultural Advancement: Racial Identity and Participation in the Arts among the Black Middle Class. *Ethnic and Racial Studies*, 33(2), 272–289. https://doi.org/10.1080/01419870903121332

Banks, R. R. (2012). *Is Marriage for White People? How the African American Marriage Decline Affects Everyone*. Penguin.

Barnes, D. M., & Bates, L. M. (2017). Do Racial Patterns in Psychological Distress Shed Light on the Black–White Depression Paradox? A Systematic Review. *Social Psychiatry and Psychiatric Epidemiology*, 52(8), 913–928. https://doi.org/10.1007/s00127-017-1394-9

Barnes, R. J. D. (2015). *Raising the Race: Black Career Women Redefine Marriage, Motherhood, and Community*. Rutgers University Press.

Barroso, A., & Brown, A. (n.d.). Gender Pay Gap in U.S. Held Steady in 2020. Pew Research Center. Accessed June 30, 2022, from www.pewresearch.org/fact-tank/2021/05/25/gender-pay-gap-facts/

Battle, J., & Wright, E. (2002). W.E.B. Du Bois's Talented Tenth: A Quantitative Assessment. *Journal of Black Studies*, 32(6), 654–672. https://doi.org/10.1177/00234702032006002

Battle, N. T. (2016). From Slavery to Jane Crow to Say Her Name: An Intersectional Examination of Black Women and Punishment. *Meridians*, 15(1), 109–136. https://doi.org/10.2979/meridians.15.1.07

(2021). Black Girls and the Beauty Salon: Fostering a Safe Space for Collective Self-Care. *Gender & Society*, 35(4), 557–566. https://doi.org/10.1177/08912432211027258

Beaman, J., & Petts, A. (2020). Towards a Global Theory of Colorblindness: Comparing Colorblind Racial Ideology in France and the United States. *Sociology Compass*, 14(4), e12774. https://doi.org/10.1111/soc4.12774

Becker, G. S. (1991). *A Treatise on the Family*. Harvard University Press.

Bell, C. N., Thorpe, R. J., Bowie, J. V., & LaVeist, T. A. (2018). Race Disparities in Cardiovascular Disease Risk Factors within Socioeconomic Status Strata. *Annals of Epidemiology*, 28(3), 147–152. https://doi.org/10.1016/j.annepidem.2017.12.007

Bennett, J., Fry, R., & Kochhar, R. (2020). Are You in the American Middle Class? Find Out with Our Income Calculator. Pew Research Center. www.pewresearch.org/fact-tank/2020/07/23/are-you-in-the-american-middle-class/.

Berger, M. T. (2018). I Do Practice Yoga! Controlling Images and Recovering the Black Female Body in "Skinny White Girl" Yoga Culture. *Race and Yoga*, 3(1), 31–49. https://doi.org/10.5070/R331034199

Berry, D. R. (2017). *The Price for their Pound of Flesh: The Value of the Enslaved, from Womb to Grave, in the Building of a Nation*. Beacon Press.

Besharov, D. J. (2005). The Economic Stagnation of the Black Middle Class. Presentation to the US Commission on Civil Rights, Washington, DC. https://policycommons.net/artifacts/1300407/the-economic-stagnation-of-the-black-middle-class-relative-to-whites/1903693/

Billingsley, A. (1968). *Black Families in White America*. Prentice-Hall. http://books.google.com/books?id=0HREAAAAIAAJ

Frazier, Franklin. (1997). *Black Bourgeoisie*. Simon and Schuster. www.simonandschuster.com/books/Black-Bourgeoisie/Franklin-Frazier/9780684832418

Blackman, L., Clayton, O., Glenn, N., Malone-Colon, L., & Roberts, A. (2005). *The Consequences of Marriage for African Americans: A Comprehensive Literature Review*. Institute for American Values.

Bobo, L., Kluegel, J. R., & Smith, R. A. (1996). Laissez-Faire Racism: The Crystallization of a Kinder, Gentler, Antiblack Ideology. *Racial Attitudes in the 1990s: Continuity and Change*, 15, 23–25.

Boen, C., Keister, L., & Aronson, B. (2020). Beyond Net Worth: Racial Differences in Wealth Portfolios and Black–White Health Inequality across the Life Course. *Journal of Health and Social Behavior*, 61(2), 153–169. https://doi.org/10.1177/0022146520924811

Bolick, K. (2011, September 30). All the Single Ladies. *The Atlantic*. www.theatlantic.com/magazine/archive/2011/11/all-the-single-ladies/308654/

(2017). Surveying the Singles Beat. *Signs: Journal of Women in Culture and Society*, 42(4), 1009–1012. https://doi.org/10.1086/690923

Bonilla-Silva, E. (2006). *Racism without Racists: Color-Blind Racism and the Persistence of Racial Inequality in the United States*. Rowman & Littlefield.

(2015). The Structure of Racism in Color-Blind, "Post-Racial" America. *American Behavioral Scientist*, 59(11), 1358–1376. https://doi.org/10.1177/0002764215586826

Bonilla-Silva, E., & Peoples, C. E. (2022). Historically White Colleges and Universities: The Unbearable Whiteness of (Most) Colleges and Universities in America. *American Behavioral Scientist*, 66(11), 1490–1504.

Bourdieu, P. (1989). Social Space and Symbolic Power. *Sociological Theory*, 7(1), 14–25. https://doi.org/10.2307/202060

(2001). *Masculine Domination*. Stanford University Press.

(2014). The Habitus and the Space of Life-Styles: (1984). In J. J. Gieseking, W. Mangold, C. Katz, S. Low, & S. Saegert (Eds.), *The People, Place, and Space Reader* (pp. 139–144). Routledge. https://doi.org/10.4324/9781315816852-27

(2018). Distinction a Social Critique of the Judgement of Taste. In D. Grusky and S. Szelenyi (Eds.), *Inequality Classic Readings in Race, Class, and Gender* (pp. 287–318). Routledge.

Bowleg, L., Lucas, K. J., & Tschann, J. M. (2004). "The Ball was Always in His Court": An Exploratory Analysis of Relationship Scripts, Sexual Scripts, and Condom Use among African American Women. *Psychology of Women Quarterly, 28*(1), 70–82. https://doi.org/10.1111/j.1471-6402.2004.00124.x

Bowser, B. P. (2022). *The Black Middle Class: Social Mobility – and Vulnerability*. Lynne Rienner Publishers. https://doi.org/10.1515/9781588269546

Braveman, P. A., Cubbin, C., Egerter, S., Williams, D. R., & Pamuk, E. (2010). Socioeconomic Disparities in Health in the United States: What the Patterns Tell Us. *American Journal of Public Health, 100*(S1), S186–S196. https://doi.org/10.2105/AJPH.2009.166082

Britton, M. L., & Goldsmith, P. R. (2013). Keeping People in Their Place? Young-Adult Mobility and Persistence of Residential Segregation in US Metropolitan Areas. *Urban Studies, 50*(14), 2886–2903. https://doi.org/10.1177/0042098013482506

Broman, C. L. (1993). Race Differences in Marital Well-Being. *Journal of Marriage and Family, 55*(3), 724–732. https://doi.org/10.2307/353352

(2005). Marital Quality in Black and White Marriages. *Journal of Family Issues, 26*(4), 431–441. https://doi.org/10.1177/0192513X04272439

Brooks, L. B. (2020). Black Joy, Black Love and COVID-19: A Reflection on Self-Care and Community in the Midst of a Pandemic. *Journal of Black Sexuality and Relationships, 7*(1), 67–72. https://doi.org/10.1353/bsr.2020.0012

Brown, D. A. (2021). *The Whiteness of Wealth: How the Tax System Impoverishes Black Americans – and How We Can Fix It*. Crown Publishing Group.

Brown, D. L. (2015, January 23). Prince George's neighborhoods make 'Top 10 List of Richest Black Communities in America'. *The Washington Post*. www.washingtonpost.com/news/local/wp/2015/01/23/prince-georges-neighborhoods-make-top-10-list-of-richest-black-communities-in-america/

Brown, T. H. (2016). Diverging Fortunes: Racial/Ethnic Inequality in Wealth Trajectories in Middle and Late Life. *Race and Social Problems, 8*(1), 29–41. https://doi.org/10.1007/s12552-016-9160-2

Brown, T. N., Williams, D. R., Jackson, J. S., Neighbors, H. W., Torres, M., Sellers, S. L., & Brown, K. T. (2000). "Being Black and Feeling Blue": The Mental Health Consequences of Racial Discrimination. *Race and Society, 2*(2), 117–131. https://doi.org/10.1016/S1090-9524(00)00010-3

Bryant, C. M., Taylor, R. J., Lincoln, K. D., Chatters, L. M., & Jackson, J. S. (2008). Marital Satisfaction Among African Americans and Black Caribbeans: Findings from the National Survey of American Life. *Family Relations, 57*(2), 239–253. https://doi.org/10.1111/j.1741-3729.2008.00497.x

Byrd, A., & Tharps, L. (2014). *Hair Story: Untangling the Roots of Black Hair in America*. Macmillan.

Byrne, A., & Carr, D. (2005). Caught in the Cultural Lag: The Stigma of Singlehood. *Psychological Inquiry, 16*(2/3), 84–91. www.jstor.org/stable/20447267

Casper, W. J., & DePaulo, B. (2012). A New Layer to Inclusion: Creating Singles-Friendly Work Environments. In N. P. Reilly, M. J. Sirgy, & C. A. Gorman (Eds.),

Work and Quality of Life: Ethical Practices in Organizations (pp. 217–234). Springer Netherlands. https://doi.org/10.1007/978-94-007-4059-4_12

Castañeda, M., Zambrana, R. E., Marsh, K., Vega, W., Becerra, R., & Pérez, D. J. (2015). Role of Institutional Climate on Underrepresented Faculty Perceptions and Decision Making in Use of Work–Family Policies. *Family Relations*, 64(5), 711–725. https://doi.org/10.1111/fare.12159

Chadiha, L. A., Adams, P., Biegel, D. E., Auslander, W., & Gutierrez, L. (2004). Empowering African American Women Informal Caregivers: A Literature Synthesis and Practice Strategies. *Social Work*, 49(1), 97–108. www.jstor.org/stable/23720783

Chaney, C. (2010). "Like Siamese Twins": Relationship Meaning Among Married African-American Couples. *Marriage & Family Review*, 46(8), 510–537. https://doi.org/10.1080/01494929.2010.543037

Chaney, C., & Marsh, K. (2008). Factors That Facilitate Relationship Entry Among Married and Cohabiting African Americans. *Marriage & Family Review*, 45(1), 26–51. https://doi.org/10.1080/01494920802537423

Charles, C. Z. (2003). The Dynamics of Racial Residential Segregation. *Annual Review of Sociology*, 29, 167–207. www.jstor.org/stable/30036965

Charles, C. Z., Massey, D. S., Torres, K. C., & Kramer, R. (2022). *Young, Gifted and Diverse: Origins of the New Black Elite*. Princeton University Press.

Charmaz, K. (2006). *Constructing Grounded Theory: A Practical Guide through Qualitative Analysis*. SAGE.

Cherlin, A. J. (1998). Marriage and Marital Dissolution Among Black Americans. *Journal of Comparative Family Studies*, 29(1), 147–158. https://doi.org/10.3138/jcfs.29.1.147

Chetty, R., & Hendren, N. (2018). The Impacts of Neighborhoods on Intergenerational Mobility I: Childhood Exposure Effects. *The Quarterly Journal of Economics*, 133(3), 1107–1162. https://doi.org/10.1093/qje/qjy007

Chetty, R., Hendren, N., Jones, M. R., & Porter, S. R. (2020). Race and Economic Opportunity in the United States: An Intergenerational Perspective. *The Quarterly Journal of Economics*, 135(2), 711–783. https://doi.org/10.1093/qje/qjz042

Chetty, R., Friedman, J. N., Hendren, N., Jones, M. R., & Porter, S. R. (2018). *The Opportunity Atlas: Mapping the Childhood Roots of Social Mobility* (Working Paper No. 25147). National Bureau of Economic Research. https://doi.org/10.3386/w25147

Chiteji, N. S., & Hamilton, D. (2002). Family Connections and the Black-White Wealth Gap among Middle-Class Families. *The Review of Black Political Economy*, 30(1), 9–28. https://doi.org/10.1007/BF02808169

Cross, C. J., Fomby, P., & Letiecq, B. (2022). Interlinking Structural Racism and Heteropatriarchy: Rethinking Family Structure's Effects on Child Outcomes in a Racialized, Unequal Society. *Journal of Family Theory & Review*.

Choi, J. H., Zhu, J., Goodman, L., Ganesh, B., & Strochak, S. (2018). Millennial Homeownership: Why Is It So Low, and How Can We Increase It? https://policycommons.net/artifacts/631053/millennial-homeownership/1612330/

Clark Cline, Krista Marie. (2010). Psychological Effects of Dog Ownership: Role Strain, Role Enhancement, and Depression. *The Journal of Social Psychology*, 150(2), 117–131.

Clarke, A. Y. (2011). *Inequalities of Love: College-Educated Black Women and the Barriers to Romance and Family*. Duke University Press.

Claytor, C. P. (2020). *Black Privilege: Modern Middle-Class Blacks with Credentials and Cash to Spend*. Stanford University Press.

Clerge, O. (2019). *The New Noir: Race, Identity, and Diaspora in Black Suburbia*. University of California Press.

Cohen, P. N. (2018). *Enduring Bonds: Inequality, Marriage, Parenting, and Everything Else That Makes Families Great and Terrible*. University of California Press.

Colen, C. G., Geronimus, A. T., Bound, J., & James, S. A. (2006). Maternal Upward Socioeconomic Mobility and Black–White Disparities in Infant Birthweight. *American Journal of Public Health, 96*(11), 2032–2039. https://doi.org/10.2105/AJPH.2005.076547

Collective, C. R. (1977). *"A Black Feminist Statement."* na.

Collins, P. H. (1998). It's All in the Family: Intersections of Gender, Race, and Nation. *Hypatia, 13*(3), 62–82. https://doi.org/10.1111/j.1527-2001.1998.tb01370.x

(2004). *Black Sexual Politics: African Americans, Gender, and the New Racism*. Routledge.

(2009). *Black Feminist Thought: Knowledge, Consciousness, and the Politics of Empowerment*. Routledge.

(2015). Intersectionality's Definitional Dilemmas. *Annual Review of Sociology, 41*(1), 1–20. https://doi.org/10.1146/annurev-soc-073014-112142

Collins, P. H., & Bilge, S. (2020). *Intersectionality*. John Wiley & Sons.

Collins, S. M. (1983). The Making of the Black Middle Class. *Social Problems 30*(4), 369–382.

(1989). The Marginalization of Black Executives. *Social Problems 36*(4), 317–331.

(1997). *Black Corporate Executives: The Making and Breaking of a Black Middle Class*. Temple University Press.

(2011). Diversity in the Post Affirmative Action Labor Market: A Proxy for Racial Progress?. *Critical Sociology 37*(5), 521–540.

Cooper, A. J. (1988). *A Voice from the South*. Oxford University Press.

Cooper, B. (2018). *Eloquent Rage: A Black Feminist Discovers Her Superpower*. St. Martin's Publishing Group.

Cooper, B. C. (2017). *Beyond Respectability: The Intellectual Thought of Race Women*. University of Illinois Press.

Corbin, J., & Strauss, A. (2008). *Basics of Qualitative Research: Techniques and Procedures for Developing Grounded Theory* (3rd ed.). SAGE Publications, Inc. https://doi.org/10.4135/9781452230153

Cottom, T. M. (2018). *Thick: And Other Essays*. The New Press.

Council, L. D. (2021). Marriage Matters for Black Middle-Class Women: A Review of Black American Marriages, Work, and Family Life. *Sociology Compass, 15*(11), e12934. https://doi.org/10.1111/soc4.12934

Cox, O. C. (1950). Max Weber on Social Stratification: A Critique. *American Sociological Review, 15*(2), 223–227. https://doi.org/10.2307/2086786

Craigie, T.-A., Myers, S. L., & Darity Jr., W. A. (2018). Racial Differences in the Effect of Marriageable Males on Female Family Headship. *Journal of Demographic Economics, 84*(3), 231–256. https://doi.org/10.1017/dem.2018.3

Crenshaw, K. (1990). Mapping the Margins: Intersectionality, Identity Politics, and Violence against Women of Color. *Stanford Law Review, 43*(6), 1241–1300. https://heinonline.org/HOL/P?h=hein.journals/stflr43&i=1257

Crowder, K., & Downey, L. (2010). Interneighborhood Migration, Race, and Environmental Hazards: Modeling Microlevel Processes of Environmental Inequality. *American Journal of Sociology, 115*(4), 1110–1149. https://doi.org/10.1086/649576

Crowder, K., & Krysan, M. (2016). Moving Beyond the Big Three: A Call for New Approaches to Studying Racial Residential Segregation. *City & Community, 15*(1), 18–22. https://doi.org/10.1111/cico.12148

Crowder, K. D., & Tolnay, S. E. (2000). A New Marriage Squeeze for Black Women: The Role of Racial Intermarriage by Black Men. *Journal of Marriage and Family, 62*(3), 792–807. https://doi.org/10.1111/j.1741-3737.2000.00792.x

Curington, C. V., Lundquist, J. H., & Lin, K.-H. (2021). *The Dating Divide: Race and Desire in the Era of Online Romance.* University of California Press.

Dancy, T. E., Edwards, K. T., & Earl Davis, J. (2018). Historically White Universities and Plantation Politics: Anti-Blackness and Higher Education in the Black Lives Matter Era. *Urban Education, 53*(2), 176–195. https://doi.org/10.1177/0042085918754328

Darity Jr., W. A., & Mullen, A. K. (2020). *From Here to Equality: Reparations for Black Americans in the Twenty-First Century.* UNC Press Books.

Darity Jr., W. A., & Myers Jr, S. L. (1995). 9 Family Structure and the Marginalization of Black Naen: Policy Implications. In M. B. Tucker, & C. Mitchell-Kernan (Eds.). *The Decline in Marriage among African Americans: Causes, Consequences, and Policy Implications.* Russell Sage Foundation, p. 263.

Darity Jr., W. A., Addo, F. R., & Smith, I. Z. (2021). A Subaltern Middle Class: The Case of the Missing "Black bourgeoisie" in America. *Contemporary Economic Policy, 39*(3), 494–502. https://doi.org/10.1111/coep.12476

Darity Jr., W. A., Hamilton, D., Paul, M., Aja, A., Price, A., Moore, A., & Chiopris, C. (2018). *What We Get Wrong About Closing the Racial Wealth Gap.* p. 67.

Darity Jr., W. A., Hamilton, D., & Stewart, J. B. (2015). A Tour de Force in Understanding Intergroup Inequality: An Introduction to Stratification Economics. *The Review of Black Political Economy, 42*(1–2), 1–6. https://doi.org/10.1007/s12114-014-9201-2

Daum, M. (2015). *Selfish, Shallow, and Self-Absorbed: Sixteen Writers on the Decision Not to Have Kids.* Picador.

Davis, A. Y. (1983). *Women, Race, and Class.* Vintage Books.

Davis, S. M. (2019). When Sistahs Support Sistahs: A Process of Supportive Communication about Racial Microaggressions among Black Women. *Communication Monographs, 86*(2), 133–157. https://doi.org/10.1080/03637751.2018.1548769

Davis, S. M., & Afifi, T. D. (2019). The Strong Black Woman Collective Theory: Determining the Prosocial Functions of Strength Regulation in Groups of Black Women Friends. *Journal of Communication, 69*(1), 1–25. https://doi.org/10.1093/joc/jqy065

Dean, P., Marsh, K., & Landry, B. (2013). Cultural Contradiction or Integration? Work–Family Schemas of Black Middle Class Mothers. In M. H. Kohlman,

D. B. Krieg, & B. J. Dickerson (Eds.), *Notions of Family: Intersectional Perspectives* (Vol. 17, pp. 137–158). Emerald Group Publishing Limited. https://doi.org/10.1108/S1529-2126(2013)0000017010

DePaulo, B. (2006). *Singled Out: How Singles Are Stereotyped, Stigmatized, and Ignored, and Still Live Happily Ever After*. Macmillan.

DePaulo, B. (May 25, 2018). Think Single People Are Selfish? The Research Proves Otherwise. *The Washington Post Blogs*. https://advance-lexis-com.proxy-um.researchport.umd.edu/api/document?collection=news&id=urn:contentItem:5SDB-3Y51-DXKP-J3ST-00000-00&context=1516831.

DePaulo, B., & DePaulo, B. M. (2015). *How We Live Now: Redefining Home and Family in the 21st Century*. Simon & Schuster.

DePaulo, B. M. (2011). *Singlism: What It Is, Why It Matters, and How to Stop It*. DoubleDoor Books.

DePaulo, B. M., & Morris, W. L. (2005). Singles in Society and in Science. *Psychological Inquiry*, *16*(2/3), 57–83. www.jstor.org/stable/20447266

Dickson, L., & Marsh, K. (2008). The Love Jones Cohort: A New Face of the Black Middle Class? *Black Women, Gender + Families*, *2*(1), 84–105. www.jstor.org/stable/10.5406/blacwomegendfami.2.1.0084

Diette, T. M., Goldsmith, A. H., Hamilton, D., & Darity, W. (2015). Skin Shade Stratification and the Psychological Cost of Unemployment: Is there a Gradient for Black Females? *The Review of Black Political Economy*, *42*(1–2), 155–177. https://doi.org/10.1007/s12114-014-9192-z

Dillaway, H., & Broman, C. (2001). Race, Class, and Gender Differences in Marital Satisfaction and Divisions of Household Labor Among Dual-Earner Couples: A Case for Intersectional Analysis. *Journal of Family Issues*, *22*(3), 309–327. https://doi.org/10.1177/019251301022003003

Dilworth-Anderson, P., Williams, I. C., & Gibson, B. E. (2002). Issues of Race, Ethnicity, and Culture in Caregiving Research: A 20-year Review (1980–2000). *The Gerontologist*, *42*(2), 237–272. https://doi.org/10.1093/geront/42.2.237

Donahoo, S., & Smith, A. D. (2022). Controlling the Crown: Legal Efforts to Professionalize Black Hair. *Race and Justice*, *12*(1), 182–203. https://doi.org/10.1177/2153368719888264

Dow, D. M. (2019). *Mothering While Black: Boundaries and Burdens of Middle-Class Parenthood*. University of California Press. https://doi.org/10.1525/9780520971776

Downey, L., Crowder, K., & Kemp, R. J. (2017). Family Structure, Residential Mobility, and Environmental Inequality. *Journal of Marriage and Family*, *79*(2), 535–555. https://doi.org/10.1111/jomf.12355

Downey, L., Dubois, S., Hawkins, B., & Walker, M. (2008). Environmental Inequality in Metropolitan America. *Organization & Environment*, *21*(3), 270–294. https://doi.org/10.1177/1086026608321327

Drake, St. C., & Cayton, H. R. (1945). *Black Metropolis* (p. 843). Harcourt, Brace.

Du Bois, W. E. B., & Eaton, I. (1899). *The Philadelphia Negro: A Social Study*. University of Pennsylvania Press.

duCille, A. (2018). Blacks of the Marrying Kind: Marriage Rites and the Right to Marry in the Time of Slavery. *Differences*, *29*(2), 21–67. https://doi.org/10.1215/10407391-6999760

Durant, T. J., & Louden, J. S. (1986). The Black Middle Class in America: Historical and Contemporary Perspectives. *Phylon* (1960-), *47*(4), 253–263. https://doi.org/10.2307/274621

Ellick, K. L. (2021). "Started From The Bottom, Now We're…Where?" A Qualitative Analysis of Stress and Coping Among Highly Educated Black Women. https://doi.org/10.13016/dnbv-51nl

Erickson, K. A. (2020). *Boundaries of Love: Interracial Marriage and the Meaning of Race*, by Chinyere K. Osuji. New York University Press, 2019. 279 pp. $32.00 paper. ISBN: 9781479831456. https://journals-sagepub-com.proxy-um.researchport.umd.edu/doi/full/10.1177/0094306120963121t

Erigha, M. (2018). Black Women Having It All. *The Black Scholar*, *48*(1), 20–30. https://doi.org/10.1080/00064246.2018.1402253

Essed, P. (1991). *Understanding Everyday Racism: An Interdisciplinary Theory*. SAGE.

Evans, S. Y. (2021). *Black Women's Yoga History: Memoirs of Inner Peace*. SUNY Press.

Evans, S. Y., Bell, K., & Burton, N. K. (2017). *Black Women's Mental Health: Balancing Strength and Vulnerability*. SUNY Press.

Faber, J. W., & Ellen, I. G. (2016). Race and the Housing Cycle: Differences in Home Equity Trends Among Long-Term Homeowners. *Housing Policy Debate*, *26*(3), 456–473. https://doi.org/10.1080/10511482.2015.1128959

Fabius, C. D., Wolff, J. L., & Kasper, J. D. (2020). Race Differences in Characteristics and Experiences of Black and White Caregivers of Older Americans. *The Gerontologist*, *60*(7), 1244–1253. https://doi.org/10.1093/geront/gnaa042

Farmer, M. M., & Ferraro, K. F. (2005). Are Racial Disparities in Health Conditional on Socioeconomic Status? *Social Science & Medicine*, *60*(1), 191–204. https://doi.org/10.1016/j.socscimed.2004.04.026

Favor, J. M. (1999). *Authentic Blackness: The Folk in the New Negro Renaissance*. Duke University Press.

Feagin, J. R., & Sikes, M. P. (1994). *Living with Racism: The Black Middle-class Experience* (pp. xii, 398). Beacon Press.

Felix, A. S., Shisler, R., Nolan, T. S., Warren, B. J., Rhoades, J., Barnett, K. S., & Williams, K. P. (2019). High-Effort Coping and Cardiovascular Disease among Women: A Systematic Review of the John Henryism Hypothesis. *Journal of Urban Health*, *96*(1), 12–22. https://doi.org/10.1007/s11524-018-00333-1

Flippen, C. (2004). Unequal Returns to Housing Investments? A Study of Real Housing Appreciation among Black, White, and Hispanic Households. *Social Forces*, *82*(4), 1523–1551. https://doi.org/10.1353/sof.2004.0069

Fordham, S. (1996). *Blacked Out: Dilemmas of Race, Identity, and Success at Capital High*. University of Chicago Press.

(2011). Racelessness as a Factor in Black Students' School Success: Pragmatic Strategy or Pyrrhic Victory? *Harvard Educational Review*, *58*(1), 54–85. https://doi.org/10.17763/haer.58.1.c5r77323145r7831

Fordham, S., & Ogbu, J. U. (1986). Black Students' School Success: Coping with the "Burden of 'Acting White.'" *The Urban Review*, *18*(3), 176–206. https://doi.org/10.1007/BF01112192

Frazier, E. F. (1957). *Black Bourgeoisie*. Free Press. http://catalog.hathitrust.org/api/volumes/oclc/402005.html

Friedman, D., Hechter, M., & Kanazawa, S. (1994). A Theory of the Value of Children. *Demography, 31*(3), 375–401. https://doi.org/10.2307/2061749

Fries-Britt, S., & Kelly, B. T. (2005). Retaining Each Other: Narratives of Two African American Women in the Academy. *The Urban Review, 3*(37), 221–242. https://doi.org/10.1007/s11256-005-0006-2

Gaines, K. K. (2012). *Uplifting the Race: Black Leadership, Politics, and Culture in the Twentieth Century.* UNC Press Books.

Geronimus, A. T., Bound, J., Waidmann, T. A., Colen, C. G., & Steffick, D. (2001). Inequality in Life Expectancy, Functional Status, and Active Life Expectancy across Selected Black and White Populations in the United States. *Demography, 38*(2), 227–251. https://doi.org/10.1353/dem.2001.0015

Giddings, P. J. (2011). Meridians, Introduction 11.1: Memory. *Meridians: Feminism, Race, Transnationalism, 11*(1), v–vii. https://muse.jhu.edu/article/463996

(2014). *When and Where I Enter.* HarperCollins e-Books. http://rbdigital.oneclickdigital.com

Gieseking, J. J., Mangold, W., Katz, C., Low, S., & Saegert, S. (Eds.) (2014). *The People, Place, and Space Reader.* Routledge.

Gill, T. M. (2010). *Beauty Shop Politics: African American Women's Activism in the Beauty Industry.* University of Illinois Press.

(2015). #TeamNatural: Black Hair and the Politics of Community in Digital Media. *Nka Journal of Contemporary African Art, 2015*(37), 70–79. https://doi.org/10.1215/10757163-3339739

Golden, E. N., & Utah, A. (2015). Getting to Joy: Emergence[s] & Experimentation/s. *Obsidian, 41*(1/2), 14–18. www.jstor.org/stable/44489408

Goldsmith, A. H., Hamilton, D., & Darity Jr, W. A. (2006). Shades of Discrimination: Skin Tone and Wages. *American Economic Review, 96*(2), 242–245. https://doi.org/10.1257/000282806777212152

Goldsmith, A. H., Hamilton, D., & Darity Jr., W. A. (2007). From Dark to Light: Skin Color and Wages Among African-Americans. *Journal of Human Resources,* XLII (4), 701–738. https://doi.org/10.3368/jhr.XLII.4.701

Goldsmith-Pinkham, P., & Shue, K. (2020). *The Gender Gap in Housing Returns* (Working Paper No. 26914). National Bureau of Economic Research. https://doi.org/10.3386/w26914

Goodwin, M. (2021). Pregnancy and the New Jane Crow. Lead Essay, *Connecticut Law Review, 53*(3), 543–570. https://heinonline.org/HOL/P?h=hein.journals/conlr53&i=569

Gould, E. (n.d.). State of Working America Wages 2019: A Story of Slow, Uneven, and Unequal Wage Growth over the Last 40 years. Accessed June 30, 2022, from https://policycommons.net/artifacts/1409577/state-of-working-america-wages-2019/2023842/

Graefe, D. R., & Lichter, D. T. (2002). Marriage among Unwed Mothers: Whites, Blacks and Hispanics Compared. *Perspectives on Sexual and Reproductive Health, 34*(6), 286–293. https://doi.org/10.2307/3097747

Green, T. L., & Darity Jr., W. A. (2010). Under the Skin: Using Theories from Biology and the Social Sciences to Explore the Mechanisms Behind the Black–White Health Gap. *American Journal of Public Health, 100*(S1), S36–S40. https://doi.org/10.2105/AJPH.2009.171140

Gregory, S. (1998). *Black Corona: Race and the Politics of Place in an Urban Community*. Princeton University Press. www.aspresolver.com/aspresolver.asp? ANTH;1671325

Griffin, K. A., & Reddick, R. J. (2011). Surveillance and Sacrifice: Gender Differences in the Mentoring Patterns of Black Professors at Predominantly White Research Universities. *American Educational Research Journal, 48*(5), 1032–1057. https://doi.org/10.3102/0002831211405025

Grossbard-Schectman, S. (2019). *On the Economics of Marriage*. Routledge.

Guy-Sheftall, B. (1995). *Words of Fire: An Anthology of African-American Feminist Thought*. The New Press.

Guzman, E., & Vulimiri, M. (2015). African American Retirement Insecurity. *Fact Sheet, 8*, 1–8.

Hall, N. M. (2022). *Sexual Health and Black College Students: Exploring the Sexual Milieu of HBCUs*. Taylor & Francis.

Hall, N. M., Lee, A. K., & Witherspoon, D. D. (2014). Factors Influencing Dating Experiences among African American Emerging Adults. *Emerging Adulthood, 2* (3), 184–194.

Hamilton, D. (2020). The Moral Burden on Economists: Darrick Hamilton's 2017 NEA Presidential Address. *The Review of Black Political Economy, 47*(4), 331–342. https://doi.org/10.1177/0034644620968104

Hamilton, D., Goldsmith, A. H. & Darity Jr., W. A. (2009). Shedding 'Light' on Marriage: The Influence of Skin Shade on Marriage for Black Females. *Journal of Economic Behavior & Organization, 72*(1), 30–50.

Hare, N. (1965). *The Black Anglo-Saxons*. Marzani & Munsell.

Harper, S. R. (2012). Race without Racism: How Higher Education Researchers Minimize Racist Institutional Norms. *The Review of Higher Education, 36*(1), 9–29. https://doi.org/10.1353/rhe.2012.0047

Harris, A. L., & Marsh, K. (2010). Is a Raceless Identity an Effective Strategy for Academic Success Among Blacks?. *Social Science Quarterly, 91*(5), 1242–1263. https://doi.org/10.1111/j.1540-6237.2010.00730.x

Harris, C. A., & Khanna, N. (2010). Black Is, Black Ain't: Biracials, Middle-Class Blacks, and the Social Construction of Blackness. *Sociological Spectrum, 30*(6), 639–670. https://doi.org/10.1080/02732173.2010.510057

Harris, K. L. (2018). Biracial American Colorism: Passing for White. *American Behavioral Scientist, 62*(14), 2072–2086. https://doi.org/10.1177/0002764218810747

Harvey Wingfield, A. (2019). "Reclaiming Our Time": Black Women, Resistance, and Rising Inequality: SWS Presidential Lecture. *Gender & Society, 33*(3), 345–362. https://doi.org/10.1177/0891243219835456

(2020). Where Work Has Been, Where It Is Going: Considering Race, Gender, and Class in the Neoliberal Economy. *Sociology of Race and Ethnicity, 6*(2), 137–145. https://doi.org/10.1177/2332649220903715

Hatchett, S. J., & Jackson, J. S. (1993). African American Extended Kin Systems: An Assessment. In H. P. McAdoo (Ed.), *Family Ethnicity: Strength in Diversity* (pp. 90–108). Sage Publications, Inc.

Haynes, B. D. (2008). *Red Lines, Black Spaces: The Politics of Race and Space in a Black Middle-Class Suburb*. Yale University Press.

Hearne, B. N. (2021). Psychological Distress across Intersections of Race/ethnicity, Gender, and Marital Status during the COVID-19 Pandemic. *Ethnicity & Health*, *0*(0), 1–20. https://doi.org/10.1080/13557858.2021.1969537

Hechter, M., & Kanazawa, S. (1997). Sociological Rational Choice Theory. *Annual Review of Sociology*, *23*, 191–214. www.jstor.org/stable/2952549

Heflin, C. M., & Pattillo, M. (2006). Poverty in the Family: Race, Siblings, and Socioeconomic Heterogeneity. *Social Science Research*, *35*(4), 804–822. https://doi.org/10.1016/j.ssresearch.2004.09.002

Henderson, A. A. (2020). *Veil and Vow: Marriage Matters in Contemporary African American Culture*. UNC Press Books.

Higginbotham, E. (2001). *Too Much to Ask: Black Women in the Era of Integration*. University of North Carolina Press.

Higginbotham, E. B. (1994). *Righteous Discontent: The Women's Movement in the Black Baptist Church, 1880–1920*. Harvard University Press.

Hill Collins, P. (2001). Like one of the Family: Race, Ethnicity, and the Paradox of US National Identity. *Ethnic and Racial Studies*, *24*(1), 3–28. https://doi.org/10.1080/014198701750052479

Hill, M. E. (2020). "You Can Have It All, Just Not at the Same Time": Why Doctoral Students are Actively Choosing Singlehood. *Gender Issues*, *37*(4), 315–339. https://doi.org/10.1007/s12147-020-09249-0

Hill, R. B. (2003). *The Strengths of Black Families*. University Press of America.

Hill, S. A. (2013). The Inequalities of Love: College-Educated Black Women and the Barriers to Romance and Family. *Contemporary Sociology*, *42*(1), 67–69. https://doi.org/10.1177/0094306112468721c

Hixson, A. B. (2022). An Examination of Black Womxn's Use of Social Media to Inform the Doctoral Journey in Higher Education and Student Affairs Graduate Programs at Historically White Institutions. [Unpublished manuscript].

Hogue, C. J. R., & Bremner, J. D. (2005). Stress Model for Research into Preterm Delivery among Black Women. *American Journal of Obstetrics and Gynecology*, *192*(5, Supplement), S47–S55. https://doi.org/10.1016/j.ajog.2005.01.073

Holder, M. (2020). The "Double Gap" and the Bottom Line: 30.

Holzberg, J. L., Ellis, R., Virgile, M., Nelson, D. V., Edgar, J., Phipps, P., & Kaplan, R. (n. d.). *Assessing the Feasibility of Asking About Gender Identity in the Current Population Survey: Results from Focus Groups with Members of the Transgender Population*. 71.

Homan, P., Brown, T. H., & King, B. (2021). Structural Intersectionality as a New Direction for Health Disparities Research. *Journal of Health and Social Behavior*, *62*(3), 350–370. https://doi.org/10.1177/00221465211032947

hooks, bell. (1986). Sisterhood: Political Solidarity between Women. *Feminist Review*, *23*(1), 125–138.

(2000). *Feminist Theory: From Margin to Center*. Pluto Press.

hooks, bell, & West, C. (2016). *Breaking Bread: Insurgent Black Intellectual Life*. Routledge. https://doi.org/10.4324/9781315437095

Horowitz, J., Graf, N., & Livingston, G. (2019). *Marriage and Cohabitation in the U.S.* 53.

Horwitz, A. V., & Wakefield, J. C. (2007). *The Loss of Sadness: How Psychiatry Transformed Normal Sorrow into Depressive Disorder*. Oxford University Press.

Houle, J. N., & Addo, F. R. (2019). Racial Disparities in Student Debt and the Reproduction of the Fragile Black Middle Class. *Sociology of Race and Ethnicity*, 5(4), 562–577. https://doi.org/10.1177/2332649218790989

Howell, J., & Korver-Glenn, E. (2018). Neighborhoods, Race, and the Twenty-first-century Housing Appraisal Industry. *Sociology of Race and Ethnicity*, 4(4), 473–490. https://doi.org/10.1177/2332649218755178

Hudson, D. L., Neighbors, H. W., Geronimus, A. T., & Jackson, J. S. (2016). Racial Discrimination, John Henryism, and Depression Among African Americans. *Journal of Black Psychology*, 42(3), 221–243. https://doi.org/10.1177/0095798414567757

Hunter, M. (2007). The Persistent Problem of Colorism: Skin Tone, Status, and Inequality. *Sociology Compass*, 1(1), 237–254. https://doi.org/10.1111/j.1751-9020 .2007.00006.x

(2016). Colorism in the Classroom: How Skin Tone Stratifies African American and Latina/o Students. *Theory into Practice*, 55(1), 54–61. https://doi.org/10.1080/ 00405841.2016.1119019

Hunter, M. L. (2005). *Race, Gender, and the Politics of Skin Tone*. Routledge. https://doi .org/10.4324/9780203620342

(2013). *Race, Gender, and the Politics of Skin Tone*. Routledge.

Hunter, T. W. (2017). *Bound in Wedlock: Slave and Free Black Marriage in the Nineteenth Century*. Harvard University Press.

Hutto, J. W., & Green, R. D. (2016). Social Movements Against Racist Police Brutality and Department of Justice Intervention in Prince George's County, Maryland. *Journal of Urban Health*, 93(1), 89–121. https://doi.org/10.1007/ s11524-015-0013-x

Hwang, W.-C. (2013). Who Are People Willing to Date? Ethnic and Gender Patterns in Online Dating. *Race and Social Problems*, 5(1), 28–40. https://doi.org/10.1007/ s12552-012-9082-6

Inc, G. (2016, May 18). Majority in U.S. Do Not Have a Will. Gallup.Com. https://news .gallup.com/poll/191651/majority-not.aspx

Jackson, J. L. (2010). *Harlemworld Doing Race and Class in Contemporary Black America*. University of Chicago Press. http://site.ebrary.com/id/10383919

Jackson, P. B., & Cummings, J. (2011). Health Disparities and the Black Middle Class: Overview, Empirical Findings, and Research Agenda. In B. A. Pescosolido, J. K. Martin, J. D. McLeod, & A. Rogers (Eds.), *Handbook of the Sociology of Health, Illness, and Healing: A Blueprint for the Twenty-first Century* (pp. 383–410). Springer. https://doi.org/10.1007/978-1-4419-7261-3_20

Jackson, P. B., & Williams, D. R. (2006). The Intersection of Race, Gender, and SES: Health Paradoxes. In A. J. Schulz & L. E. Mullings (Eds.), *Gender, Race, Class, & Health: Intersectional Approaches* (pp. 131–162). Jossey-Bass/Wiley.

Jacobs-Huey, L. (2006). *From the Kitchen to the Parlor: Language and Becoming in African American Women's Hair Care*. Oxford University Press.

James, A. D., Tucker, M. B., & Mitchell-Kernan, C. (1996). Marital Attitudes, Perceived Mate Availability, and Subjective Well-Being among Partnered African American Men and Women. *Journal of Black Psychology*, 22(1), 20–36. https://doi.org/10 .1177/00957984960221003

James, J. (2014). *Transcending the Talented Tenth: Black Leaders and American Intellectuals*. Routledge.

James, S. A. (1994). John Henryism and the health of African-Americans. *Culture, Medicine and Psychiatry, 18*(2), 163–182. https://doi.org/10.1007/BF01379448

James, S. A., Hartnett, S. A., & Kalsbeek, W. D. (1983). John Henryism and Blood Pressure Differences among Black Men. *Journal of Behavioral Medicine, 6*(3), 259–278. https://doi.org/10.1007/BF01315113

Jefferson, M. (2016). *Negroland: A Memoir.* Vintage Books, a division of Penguin Random House LLC.

Jenkins, A. I. C., Fredman, S. J., Le, Y., Sun, X., Brick, T. R., Skinner, O. D., & McHale, S. M. (2020). Prospective Associations between Depressive Symptoms and Marital Satisfaction in Black Couples. *Journal of Family Psychology, 34*(1), 12–23. https://doi.org/10.1037/fam0000573

Jenkins, C. M. (2019). *Black Bourgeois: Class and Sex in the Flesh.* University of Minnesota Press.

Jennings, J. (2022). Society's True Colors: Reviewing the Genesis and Outcomes of Colorism in Existing Works. [Unpublished manuscript].

Johnson, C. M. E. (2019). "Each New Curl Howling a War Cry": Black Women, Embodiment, and Gendered Racial Formation. Doctoral dissertation. University of Southern California.

Johnson, E. P. (2003). *Appropriating Blackness: Performance and the Politics of Authenticity.* Duke University Press.

Johnson, K. R., & Loscocco, K. (2015). Black Marriage through the Prism of Gender, Race, and Class. *Journal of Black Studies, 46*(2), 142–171.

Johnson, J. H., & Roseman, C. C. (1990). Increasing Black Outmigration from Los Angeles: The Role of Household Dynamics and Kinship Systems. *Annals of the Association of American Geographers, 80*(2), 205–222. https://doi.org/10.1111/j.1467-8306.1990.tb00288.x

Johnson, M. S. (2013). Strength and Respectability: Black Women's Negotiation of Racialized Gender Ideals and the Role of Daughter-Father Relationships. *Gender and Society, 27*(6), 889–912. www.jstor.org/stable/43669842

Jones, J. (2006, March 26). Marriage Is for White People. *The Washington Post.* www.washingtonpost.com/archive/opinions/2006/03/26/marriage-is-for-white-people/095b1136-1440-4380-ac23-64beeeac3df4/

Jones, J., & Mosher, W. D. (2013). Fathers' Involvement with their Children: United States, 2006–2010. *National Health Statistics Reports, 71.* https://jhu.pure.elsevier.com/en/publications/fathers-involvement-with-their-children-united-states-2006-2010-9

Justin, T. (2021). Fear, Freaks, and Fat Phobia: An Examination of How My 600 Lbs Life Displays "Fat" Black Women. *Feminist Media Studies, 0*(0), 1–14. https://doi.org/10.1080/14680777.2021.1999296

Justin, T. A., & Jette, S. (2022). "That Chart Ain't for Us": How Black Women Understand "Obesity," Health, and Physical Activity. *Health, 26*(5), 605–621. https://doi.org/10.1177/13634593211046844

Kalmijn, M. (1998). Intermarriage and Homogamy: Causes, Patterns, Trends. *Annual Review of Sociology, 24,* 395–421. www.jstor.org/stable/223487

Kawachi, I., Adler, N. E., & Dow, W. H. (2010). Money, Schooling, and Health: Mechanisms and Causal Evidence. *Annals of the New York Academy of Sciences, 1186*(1), 56–68. https://doi.org/10.1111/j.1749-6632.2009.05340.x

Kelly, B. T., Gardner, P. J., Stone, J., Hixson, A., & Dissassa, D.-T. (2021). Hidden in Plain Sight: Uncovering the Emotional Labor of Black Women Students at Historically White Colleges and Universities. *Journal of Diversity in Higher Education, 14*(2), 203–216. https://doi.org/10.1037/dhe0000161

Kelly, K., Sullivan, J., & Rich, S. (2015). In Fairwood, Dreams of Black Wealth Foundered Amid the Mortgage Meltdown. *The Washington Post.* www.washingtonpost.com/sf/investigative/2015/01/25/in-fairwood-dreams-of-black-wealth-foundered-amid-the-mortgage-meltdown/

Khunou, G. (2015). What Middle Class? The Shifting and Dynamic Nature of Class Position. *Development Southern Africa, 32*(1), 90–103. https://doi.org/10.1080/0376835X.2014.975889

Khunou, G., Marsh, K., Chauke, P., Plank, L., Igbanoi, L., & Kgosiemang, M. (2019). *Does the Black Middle Class Exist and Are We Members?: Reflections from a Research Team.* Emerald Publishing Limited. https://doi.org/10.1108/9781838673536

Kilomba, G. (2021). *Plantation Memories: Episodes of Everyday Racism.* Between the Lines.

Kinder, D. R., & Sanders, L. M. (1996). *Divided by Color: Racial Politics and Democratic Ideals* (pp. xi, 391). University of Chicago Press.

King, D. K. (1988). Multiple Jeopardy, Multiple Consciousness: The Context of a Black Feminist Ideology. *Signs: Journal of Women in Culture and Society, 14*(1), 42–72.

Kislev, Elyakim. (2019). *Happy Singlehood: The Rising Acceptance and Celebration of Solo Living.* University of California Press.

(2022a). Aging, Marital Status, and Loneliness: Multilevel Analyses of 30 Countries. *Research on Ageing and Social Policy, 10*(1), 77–103.

(2022b). Relationship Desire and Life Satisfaction among Never-Married and Divorced Men and Women. *Sexual and Relationship Therapy,* 1–13.

Klinenberg, E. (2013). *Going Solo: The Extraordinary Rise and Surprising Appeal of Living Alone.* Penguin.

(2016). Social Isolation, Loneliness, and Living Alone: Identifying the Risks for Public Health. *American Journal of Public Health, 106*(5), 786–787. https://doi.org/10.2105/AJPH.2016.303166

Kochhar, R., & Fry, R. (2014, December 12). Wealth Inequality Has Widened along Racial, Ethnic Lines since End of Great Recession. Pew Research Center. www.pewresearch.org/fact-tank/2014/12/12/racial-wealth-gaps-great-recession/

Korver-Glenn, E. (2018). Compounding Inequalities: How Racial Stereotypes and Discrimination Accumulate across the Stages of Housing Exchange. *American Sociological Review, 83*(4), 627–656. https://doi.org/10.1177/0003122418781774

Koss, C. S., & Baker, T. A. (2018). Where There's a Will: The Link Between Estate Planning and Disparities in Advance Care Planning by White and Black Older Adults. *Research on Aging, 40*(3), 281–302. https://doi.org/10.1177/0164027517697116

Krivo, L. J., & Kaufman, R. L. (2004). Housing and Wealth Inequality: Racial-Ethnic Differences in Home Equity in the United States. *Demography, 41*(3), 585–605. www.jstor.org/stable/1515194

Krueger, J., Heckhausen, J., & Hundertmark, J. (1995). Perceiving Middle-aged Adults: Effects of Stereotype-congruent and Incongruent Information. *The Journals of*

Gerontology: Series B: Psychological Sciences and Social Sciences, 50(2), P82–P93. https://doi.org/10.1093/geronb/50B.2.P82

Krysan, M., & Bader, M. (2007). Perceiving the Metropolis: Seeing the City through a Prism of Race. *Social Forces*, 86(2), 699–733.

Krysan, M., & Bader, M. D. M. (2009). Racial Blind Spots: Black-White-Latino Differences in Community Knowledge. *Social Problems*, 56(4), 677–701. https://doi.org/10.1525/sp.2009.56.4.677

Krysan, M., & Crowder, K. (2017). *Cycle of Segregation: Social Processes and Residential Stratification*. Russell Sage Foundation.

Kung, H.-C., Hoyert, D. L., Xu, J., & Murphy, S. L. (2008). Deaths: Final Data for 2005. *National Vital Statistics Reports : From the Centers for Disease Control and Prevention, National Center for Health Statistics, National Vital Statistics System*, 56(10), 1–120. www.safetylit.org/citations/index.php?fuseaction=citations .viewdetails&citationIds[]=citjournalarticle_87997_22

Lacy, K. (2012). All's Fair? The Foreclosure Crisis and Middle-Class Black (In)Stability. *American Behavioral Scientist*, 56(11), 1565–1580. https://doi.org/10.1177/ 0002764212458279

Lacy, K. R. (2004). Black Spaces, Black Places: Strategic Assimilation and Identity Construction in Middle-class Suburbia. *Ethnic and Racial Studies*, 27(6), 908–930. https://doi.org/10.1080/0141987042000268521

(2007). *Blue-Chip Black: Race, Class, and Status in the New Black Middle Class*. University of California Press.

Lahad, K. (2012). Singlehood, Waiting, and the Sociology of Time. *Sociological Forum*, 27(1), 163–186. https://doi.org/10.1111/j.1573-7861.2011.01306.x

Landor, A., & Barr, A. (2018). Politics of Respectability, Colorism, and the Terms of Social Exchange in Family Research. *Journal of Family Theory & Review*, 10(2), 330–347. https://doi.org/10.1111/jftr.12264

Landor, A. M., & McNeil Smith, S. (2019). Skin-Tone Trauma: Historical and Contemporary Influences on the Health and Interpersonal Outcomes of African Americans. *Perspectives on Psychological Science*, 14(5), 797–815. https://doi.org/ 10.1177/1745691619851781

Landry, B. (1987). *The New Black Middle Class*. University of California Press.

(2002). *Black Working Wives: Pioneers of the American Family Revolution*. University of California Press

(2018). *The New Black Middle Class in the Twenty-First Century*. Rutgers University Press.

Landry, B., & Marsh, K. (2011). The Evolution of the New Black Middle Class. *Annual Review of Sociology*, 37, 373–394. www.jstor.org/stable/41288613

LaPierre, T. A., & Hill, S. A. (2013). Examining Status Discrepant Marriages and Marital Quality at the Intersections of Gender, Race, and Class. In M. H. Kohlman, D. B. Krieg, & B. J. Dickerson (Eds.), *Notions of Family: Intersectional Perspectives* (Vol. 17, pp. 113–136). Emerald Group Publishing Limited. https:// doi.org/10.1108/S1529-2126(2013)0000017009

LaVeist, T. A., Thorpe Jr., R. J., Pierre, G., Mance, G. A., & Williams, D. R. (2014). The Relationships among Vigilant Coping Style, Race, and Depression. *Journal of Social Issues*, 70(2), 241–255. https://doi.org/10.1111/josi.12058

Lee, H., & Hicken, M. T. (2016). Death by a Thousand Cuts: The Health Implications of Black Respectability Politics. *Souls*, *18*(2–4), 421–445. https://doi.org/10.1080/10999949.2016.1230828

Lee, K. O., & Painter, G. (2013). What Happens to Household Formation in a Recession? *Journal of Urban Economics*, *76*, 93–109. https://doi.org/10.1016/j.jue.2013.03.004

Lenhardt, R. A. (2014). Marriage as Black Citizenship. *Hastings Law Journal*, *66*(5), 1317–1364. https://heinonline.org/HOL/P?h=hein.journals/hastlj66&i=1423

Letherby, G. (2002). Childless and Bereft?: Stereotypes and Realities in Relation to 'Voluntary' and 'Involuntary' Childlessness and Womanhood. *Sociological Inquiry*, *72*(1), 7–20. https://doi.org/10.1111/1475-682X.00003

Lewis, J. A., Mendenhall, R., Harwood, S. A., & Browne Huntt, M. (2013). Coping with Gendered Racial Microaggressions among Black Women College Students. *Journal of African American Studies*, *17*(1), 51–73. https://doi.org/10.1007/s12111-012-9219-0

Lichter, D. T., McLaughlin, D. K., Kephart, G., & Landry, D. J. (1992). Race and the Retreat From Marriage: A Shortage of Marriageable Men? *American Sociological Review*, *57*(6), 781–799. https://doi.org/10.2307/2096123

Livingston, G., & Brown, A. (2017, May 18). Intermarriage in the U.S. Fifty Years After Loving v. Virginia. Pew Research Center's Social & Demographic Trends Project. www.pewresearch.org/social-trends/2017/05/18/intermarriage-in-the-u-s-50-years-after-loving-v-virginia/

Lloyd, S. (2013). Sara Baartman and the "Inclusive Exclusions" of Neoliberalism. *Meridians*, *11*(2), 212–237. https://doi.org/10.2979/meridians.11.2.212

Lorde, A. (1988). A Burst of Light: Essays. Firebrand Books. www.aspresolver.com/aspresolver.asp?BLWW;1000056509

Lu, J. H., & Steele, C. K. (2019). 'Joy is Resistance': Cross-platform Resilience and (Re)Invention of Black Oral Culture Online. *Information, Communication & Society*, *22*(6), 823–837. https://doi.org/10.1080/1369118X.2019.1575449

Luhmann, M., Hofmann, W., Eid, M., & Lucas, R. E. (2012). Subjective Well-being and Adaptation to Life Events: A Meta-Analysis. *Journal of Personality and Social Psychology*, *102*(3), 592–615. https://doi.org/10.1037/a0025948

Luna, Z., & Pirtle, W. (2021). *Black Feminist Sociology: Perspectives and Praxis*. Routledge.

Lundquist, J. H., Budig, M. J., & Curtis, A. (2009). Race and Childlessness in America, 1988–2002. *Journal of Marriage and Family*, *71*(3), 741–755. https://doi.org/10.1111/j.1741-3737.2009.00630.x

Marks, L. D., Hopkins, K., Chaney, C., Monroe, P. A., Nesteruk, O., & Sasser, D. D. (2008). "Together, We Are Strong": A Qualitative Study of Happy, Enduring African American Marriages. *Family Relations*, *57*(2), 172–185. https://doi.org/10.1111/j.1741-3729.2008.00492.x

Marsh, K. (2013). "Staying Black": The Demonstration of Racial Identity and Womanhood among a Group of Young High-achieving Black Women. *International Journal of Qualitative Studies in Education*, *26*(10), 1213–1237. https://doi.org/10.1080/09518398.2012.731536

Marsh, K., Chaney, C., & Jones, D. (2012). The Strengths of High-achieving Black High School Students in a Racially Diverse Setting. *The Journal of Negro Education*, *81*(1), 39–51.

Marsh, K., Darity Jr., W. A., Cohen, P. N., Casper, L. M., & Salters, D. (2007). The Emerging Black Middle Class: Single and Living Alone. *Social Forces, 86*(2), 735–762. https://doi.org/10.1093/sf/86.2.735

Marsh, K., & Iceland, J. (2010). The Racial Residential Segregation of Black Single Adults Living Alone. *City & Community, 9*(3), 299–319. https://doi.org/10.1111/j.1540-6040.2010.01338.x

Marsh, K., & Peña, J. (2020). Marriage, Household Composition, Class Status by Nativity for Women of Color: 1980–2014. In C. Suter, S. Madheswaran, & B.P. Vani (Eds.), *The Middle Class in World Society* (pp. 135–149). Routledge. https://doi.org/10.4324/9781003049630-7

Marsh, K., & von Lockette, N. D. (2011). Racial and Ethnic Differences in Women's Marriage, Household Composition and Class Status: 1980–2008. *Race, Gender & Class, 18*(1/2), 314–330. www.jstor.org/stable/23884881

Martin, L. L. (2010). Strategic Assimilation or Creation of Symbolic Blackness: Middle-Class Blacks in Suburban Contexts. *Journal of African American Studies, 14*(2), 234–246. https://doi.org/10.1007/s12111-008-9075-0

Massey, D. S., & Denton, N. A. (1993). *American Apartheid: Segregation and the Making of the Underclass*. Harvard University Press.

Massey, D. S., Rugh, J. S., Steil, J. P., & Albright, L. (2016). Riding the Stagecoach to Hell: A Qualitative Analysis of Racial Discrimination in Mortgage Lending. *City & Community, 15*(2), 118–136. https://doi.org/10.1111/cico.12179

McAdoo, H. P. (2007). *Black Families*. SAGE.

McCluney, C. L., Durkee, M. I., Smith II, R. E., Robotham, K. J., & Sai-Lai Lee, S. (2021). To Be, Or Not to Be … Black: The Effects of Racial Codeswitching on Perceived Professionalism in the Workplace. *Journal of Experimental Social Psychology, 97*, 104199.

McMullen, J. H., & Natalia, J. (February 28, 2019, Thursday). The 'Heartbreaking' Decrease in Black Homeownership: Racism and Rollbacks in Government Policies Are Taking Their Toll. *The Washington Post Blogs*. www.washingtonpost.com/news/business/wp/2019/02/28/feature/the-heartbreaking-decrease-in-black-homeownership/

McNicholas, J., Gilbey, A., Rennie, A., Ahmedzai, S., Dono, J., & Ormerod, E. (2005). Pet Ownership and Human Health: A Brief Review of Evidence and Issues. *BMJ, 331*(7527), 1252–1254.

Meghji, A. (2019). *Black Middle-Class Britannia: Identities, Repertoires, Cultural Consumption*. Manchester University Press.

Melber, H. (2016). *The Rise of Africa's Middle Class: Myths, Realities and Critical Engagements*. Bloomsbury Publishing.

Mesch, D., Osili, U., Ackerman, J., Bergdoll, J., Williams-Pulfer, K., Pactor, A., & Thayer, A. (2019). Women Give. Lilly Family School of Philanthropy. https://philanthropy.iupui.edu/institutes/womens-philanthropy-institute/research/women-give19.html

Miles, M. B., & Huberman, A. M. (1994). *Qualitative Data Analysis: An Expanded Sourcebook*. SAGE.

Monk, E. P., Jr. (2014). Skin Tone Stratification among Black Americans, 2001–2003. *Social Forces, 92*(4), 1313–1337. https://doi.org/10.1093/sf/sou007

Monk Jr, E. P., Esposito, M. H., & Lee, H. (2021). Beholding Inequality: Race, Gender, and Returns to Physical Attractiveness in the United States. *American Journal of Sociology*, 127(1), 194–241.

Moody-Turner, S. (2015). "Dear Doctor Du Bois": Anna Julia Cooper, W. E. B. Du Bois, and the Gender Politics of Black Publishing. *MELUS*, 40(3), 47–68. https://doi.org/10.1093/melus/mlv029

Moore, J. A., & Radtke, H. L. (2015). Starting "Real" Life: Women Negotiating a Successful Midlife Single Identity. *Psychology of Women Quarterly*, 39(3), 305–319. https://doi.org/10.1177/0361684315573244

Moore, K. S. (2005). What's Class Got to Do with It? Community Development and Racial Identity. *Journal of Urban Affairs*, 27(4), 437–451. https://doi.org/10.1111/j.0735-2166.2005.00245.x

———. (2008). Class formations: Competing Forms of Black Middle-class Identity. *Ethnicities*, 8(4), 492–517. https://doi.org/10.1177/1468796808097075

Moore, M. (2011). *Invisible Families: Gay Identities, Relationships, and Motherhood Among Black Women*. University of California Press.

Moorman, J. D. (2020). Socializing Singlehood: Personal, Interpersonal, and Sociocultural Factors Shaping Black Women's Single Lives. *Psychology of Women Quarterly*, 44(4), 431–449. https://doi.org/10.1177/0361684320939070

Morison, T., Macleod, C., Lynch, I., Mijas, M., & Shivakumar, S. T. (2016). Stigma Resistance in Online Childfree Communities: The Limitations of Choice Rhetoric. *Psychology of Women Quarterly*, 40(2), 184–198. https://doi.org/10.1177/0361684315603657

Morris, W. L., DePaulo, B. M., Hertel, J., & Taylor, L. C. (2008). Singlism – Another Problem that Has No Name: Prejudice, Stereotypes and Discrimination against Singles. In M. A. Morrison & T. G. Morrison (Eds.), *The Psychology of Modern Prejudice* (pp. 165–194). Nova Science Publishers.

Morris, W. L., Sinclair, S., & DePaulo, B. M. (2007). No Shelter for Singles: The Perceived Legitimacy of Marital Status Discrimination. *Group Processes & Intergroup Relations*, 10(4), 457–470. https://doi.org/10.1177/1368430207081535

Moultrie, M. (2021). "Making Myself." *Journal of Religious Ethics*, 49(2), 314–336. https://doi.org/10.1111/jore.12353

Mouzon, D. (2014). "Blacks Don't Value Marriage as Much as Other Groups": Structural Inequality in Black Family Patterns. In S. M. McClure & C. A. Harris (Eds.), *Getting Real About Race: Hoodies, Mascots, Model Minorities, and Other Conversations* (pp. 145–155). Sage Publications.

Mouzon, D. M. (n.d.). *Why Has Marriage Declined Among Black Americans?* https://scholars.org/brief/why-has-marriage-declined-among-black-americans

Mouzon, D. M., Taylor, R. J., & Chatters, L. M. (2020). Gender Differences in Marriage, Romantic Involvement, and Desire for Romantic Involvement among Older African Americans. *PLoS ONE*, 15(5), 1–16. https://doi.org/10.1371/journal.pone.0233836

Mui, Y. Q., & Jenkins, C. L. (2012, February 5). For Some Black Women, Economy and Willingness to Aid Family Strains Finances. *The Washington Post*. www.washingtonpost.com/business/economy/for-some-black-women-economy-and-willingness-to-aid-family-strains-finances/2012/01/24/gIQAGIWksQ_story.html

Murray, J. L., & Bernfield, M. (2010, January 14). The Differential Effect of Prenatal Care on the Incidence of Low Birth Weight among Blacks and Whites in a Prepaid Health Care Plan (world) [Research-article]. Http://Dx.Doi.Org/10.1056/NEJM198811243192105; Massachusetts Medical Society. https://doi.org/10.1056/NEJM198811243192105

Myrdal, G. & et al. (1944). *An American Dilemma; the Negro Problem and Modern Democracy* (2 vols., p. 1550). Harper.

Nash, J. C. (2008). Re-Thinking Intersectionality. *Feminist Review, 89*(1), 1–15. https://doi.org/10.1057/fr.2008.4

Ndlovu, S. G. (2011). "Body" of Evidence: Saartjie Baartman and the Archive. In N. Gordon-Chipembere (Ed.), *Representation and Black Womanhood: The Legacy of Sarah Baartman* (pp. 17–30). Palgrave Macmillan US. https://doi.org/10.1057/9780230339262_2

Neil, L., & Mbilishaka, A. (2019). "Hey Curlfriends!": Hair Care and Self-Care Messaging on YouTube by Black Women Natural Hair Vloggers. *Journal of Black Studies, 50*(2), 156–177. https://doi.org/10.1177/0021934718819411

Nembhard, J. G., & Marsh, K. (2012). Wealth Affirming Policies for Women of Color. *The Review of Black Political Economy, 39*(3), 353–360. https://doi.org/10.1007/s12114-012-9144-4

Norwood, K. J. (2015). If You Is White, You's Alright: Stories about Colorism in America Global Perspectives on Colorism. *Washington University Global Studies Law Review, 14*(4), 585–608. https://heinonline.org/HOL/P?h=hein.journals/wasglo14&i=606

Nisbett, R. E., & Wilson, T. D. (1977). The Halo Effect: Evidence for Unconscious Alteration of Judgments. *Journal of Personality and Social Psychology 35*(4), 250.

Oliver, M. L., & Shapiro, T. M. (1997). Black Wealth/White Wealth: A New Perspective on Racial Inequality.

Oliver, M., & Shapiro, T. (2013). *Black Wealth/White Wealth: A New Perspective on Racial Inequality.* Routledge.

Osuji, C. K. (2019). *Boundaries of Love: Interracial Marriage and the Meaning of Race.* NYU Press.

Page, N. (2020). The Singleness Tradition and the Collective: A Literary Analysis of "for colored girls" [Unpublished Undergraduate Thesis]. University of Maryland.

Pager, D. (2003). The Mark of a Criminal Record. *American Journal of Sociology, 108*(5), 937–975. https://doi.org/10.1086/374403

Pais, J., Crowder, K., & Downey, L. (2014). Unequal Trajectories: Racial and Class Differences in Residential Exposure to Industrial Hazard. *Social Forces, 92*(3), 1189–1215. https://doi.org/10.1093/sf/sot099

Park, K. (2002). Stigma Management among the Voluntarily Childless. *Sociological Perspectives, 45*(1), 21–45. https://doi.org/10.1525/sop.2002.45.1.21

Park, R. E., Burgess, E. W., McKenzie, R. D., & Wirth, L. (1925). *The Ccity.* The University of Chicago Press.

Pattillo, M. (2005). Black Middle-Class Neighborhoods. *Annual Review of Sociology, 31,* 305–329. www.jstor.org/stable/29737722

(2010). *Black on the Block: The Politics of Race and Class in the City.* University of Chicago Press.

(2013). *Black Picket Fences: Privilege and Peril among the Black Middle Class*. Second edition. University of Chicago Press.

Pattillo-McCoy, M. (2000). The Limits of Out-Migration for the Black Middle Class. *Journal of Urban Affairs*, *22*(3), 225–241. https://doi.org/10.1111/0735-2166.00054

Payton, A. R. (2009). Mental Health, Mental Illness, and Psychological Distress: Same Continuum or Distinct Phenomena? *Journal of Health and Social Behavior*, *50*(2), 213–227. https://doi.org/10.1177/002214650905000207

Pearlin, L. I., Menaghan, E. G., Lieberman, M. A., & Mullan, J. T. (1981). The Stress Process. *Journal of Health and Social Behavior*, *22*(4), 337–356. https://doi.org/10.2307/2136676

Pearson, J. A. (2008). Can't Buy Me Whiteness: New Lessons from the Titanic on Race, Ethnicity, and Health. *Du Bois Review: Social Science Research on Race*, *5*(1), 27–47. https://doi.org/10.1017/S1742058X0808003X

Pepping, C. A., MacDonald, G., & Davis, P. J. (2018). Toward a Psychology of Singlehood: An Attachment-Theory Perspective on Long-Term Singlehood. *Current Directions in Psychological Science*, *27*(5), 324–331. https://doi.org/10.1177/0963721417752106

Pfeffer, F. T., & Killewald, A. (2019). Intergenerational Wealth Mobility and Racial Inequality. *Socius*, *5*, 1–2. https://doi.org/10.1177/2378023119831799

Pitts, B. (2021). "Uneasy Lies the Head that Wears a Crown": A Critical Race Analysis of the CROWN Act. *Journal of Black Studies*, *52*(7), 716–735. https://doi.org/10.1177/00219347211021096

Plott, M., & Umansky, L. (Eds.) (2000). *Making Sense of Women's Lives: An Introduction to Women's Studies*. Rowman & Littlefield.

Portes, A., & Rumbaut, R. G. (2001). *Legacies: The Story of the Immigrant Second Generation*. University of California Press.

Portes, A., & Zhou, M. (1993). The New Second Generation: Segmented Assimilation and its Variants. *The ANNALS of the American Academy of Political and Social Science*, *530*(1), 74–96. https://doi.org/10.1177/0002716293530001006

Pudrovska, T., Schieman, S., & Carr, D. (2006). Strains of Singlehood in Later Life: Do Race and Gender Matter? *The Journals of Gerontology: Series B*, *61*(6), S315–S322. https://doi.org/10.1093/geronb/61.6.S315

Purnell, D. (2019, February 23). Opinion | Why Does Obama Scold Black Boys? *The New York Times*. www.nytimes.com/2019/02/23/opinion/my-brothers-keeper-obama.html

Qian, Z. (1997). Breaking the Racial Barriers: Variations in Interracial Marriage between 1980 and 1990. *Demography*, *34*(2), 263–276. https://doi.org/10.2307/2061704

Quillian, L. (2002). Why Is Black–White Residential Segregation So Persistent?: Evidence on Three Theories from Migration Data. *Social Science Research*, *31*(2), 197–229. https://doi.org/10.1006/ssre.2001.0726

Quillian, L., Lee, J. J., & Honoré, B. (2020). Racial Discrimination in the U.S. Housing and Mortgage Lending Markets: A Quantitative Review of Trends, 1976–2016. *Race and Social Problems*, *12*(1), 13–28. https://doi.org/10.1007/s12552-019-09276-x

Reynolds, B. (2015, January 19). The Biggest Problem with 'Selma' Has Nothing to Do with LBJ or the Oscars, *The Washington Post*. www.washingtonpost.com/

posteverything/wp/2015/01/19/the-biggest-problem-with-selma-has-nothing-to-do-with-lbj-or-the-oscars/

Rhee, N. (n.d.). *Race and Retirement Insecurity in the United States*. 22.

Romano, R. (2018). Something Old, Something New: Black Women, Interracial Dating, and the Black Marriage Crisis. *Differences*, *29*(2), 126–153. https://doi.org/10.1215/10407391-6999802

Roseman, C. C., & Lee, S. W. (1998). Linked and Independent African American Migration from Los Angeles. *The Professional Geographer*, *50*(2), 204–214. https://doi.org/10.1111/0033-0124.00115

Rosenblum, A., Darity Jr., W. A., Harris, A. L., & Hamilton, T. G. (2016). Looking through the Shades: The Effect of Skin Color on Earnings by Region of Birth and Race for Immigrants to the United States. *Sociology of Race and Ethnicity*, *2*(1), 87–105. https://doi.org/10.1177/2332649215600718

Ross, S. L., & Turner, M. A. (2005). Housing Discrimination in Metropolitan America: Explaining Changes between 1989 and 2000. *Social Problems*, *52*(2), 152–180. https://doi.org/10.1525/sp.2005.52.2.152

Rothstein, R. (2017). *The Color of Law: A Forgotten History of How Our Government Segregated America*. Liveright Publishing.

Ruggles, Steven, Flood, Sarah, Goeken, Ronald, Schouweiler, Megan, & Sobek, Matthew. (2022). *IPUMS USA: Version 12.0 (12.0) [Data set]*. IPUMS. https://doi.org/10.18128/D010.V12.0

Rumbaut, R. G., & Portes, A. (2001). *Ethnicities: Children of Immigrants in America*. University of California Press.

Sacks, T. K. (2018). *Invisible Visits: Black Middle-Class Women in the American Healthcare System*. Oxford University Press.

Sacks, T. K., Sewell, W. A., Asher, A. E., & Hudson, D. (2020). 'It Fell on Me to Help Everybody': Financial Precariousness and Costs of Upward Social Mobility among Black Middle-Class Women. *Issues in Race and Society: An Interdisciplinary Global Journal*, Spring 2020, *on Manifold*. (n.d.). Manifold Scholarship. Retrieved June 29, 2022. https://ucincinnatipress.manifoldapp.org/read/issues-in-race-and-society-an-interdisciplinary-global-journal-spring-2020-edition/section/44811de1-c72a-4f95-9771-ca6b3cfd3b06

Sanders, M. G. (1997). Overcoming Obstacles: Academic Achievement as a Response to Racism and Discrimination. *Journal of Negro Education*, *66*(1), 83–93.

Sarkisian, N., & Gerstel, N. (2016). Does Singlehood Isolate or Integrate? Examining the Link between Marital Status and Ties to Kin, Friends, and Neighbors. *Journal of Social and Personal Relationships*, *33*(3), 361–384. https://doi.org/10.1177/0265407515597564

Schoendorf, K. C., Hogue, C. J. R., Kleinman, J. C., & Rowley, D. (1992). Mortality among Infants of Black as Compared with White College-Educated Parents. *New England Journal of Medicine*, *326*(23), 1522–1526. https://doi.org/10.1056/NEJM199206043262303

Schwartz, C. R. (2013). Trends and Variation in Assortative Mating: Causes and Consequences. *Annual Review of Sociology*, *39*(1), 451–470. https://doi.org/10.1146/annurev-soc-071312-145544

Shantu Riley, S. (2004). "Ecology Is a Sistah's Issue Too: The Politics of Emergent Afrocentric Ecowomanism." In R. S. Gottlieb (Ed.), *This Sacred Earth: Religion, Nature, Environment* (pp. 368–381). Routledge.

Shiovitz-Ezra, S., & Ayalon, L. (2010). Situational versus Chronic Loneliness as Risk Factors for All-cause Mortality. *International Psychogeriatrics, 22*(3), 455–462. https://doi.org/10.1017/S1041610209991426

Simms, A. (2019). The "Veil" of Racial Segregation in the Twenty-First Century: The Suburban Black Middle Class, Public Schools, and Pursuit of Racial Equity. *Phylon (1960-), 56*(1), 81–110. www.jstor.org/stable/26743832

Simms, A. (2021). COVID-19, Black Jurisdictions, and Budget Constraints: How Fiscal Footing Shapes Fighting the Virus. *Ethnic and Racial Studies, 44*(5), 836–850. https://doi.org/10.1080/01419870.2020.1859576

Simpson, R. (2016). Singleness and Self-identity: The Significance of Partnership Status in the Narratives of Never-Married Women. *Journal of Social and Personal Relationships, 33*(3), 385–400. https://doi.org/10.1177/0265407515611884

Smith, C. A., Williams, E. L., Wadud, I. A., Pirtle, W. N. L., & Collective, T. C. B. W. (2021). Cite Black Women: A Critical Praxis (A Statement). *Feminist Anthropology, 2*(1), 10–17. https://doi.org/10.1002/fea2.12040

Smith, H. L. (1989). Integrating Theory and Research on the Institutional Determinants of Fertility. *Demography, 26*(2), 171–184. https://doi.org/10.2307/2061518

Smith, W. A., Allen, W. R., & Danley, L. L. (2007). "Assume the Position . . . You Fit the Description": Psychosocial Experiences and Racial Battle Fatigue Among African American Male College Students. *American Behavioral Scientist, 51*(4), 551–578. https://doi.org/10.1177/0002764207307742

Smith-Tran, A. (2021). "Finally Something for Us": Black Girls Run! and Racialized Space-Making in Recreational Running. *Journal of Sport and Social Issues, 45*(3), 235–250. https://doi.org/10.1177/0193723519899241

South, S. J. (1993). Racial and Ethnic Differences in the Desire to Marry. *Journal of Marriage and Family, 55*(2), 357–370. https://doi.org/10.2307/352807

South, S. J., Huang, Y., Spring, A., & Crowder, K. (2016). Neighborhood Attainment over the Adult Life Course. *American Sociological Review, 81*(6), 1276–1304. https://doi.org/10.1177/0003122416673029

Southall, R. (2016). *The New Black Middle Class in South Africa.* Boydell & Brewer.

Spillers, H. J. (1987). Mama's Baby, Papa's Maybe: An American Grammar Book. *Diacritics, 17*(2), 65–81. https://doi.org/10.2307/464747

(1994). *Mamas Baby, Papas Maybe: An American Grammar Book* (pp. 454–481). Duke University Press. https://doi.org/10.1515/9780822399889-036

Springer, K. (2007). *10. Divas, Evil Black Bitches, and Bitter Black Women: African American Women in Postfeminist and Post-Civil-Rights Popular Culture* (pp. 249–276). Duke University Press. https://doi.org/10.1515/9780822390411-012

St. Vil, N. M., McDonald, K. B., & Cross-Barnet, C. (2018). A Qualitative Study of Black Married Couples' Relationships with Their Extended Family Networks. *Families in Society, 99*(1), 56–66. https://doi.org/10.1177/1044389418756847

Staples, R. (1981). *The World of Black Singles: Changing Patterns of Male/Female Relations.* Greenwood Press.

Steele, Claude M. (2011). *Whistling Vivaldi: How Stereotypes Affect Us and What We Can Do.* W. W. Norton & Company.

Stewart, Q. T., Cobb, R. J., & Keith, V. M. (2020). The Color of Death: Race, Observed Skin Tone, and All-Cause Mortality in the United States. *Ethnicity & Health, 25* (7), 1018–1044.

Strauss, A., & Corbin, J. M. (1997). *Grounded Theory in Practice*. SAGE.

Strings, S. (2019). *Fearing the Black Body: The Racial Origins of Fat Phobia*. New York University Press. https://doi.org/10.18574/9781479891788\

Taylor, E. D. (2017). *The Original Black Elite: Daniel Murray and the Story of a Forgotten Era*. HarperCollins.

Taylor, J., & Turner, R. J. (2002). Perceived Discrimination, Social Stress, and Depression in the Transition to Adulthood: Racial Contrasts. *Social Psychology Quarterly*, 65(3), 213–225. https://doi.org/10.2307/3090120

Taylor, K.-Y. (2017). *How We Get Free: Black Feminism and the Combahee River Collective*. Haymarket Books.

Taylor, R. J., James, S. J., & Chatters, L. M. (Eds.) (1997). *Family Life in Black America*. Sage Publications, Inc.

Taylor, S. R. (2021). *The Body Is Not an Apology, Second Edition: The Power of Radical Self-Love*. Berrett-Koehler Publishers.

The Combahee River Collective Statement. (2018). *Theorizing Feminism* (pp. 29–37). Routledge. https://doi.org/10.4324/9780429494277-3

Thoits, P. A. (1983). Multiple Identities and Psychological Well-Being: A Reformulation and Test of the Social Isolation Hypothesis. *American Sociological Review*, 48(2), 174–187. https://doi.org/10.2307/2095103

(1999). Sociological Approaches to Mental Illness. In A. V. Horwitz & T. L. Scheid (Eds.), *A Handbook for the Study of Mental Health: Social Contexts, Theories, and Systems* (pp. 121–138). Cambridge University Press.

Thomas, M. E., Moye, R., Henderson, L., & Horton, H. D. (2018). Separate and Unequal: The Impact of Socioeconomic Status, Segregation, and the Great Recession on Racial Disparities in Housing Values. *Sociology of Race and Ethnicity*, 4(2), 229–244. https://doi.org/10.1177/2332649217711457

Thompson, K. (2012, January 22). Survey Paints Portrait of Black Women in America. *The Washington Post*. www.washingtonpost.com/politics/survey-paints-portrait-of-black-women-in-america/2011/12/22/gIQAvxFcJQ_story.html

Tippett, R., Jones-DeWeever, A., Rockeymoore, M., Hamilton, D., & Darity Jr., W. A. (2014). *Beyond Broke: Why Closing the Racial Wealth Gap is a Priority for National Economic Security*. Center for Global Policy Solutions.

Traister, R. (2016). *All the Single Ladies: Unmarried Women and the Rise of an Independent Nation*. Simon & Schuster.

Tucker, M. B. (2000). Marital Values and Expectations in Context: Results from a 21-City Survey. In L. Waite, C. Bacharach, M. Hindin, E. Thomson, & A. Thornton (Eds.), *The Ties That Bind: Perspectives on Marriage and Cohabitation* (pp. 166–187). Aldine de Gruyter.

Tucker, M. B., & Mitchell-Kernan, C. (1990). New Trends in Black American Interracial Marriage: The Social Structural Context. *Journal of Marriage and Family*, 52(1), 209–218. https://doi.org/10.2307/352851

(1995). *The Decline in Marriage Among African Americans: Causes, Consequences, and Policy Implications*. Russell Sage Foundation.

Turner, J. B., & Turner, R. J. (2013). Social Relations, Social Integration, and Social Support. In C. S. Aneshensel, J. C. Phelan, & A. Bierman (Eds.), *Handbook of the Sociology of Mental Health* (pp. 341–356). Springer Netherlands. https://doi.org/10.1007/978-94-007-4276-5_17

Turner, J. C. (2010). *Social Categorization and the Self-concept: A Social Cognitive Theory of Group Behavior* (p. 272). Psychology Press.

Turner, R. J., & Avison, W. R. (2003). Status Variations in Stress Exposure: Implications for the Interpretation of Research on Race, Socioeconomic Status, and Gender. *Journal of Health and Social Behavior*, 44(4), 488–505. https://doi.org/10.2307/1519795

Turner, R. J., Scheid, T. L., & Brown, R. L. (2010). Social Support and Mental Health. In *A Handbook for the Study of Mental Health: Social Contexts, Theories, and Systems*, 2nd ed (pp. 200–212). Cambridge University Press.

U.S. Bureau of Labor Statistics. Household Data, Annual Averages. Table 11. Employed Persons by Detailed Occupation, Sex, Race, and Hispanic or Latino Ethnicity. 2020. www.bls.gov/cps/cpsaat11.htm.

U.S. Census Bureau and National Center for Science and Engineering Statistics, 2020 Annual Business Survey, data year 2019.

U.S. Census Bureau. Current Population Survey, 2019 Annual Social and Economic Supplement. Table 3. Detailed Years of School Completed by People 25 Years and Over by Sex, Age Groups, Race and Hispanic Origin: 2019.

U.S. Census Bureau, Current Population Survey. 2020 and 2021 Annual Social and Economic Supplements (CPS ASEC). Table A-1. Table A-1. Income Summary Measures by Selected Characteristics: 2019 and 2020.

U.S. Census Bureau, Current Population Survey, Annual Social and Economic Supplement. (2020). Table A1. Marital Status of People 15 Years and Over, by Age, Sex, and Personal Earnings: 2020.

U.S. Census Bureau, Current Population Survey, Annual Social and Economic Supplements. (2018). Table H-5. Race and Hispanic Origin of Householder–Households by Median and Mean Income: 1967 to 2018.

U.S. Census Bureau, Current Population Survey/Housing Vacancy Survey. (February 27, 2018).

(April 2020). Table 3. Estimates of the Total Housing Inventory for the United States: First Quarter 2019 and 2020a.

U.S. Census Bureau, Historical Census of Housing Tables. (October 31, 2011).

U.S. Census Bureau, Population Division, Annual Estimates of the Resident Population: April 1, 2010 to July 1, 2018.

U.S. Census Bureau, Population Division. (2021). Table CBSA-EST2020-alldata: Annual Resident Population Estimates and Estimated Components of Resident Population Change for Metropolitan and Micropolitan Statistical Areas and their Geographic Components: April 1, 2010 to July 1, 2020. Release date: May 2021.

U.S. Census Bureau. (2015). "Housing Vacancies and Homeownership (CPS/HVS): Table 16. Homeownership Rates by Race and Ethnicity of Householder: 1994 to Present." Retrieved February 15, 2016. www.census.gov/housing/hvs/data/histtabs.html.

Veblen, T. (2009). *The Theory of the Leisure Class*. Oxford University Press.

Waite, L. J., & Bachrach, C. (2000). *The Ties That Bind: Perspectives on Marriage and Cohabitation*. Transaction Publishers.

Walker, A. (1983a). *Search of Our Mothers' Gardens: Womanist Prose*. Houghton Mifflin Harcourt.

(1983b). *The Color Purple*. Womens Press Ltd.

Washington, M. H. (1982). Working at Single Bliss. In M. Plott & L. Umansky (Eds.), *Making Sense of Women's Lives: An Introduction to Women's Studies* (pp. 185–191). Rowman & Littlefield.

Washington, Mary Helen. (1995). Working at Single Bliss. In Amy Kesselman & Lily D. McNair (Eds.), *Women: Images and Realities: A Multicultural Anthology* (pp. 356–361). Mayfield.

Watkins-Hayes, C. (2009). The New Welfare Bureaucrats. In *The New Welfare Bureaucrats*. University of Chicago Press.

Watters, E. (2004). *Urban Tribes: A Generation Redefines Friendship, Family, and Commitment*. Holtzbrinck Publishers.

Weiss, R. S. (1973). *Loneliness: The Experience of Emotional and Social Isolation*. The MIT Press.

Wilder, C. S. (2013). *Ebony and Ivy: Race, Slavery, and the Troubled History of America's Universities*. Bloomsbury Publishing USA.

Williams, D. R., & Mohammed, S. A. (2009). Discrimination and Racial Disparities in Health: Evidence and Needed Research. *Journal of Behavioral Medicine, 32*(1), 20–47. https://doi.org/10.1007/s10865-008-9185-0

Williams, D. R., Priest, N., & Anderson, N. B. (2016). Understanding Associations among Race, Socioeconomic Status, and Health: Patterns and Prospects. *Health Psychology, 35*(4), 407–411. https://doi.org/10.1037/hea0000242

Williams, D. R., Yu, Y., Jackson, J. S., & Anderson, N. B. (1997). Racial Differences in Physical and Mental Health: Socio-economic Status, Stress and Discrimination. *Journal of Health Psychology, 2*(3), 335–351. https://doi.org/10.1177/135910539700200305

Williams, S. W., & Dilworth-Anderson, P. (2002). Systems of Social Support in Families Who Care for Dependent African American Elders. *The Gerontologist, 42*(2), 224–236. https://doi.org/10.1093/geront/42.2.224

Wilson, K. B., Thorpe, R. J., & LaVeist, T. A. (2017). Dollar for Dollar: Racial and Ethnic Inequalities in Health and Health-related Outcomes among Persons with Very High Income. *Preventive Medicine, 96*, 149–153. https://doi.org/10.1016/j.ypmed.2016.08.038

Wilson, W. J. (2012a). *The Truly Disadvantaged: The Inner City, the Underclass, and Public Policy* (2nd ed). University of Chicago Press.

(2012b). *The Declining Significance of Race: Blacks and Changing American Institutions*. University of Chicago Press.

Wilson, W. J., & Taub, R. P. (2011). *There Goes the Neighborhood: Racial, Ethnic, and Class Tensions in Four Chicago Neighborhoods and Their Meaning for America*. Knopf Doubleday Publishing Group.

Wingfield, A. H. (2007). The Modern Mammy and the Angry Black Man: African American Professionals' Experiences with Gendered Racism in the Workplace. *Race, Gender & Class, 14*(1/2), 196–212. www.jstor.org/stable/41675204

(2008). *Doing Business with Beauty: Black Women, Hair Salons, and the Racial Enclave Economy*. Rowman & Littlefield.

(2012). *Changing Times for Black Professionals*. Routledge. https://doi.org/10.4324/9780203834237

Wingfield, A. H., & Alston, R. S. (2012). The Understudied Case of Black Professional Men: Advocating an Intersectional Approach. *Sociology Compass, 6*(9), 728–739. https://doi.org/10.1111/j.1751-9020.2012.00503.x

Woods-Giscombé, C. L. (2010). Superwoman Schema: African American Women's Views on Stress, Strength, and Health. *Qualitative Health Research, 20*(5), 668–683. https://doi.org/10.1177/1049732310361892

Zambrana, R. E., Harvey Wingfield, A., Lapeyrouse, L. M., Dávila, B. A., Hoagland, T. L., & Valdez, R. B. (2017). Blatant, Subtle, and Insidious: URM Faculty Perceptions of Discriminatory Practices in Predominantly White Institutions. *Sociological Inquiry, 87*(2), 207–232. https://doi.org/10.1111/soin.12147

Zaw, K., Bhattacharya, J., Price, A., Hamilton, D., & Darity Jr., W. A. (2017). Women, Race and Wealth. Samuel DuBois Cook Center on Social Equity and Insight Center for Community Economic Development.

Index

Made in United States
North Haven, CT
10 July 2023

38781607R10148